# Ethics and Risk Management

A Volume in
Ethics in Practice

Series Editors
Robert A. Giacalone, *Daniels College of Business at University of Denver*
Carole L. Jurkiewicz, *Hofstra University*

# Ethics in Practice

Robert A. Giacalone and Carole L. Jurkiewicz, Series Editors

# Ethics and Risk Management

edited by

**Lina Svedin**
*University of Utah*

**INFORMATION AGE PUBLISHING, INC.**
Charlotte, NC • www.infoagepub.com

**Library of Congress Cataloging-in-Publication Data**

IP record for this book is available from the Library of Congress
http://www.loc.gov

ISBN: 978-1-68123-093-1 (Paperback)
       978-1-68123-094-8 (Hardcover)
       978-1-68123-095-5 (ebook)

# CONTENTS

# FOREWORD

This collection of studies on ethics and risk management provides both a welcome pause in the hectic practice of risk management to reflect on the values at stake, and an important contribution to the foundation of a much-needed subfield of serious scholarly study.

We may at first glance think of ethics and risk management as the province of distinct specialists. And, indeed, there are scholars and other experts who devote their lives to studying and practicing ethics and risk management. Thus, we may look to philosophers and theologians specialized on ethics for guidance on ethics, and to those who have some variant of risk management in their job titles or descriptions as experts on that topic. This view is not wrong, but it is incomplete. For while there are experts devoted to ethics, and experts devoted to risk management, ethics and risk management are intertwined activities not confined to specialists. The reality is that we all do ethics and risk management, and we do them all the time. Ethics and risk management are ubiquitous, highly democratic activities rather than the exclusive area of designated experts; although of course, experts engage in them as well. So, this collection of studies of ethics and risk management should be of interest to everyone, including specialists. In fact, it may serve specialists particularly well in helping them deepen and broaden their understanding of ethics and risk management.

Several contributions to this volume drive home the fact that we are all ethicists and risk managers, simply because we all inhabit one or more cultures; and these cultures teach us what to value, what to fear, and how to implement our values to deal with our fears. Thus, by virtue of being embedded in cultures, we all are constantly engaged in learning

*Ethics and Risk Management,* pp. vii–ix
Copyright © 2015 by Information Age Publishing
All rights of reproduction in any form reserved.

and applying values, managing fears, and pursuing the activities that our cultures lead us to consider risky or dangerous. Thus, even in, or especially in, cultures where there are successful efforts to assign ethics and risk management to experts, we need to become aware of the ethical work and risk-management work done by other actors, up to and including everyone else in those cultures. The contributions to this volume help us do that. For example, in the United States it has become common to segregate risk assessment and risk management. Different actors and often different institutions are assigned the job of assessing risks, figuring out which hazards exist, how dangerous they are to whom under what conditions, and what to do to reduce these risks. In the United States, risk assessors are not supposed to apply values, they are just supposed to determine the types and extent of risk. It is left to risk managers to apply professional, and perhaps societal, values to determine which risks to reduce or mitigate, and by how much (using what means).

Looking at the United States, we do not necessarily have a problem seeing ethics and risk management as being intertwined activities; because in the United States we have an expectation that risk managers will use values to make choices about how to manage risks. However, in the United States we have a problem with risk assessors doing risk management and applying values. The way these practices have been developed, American risk assessors are not supposed to be engaged in risk *management*, including the application of values. Studies, including some in this volume, of course show that risk assessment and risk management are not so neatly segregated in practice, and that values guide both activities. Risk assessors necessarily rely on values in guiding them toward what risks to assess, and how to go about assessing them. These are important, hard won insights, but we should not stop there.

A further significant insight is that risks are assessed and regulated by both governmental and non-governmental actors, who rely on their values to participate in the regulatory regimes for particular risks. Thus, in the U.S. system, regulatory regimes often consist of multiple layers of governance, with international, federal, state, and local actors. Presidents, legislators, justices, and judges are among the regime risk managers at the federal level, as are interest-group representatives, voters, and the producers and consumers of everyday products and services. All these actors make use of their cultural values to assess and manage risks.

It is important to note here, that while countries, states, localities, and the institutions, organizations, and people in them may have cultural orientations that tend in particular directions, there are few social units, large or small, that are culturally monolithic in their values or risk-management behaviors. Rather, as several contributions to this volume attest, social units tend to be multi-cultural and value-pluralized, and so are their risk-assessment and management activities. Cultural-value differences lead to differences in risk concerns and to differences in risk perceptions, assessments, and management. These differences are a significant source of political conflict and coalition, as they flow through and animate political institutions with different rules for aggregating value preferences regarding risk assessment and management. As institutions come to embody particular cultural values regarding risk assessment and management, they themselves become significant, and in some cases determinative, actors shaping these activities.

Relatedly, it is important to note, that it is our cultural values that risk management ultimately seeks to protect and defend. Thus, while we may think that human well-being and the preservation of human life are the goals of most risk management, we are forced to realize this is not the case when we sacrifice human life to advance values like liberty, equality, or order. Our prioritizing of values over life itself is brought home to us most dramatically when we go to war; but this occurs less visibly and more subtly in the myriad ways we expend resources on activities, rather than on promoting human well-being and the preservation of human life. Systematic efforts to study what we value and the value trade-offs we make in upholding one value at the expense of another, should be at the center of the research on ethics and risk management.

The contributions to this volume provide multiple windows and multiple insights into the ubiquity and complexity of the intersection of ethics and risk management. The chapters herein also significantly contribute toward laying the foundation for a systematic study of ethics and risk management. Read on; the good work within will guide us in the good work that needs to be done.

Brendon Swedlow
DeKalb, IL
December 2014

# ACKNOWLEDGMENTS

While I am responsible for any shortcomings this volume may exhibit, I would like to express my gratitude to the many people and institutions that had a hand in its coming together. First and foremost, I would like to thank Carole Jurkiewicz and Robert Giacalone for their excitement about this book, and for encouraging me to put it together. As the instigator and editor of this project, I would also sincerely like to thank all of the chapter contributors for saying yes, despite not having time to do this, and supporting a line of research that was not always a familiar fit for them. This book features some remarkable scholars from quite different disciplines and at various stages of their academic journey. Their reflections on ethics and topics they are rather more familiar with was, in many ways, a leap of faith they agreed to take with me; and for that, and their resulting insights, I am both thrilled and forever grateful.

I would like to thank David Vogel and the European Union Center for Excellence at Berkeley for hosting the Comparative Risk Regulation Workshop in December 2012. The constructive discussion with the scholars who participated there sparked my interest in the ethics of risk regulation and the psychology of risk management. I am very grateful for the chance to present some of my ideas there, and to get to know a group of incredible and generous people way above my pay grade.

Brendon Swedlow was one of the participants at the Berkeley workshop whose work has really inspired me. His helpful feedback on early ideas and his encouragement were instrumental in motivating me to pursue this project. Brendon was also gracious enough to take time to write the

*Ethics and Risk Management*, pp. xi–xii
Copyright © 2015 by Information Age Publishing
All rights of reproduction in any form reserved.

foreword to the book, and I am very excited to have him participate in the volume in this capacity.

My colleagues in the MPA program and the political science department at the University of Utah continue to give me great emotional and professional support. Special thanks to Thad Hall, Mark Button, and Cindy Berg who, in their leadership capacities within the College of Social and Behavioral Science at the University of Utah, did everything within their power to keep me funded and well-traveled, but institutionally grounded. They are great role models, and I keep walking one step behind them trying to figure out how they do it.

Heartfelt thanks to Daniel Patterson for his unending encouragement and excellent copy editing support. A special thanks also to my mom, Harriet Svedin, who made sure children were picked up and meatballs were made when the compilation of this book made me particularly absentminded.

Lina Svedin
Salt Lake City, Utah

# CHAPTER 1

# INTRODUCTION

## Lina Svedin

This book centers on how we as a society perceive risk; more specifically what risks we find objectionable, what risks we think the government should intervene to reduce, and what risk levels we find acceptable when individuals engage in different types of perceived risky behaviors and activities. Our fear or dislike of certain types of risks or risk-taking groups is based on perceptions, values, and culture. Thus, mitigating and managing risk inherently means dealing with values, priorities, choices and perceptions; i.e., politics and ethics in practice. The fair or equitable distribution of risk in society—the balance between those who take risks and those who benefit from the risk taking—is one of the deeply political and ethical questions that should be continually addressed throughout the policy process. Furthermore, culturally shaped and value-driven perceptions of risk make up the uneven context in which policy regarding risk mitigation and risk management develops and needs to work. Consequently, researchers and policymakers need to better understand risk culture and public perceptions of risks in order to create more effective mitigative policies and more effective management strategies for when these risks materialize. There are several management challenges associated with risk mitigation and management that can lead governments (as well as both private and non-profit sectors) down a path to unethical behavior and communication.

Unethical management resonates with and follows other underlying chasms of inequality, prejudice, and injustice that exist in societies at a fundamental level, and serves to further solidify these existing cleavages. Ultimately this book is about the roles governments, corporations, and individuals play with regard to the identification, mitigation and management of risk in our society. It poses questions about justice, fairness, equitability, and appropriateness in relation to real and perceived risks that we as a collective and as individuals produce and engage with. It aspires to do what is seldom done in policy and public management books, which is to present practitioners with tools for making better, more ethical, analyses and decisions with regard to the inherently political and controversial topic of risk.

## WHY A BOOK ON ETHICS AND RISK MANAGEMENT?

The underlying rationale for this book is two-fold: first, to address the empirical deficit and theoretical challenges associated with societal risk management. All of the contributing authors are well established within the academic community and have published extensively on risk perception, risk management, and risk regulation. In this volume, however, I have asked them to shift their focus to specifically address the ethics of risk management and risk culture. This approach allows us to fill a gap in prior research and, as such, present a focused selection of papers and an informed discussion of a previously neglected aspect of risk management and ethics research.

The second rationale behind this work is the recognition that there is very little current research highlighting the explosively political and deeply divisive issues involved in approaching and managing risk ethically. Research on risk management in the public sector borrows heavily in its ontological approach from engineering, systems theory, and business management. Consequently, much of the current research on risk management is focused on probabilities, modeling, and abstractions of the value of mitigative action. This body of research, with its accompanying teaching materials and application in practice, is inherently structure oriented and both quantitatively and economically centered. This engenders a false sense of objectivity and makes possible a de-politicization of fundamental political and democratic questions about the allocation of society's scarce resources, the balance between governing institutions and personal risk, as well as the consequences of these distributions for real people outside of the primary decision-making circles.

While this predominant approach to research has made a comprehensive discussion of ethical foundations and implications difficult, a growing body of scholars have begun to identify the deeply political nature of managing identified and unidentified risks in society. The contributors to this volume seek to add their voices to this important debate; they are motivated by the understanding that the core political decisions we make about how to govern the risks we are exposed to, carry very real practical and personal consequences for average citizens. Our hope is that our scholarly contribution will prompt and support ongoing conversations in agency and department hallways, in classrooms and academic conferences, and in policy think-tanks about the fundamental ethical challenges that managing risk entails.

## TO OUR READERS

This book turns toward scholars and practitioners working in fields that deal implicitly or explicitly with risk. This would include, but is not limited to, scholars and students of public management, public-sector ethics, public policy, risk regulation, and risk management. This book deals directly with core problems of management in the public sector, with value conflicts, with multiple principals and stakeholders, as well as in information analysis and the application of sound and valid decision-making processes.

For those of us who are active in the field, who work with this stuff on a daily basis, the book pinpoints the ethical stakes, the analytical and managerial challenges, and the tools needed to meet the many risks that societies face. *Ethics and Risk Management* provides a unique take on the realities of cost-benefit analysis, of efforts to control and regulate risk and risky behavior, as well as the decidedly bounded rationality with which we, as decision makers and citizens, perceive and take risks. The work of identifying, understanding, prioritizing, and designing effective tools to mitigate and manage risk is an inherently analytical and strategic process, best suited to take place before and between crises.

Successful risk analysis and management reduces the general occurrence of crises, while the ethical analysis and management of risk serves to reduce the likelihood of subsequent sociopolitical turmoil, should a crisis occur. Thus, the investment that any practitioner makes in risk management has the potential to yield both social and political benefits, if the analysis and work is done with an eye toward ethics and stakeholder analysis.

One result of the increasingly interdependent risk-management relationship between public-sector actors and private contractors is the growing need to better understand the ethical dimensions of corporate risk analysis and risk management. This volume also provides a bridge for business scholars and corporate executives to identify and understand how corporate risk taking can produce both a credibility and production crisis for companies when this calculation is perceived as unethical or unfair in the public eye.

## OUTLINE OF THE CHAPTERS

Of the chapters in this book, the second chapter written by Matthew Adler takes the most philosophical and formal look at the ethics of risk. This chapter outlines, compares, and questions the formula most frequently used in the United States for allocating resources and solutions to problems in public policy: cost-benefit analysis. Adler gets to the bottom of the assumptions, choices, and distributional consequences of four different benefit formulas, including cost-benefit analysis, that policymakers can use as they consider risk and risk management. While each benefit formula has its own advantages and drawbacks that warrant ethical choices, U.S. policymakers are also unwilling to point out and differentiate among beneficiaries or target populations when they calculate risk-mitigation measures. Adler's chapter shows that this leads U.S. policymakers in practice to virtually be attacking societal risk blindfolded and armed with the bluntest tool available.

The third chapter of the book explores the ethics of risk management in the United States and the European Union, taking a comparative historical approach to the regulation of risk and the politics that have surrounded it. David Vogel looks at a number of policy areas where the United States and the European Union have gone decidedly different ways with regard to how they view the science of risk, how they protect citizens, and the extent to which the government assumes a protective or paternalistic role. Vogel also shows that for the many differences that can be seen today in the risk regulation of genetically modified foods, chemicals, and pharmaceuticals, there was a time not too long ago when the two continents stood on the opposite foot; when the EU was more laissez faire and the United States was heavily regulated. The swings in regulation culture seem to have been closely tied to bad experiences and public perceptions of the government's role in these events, leaving the future of risk regulation open to change.

In Chapter 4, Leslie Francis presents the conundrum that risk management poses for caring professions. Risk management, she states, aims to reduce the costs of adverse events. That being said, entities such as hospitals and their risk managers work to reduce the likelihood of accidents and maltreatment. However, when these adverse events happen, the very same risk managers, are charged by their employer to reduce, or preferably minimize, the costs of the events. This double responsibility places risk managers and care providers, such as nurses and doctors, in an ethical dilemma with regards to the persons affected (staff or patients). The conflict of interest presented by these situations can turn out unfavorably to those affected by the event, once formal proceedings start taking place, something that Francis has a number of ways of remedying.

Chapter 5 is written by Chris Simon, who looks closer at the ethics of energy development and the praxis of its extraction in the United States and Canada. The social and environmental costs associated with both fossil-fuel extraction, nuclear power generation, and renewable-energy development are substantial for this generation and those to come. Shale gas and oil hydraulic fracturing, as well as uranium mining have many known risks, but the risks associated with renewable energy development and its impact on public lands, water, and wildlife are often underestimated. Lessons from our historical use and development of energy sources can teach us a lot about our current values and serve as a basis for making informed and ethical decisions about our energy consumption, including making the difficult changes that need to be made to our culture if we are to leave future generations in a viable, energy-secure, environment.

Continuing previous chapters' quest to see if society manages sometimes new, sometimes somewhat-uncertain risks in a scientific, ethical, or legally defensible ways, Chapter 6 dives into biomass and its conversion into energy. Kristin Shrader-Frechette argues that risk management, with regard to biomass has largely failed and ought to include three specific strategies: human-health and ecological risk assessments and cost-benefit analysis. Tying back to the focus of Adler's chapter, she shows that empirical analysis and a cost-benefit framework would reveal to policymakers that the plans for biomass incineration to create energy would cost more in terms of harm than the good they would produce. Failure to use accurate assessments and making policy choices based on evidence and analysis, Shrader-Frechette, argues will create a "perfect storm" of three worrisome trends: massive government subsidies for biomass crop-growing/incineration; dangerous, mostly ultrafine or nanoparticle, emissions from biomass-incineration plants; and the absence of ultrafine-particulate regulations. The ethics of renewable energy development, with poor analysis and unintended consequences, is hence yet again put in question.

Chapter 7 takes a serious look at ethics and risk management from a cultural perspective. Using *Grid Group Cultural Theory* as a tool, Ásthildur Bernharðsdóttir examines the relationship between ethics and culture, and how this plays out in the management of societal risk. Iceland serves as the case example, where Bernharðsdóttir explains how several different crises occurred and were managed as a result of cultural preferences and perceptions. Cultural types can influence the way in which decision makers perceive threat and manage risk reduction efforts in both the public and private sectors. In order to manage risk ethically it is necessary to understand the most important values at stake for the public, and to recognize the variation in emphasis of certain values in different cultures. Bernharðs-dóttir's chapter presents a theoretically rich counterpoint to the rational choice benefit frameworks that were presented in Adler's chapter and complements the dualistic picture of continental preferences presented in Vogel's chapter.

Written by Aya Okada, Chapter 8 documents the impact of civil society organizations' in risk management and mitigation. Looking specifically at the triple disaster of 2011, when the eastern coast of Japan was hit by an earthquake, a tsunami, and the subsequent breakdown of the nuclear power plant in Fukushima, Okada maps new research territory. Okada argues that civil society organizations—such as neighborhood associations, residents groups, voluntary organizations, and nonprofit organizations—play a vital role in forming public perceptions in crises. The ethical aspects that Okada discusses in the Japanese case include: (1) spreading knowledge and ideas; (2) providing expert advice; and (3) helping communities to learn for future disasters. Okada discusses actor-centered ethics: the value conflicts and judgments that civil-society organizations face when making decisions that influence individuals' risk management behaviors.

In Chapter 9, Erna Danielsson, Erika Wall, and Susanna Öhman discuss the ethical aspects of using volunteers in live training exercises such as emergency manager's training for chemical, biological, radiological, and nuclear (CBRN) incidents. The authors liken live exercises to research experiments in academic settings, which normally require extensive ethical review before they are conducted if they involve human beings. By examining CBRN exercises in Great Britain and Sweden, and the volunteer's experience in these authentic live trainings of professionals, they cover new ground in research on risk mitigation and crisis management. The shift in perspective required for an ethical treatment of the volunteers could easily happen in the trainings, but are needed far earlier in the planning of the exercises. Danielsson, Wall, and Öhman also talk about the selection bias that occurs as volunteers are selected for exercises, and the unintended consequences this bias may have on policy formation and on rescue workers' actual preparedness to deal with diverse and vulnerable populations.

Adam Luedtke has written the final empirical chapter of the book, Chapter 10, in which he explores the possibilities of an ethical way of addressing the social and economic risks that global migration poses for both migrant-sending and migrant-receiving states. Luedtke's visionary chapter outlines the ethical basis for a negotiation and dispute-settlement mechanism forum for migration, functionally similar to the World Trade Organization. Luedtke argues that the proposed institution, the "World Migration Organization" (WMO), would produce ethical and practical gains while reducing the wide variety of acute risks that threaten people involved in economically or ethno-religiously based migration. Chapter 10 shows how this regulatory scheme would satisfy utilitarian ethical concerns, by optimizing practical benefits and minimizing immigration-related risks; but it also could make world migration outcomes align better with other ethical frameworks, like human rights.

The concluding chapter, Chapter 11, pulls out threads that run deep beneath the individual chapter authors' questions and empirical examples. We return to a discussion about risk and culture; about how and why policymakers and citizens perceive and value risk differently; how our value priorities, with regard to risk, has shifted across time and cultures; and the management challenges these differences pose. We also talk about the empirical examples presented throughout the book of how risks in different policy areas might be successfully and ethically managed, and the communication with stakeholders that this may need to entail. Finally we look forward, to the risks of tomorrow that are shaped in part by how we deal with the risks of today, including the ethics of the choices we make. Policy is ethics in practice, but it is also politics; so when deciding what values are going to be prioritized policymakers would do well to engage communities and stakeholder, not just experts, in the conversation that shapes ethics and risk management.

We hope you will enjoy the book and join us in the emerging conversation.

CHAPTER 2

# THE ETHICAL VALUE OF RISK REDUCTION

## Utilitarianism, Prioritarianism and Cost-Benefit Analysis

**Matthew D. Adler**

In the United States, cost-benefit analysis (CBA) has become the dominant methodology for evaluating regulatory policy. Since 1981, executive-branch agencies have been required by presidential order to assess proposed regulations using CBA. Agencies' assessments of costs and benefits are reviewed by OIRA (Office of Information and Regulatory Affairs), an oversight body within the White House that has thereby come to play a pivotal role in supervising the issuance of regulations (Renda, 2011). CBA is also widely used in scholarship by applied economists. For example, the "value of statistical life" (VSL)—the number used by CBA in assigning a benefit to risk-reduction policies, as discussed below—is the topic of much academic work (Cropper, Hammitt, & Robinson, 2011).

CBA comes in different versions, to be described momentarily. Unweighted CBA—CBA without adjustment via distributional weights—

*Ethics and Risk Management,* pp. 9–29
Copyright © 2015 by Information Age Publishing
All rights of reproduction in any form reserved.

is the version that is most commonly used in the United States. However, this approach to policy evaluation lacks a firm ethical justification.

In this chapter, I will contrast unweighted CBA with three alternative approaches to policy evaluation: utilitarianism, ex ante prioritarianism (EAP), and ex post prioritarianism (EPP). Utilitarianism, of course, is an ethical view whose intellectual history is centuries long. Many distinguished thinkers, from Bentham up to the present, have endorsed utilitarianism. While many others have emphatically rejected it, utilitarianism is surely a view worth serious consideration (Sen & Williams, 1982). Prioritarianism —although appearing much more recently in the march of ideas—also has substantial ethical appeal. It was introduced a generation ago by Parfit, and since then has been discussed extensively by moral philosophers (as cited in Adler, 2012, Ch. 5). EAP and EPP are, in turn, different specifications of prioritarianism under conditions of uncertainty.

The chapter first will describe and critique unweighted CBA. Then I will present the trio of utilitarianism, EAP, and EPP, and survey the pros and cons of each. Finally, I will use risk regulation as a concrete example of the differences between the four approaches.[1] As a shorthand, I will use the term "CBA" to mean *unweighted CBA*. The absence of weights will be implicit, while their presence will be signaled explicitly by the term "distributionally weighted CBA."

One key observation is that utilitarianism, EAP, and EPP (like CBA) are *welfarist* methodologies. All four see individual well-being as the touchstone for policy evaluation (Adler 2012, Ch. 1). This is by way of contrast with rights-based (deontological) approaches, which see individual rights as constraints on the maximization or equalization of well-being. Utilitarianism, EAP, EPP, and CBA can also be contrasted with methodologies such as cost-effectiveness analysis, or a "capabilities" approach, which are hesitant about commensurating the different dimensions of individual well-being (Abellan-Perpinan, Herrero-Blanco, & Pinto-Prades, in press; Alkire, in press).

What this chapter will show, therefore, is that there is considerable room for refinement *within* the "space" of welfarism. Critics of CBA or welfarism regularly conflate the two. But one can improve substantially on unweighted CBA—via utilitarianism, or via prioritarianism in either its "ex ante" or "ex post" specifications—while still hewing to the powerful welfarist insight that the pattern of effects on individual well-being (on the goodness of individuals' lives) should be the fundamental basis for determining which policies government ought to enact.

## Cost-Benefit Analysis

The version of (unweighted) cost-benefit analysis (CBA) that will be described momentarily, and will be generally discussed in this chapter, is the version set forth in the academic literature and employed by many academic economists.[2] CBA in governmental practice, in turn, is grounded upon this academic work—with one important exception, which I will leave aside for now and return to at the end of the chapter.

CBA evaluates policies by summing *money equivalents* (also known as "willingness to pay"/"willingness to accept" amounts). A given person's money equivalent, for a given policy,[3] is the dollar amount that just suffices to counterbalance the policy's impact on her well-being. Assume that, in the status quo,[4] this individual (denoted as individual "$i$") has income $c_i$. Market prices for goods and services are denoted as "$\mathbf{p}$." The usefulness of a given sum of money depends, of course, on these prices—both the overall price level (inflation), and the relative prices of specific goods and services that the individual desires. Finally, individual $i$ has non-income attributes, denoted "$\mathbf{a}_i$," including the state of her health, the quality of her living environment, the amount of free time she has, and so forth. A policy of some sort may change market prices, individuals' incomes, and/ or non-income attributes. Assume that, were a particular policy P to be adopted, individual $i$'s income would be $c_i{}^*$, market prices would be $\mathbf{p}^*$, and this individual's non-income attributes would be $\mathbf{a}_i{}^*$ (as opposed to $c_i$, $\mathbf{p}$, and $\mathbf{a}_i$ with the status quo). Then individual $i$'s money equivalent for policy P, $\Delta c_i$, is the amount such that: individual $i$ is indifferent between $(c_i + \Delta c_i, \mathbf{p}, \mathbf{a}_i)$ and $(c_i{}^*, \mathbf{p}^*, \mathbf{a}_i{}^*)$.[5]

Observe that CBA, as just described, involves a *preference-based* view of well-being. Such a view says: someone is better off with one outcome as compared to second iff[6] she prefers the first outcome; and she is equally well off with the first as compared to the second iff she is indifferent between them. This preference-based view of welfare is pervasive in traditional economics. Its specific role in CBA can be seen by the definition of $\Delta c_i$ as that amount that just suffices to make an individual $i$ indifferent between the two bundles $(c_i + \Delta c_i, \mathbf{p}, \mathbf{a}_i)$ and $(c_i{}^*, \mathbf{p}^*, \mathbf{a}_i{}^*)$.

The preference-based view of well-being, although controversial, has much merit (Adler, 2012, Ch. 3). Moreover, those who embrace competing views, e.g., a hedonic account of well-being, should note that CBA can be revised to mirror these views (Fujiwara & Dolan, in press). For the remainder of the chapter, I take as given the preference view. That is, my critique of CBA and comparison with the trio of alternatives—utilitarianism, EAP, and EPP—will work within the overall framework of *preference welfarism*.

Return to the definition of money equivalents. The definition I provided above presumed that the policymaker was choosing under conditions of certainty. She knew for certain what incomes various people would have; how healthy they would be; how many leisure hours would be available to them; what market prices would be, and so forth, were government to put in place any given policy, or leave in place the status quo. The definition readily generalizes to the case of *uncertainty* (which is of course much more realistic), where government may not know for sure what incomes, health states, and so forth, would result from a given policy. In the case of policy choice under uncertainty, CBA proceeds as follows: Each policy being considered, as well as the status quo, is associated with a *probability distribution* over individuals' incomes, health states, prices, and so forth. Now, $\Delta c_i$ for policy P is the following: the amount of money, added to each possible income amount that $i$ might receive were the status-quo probability distribution over $(c_i, \mathbf{p}, \mathbf{a}_i)$ bundles to be kept in place, that makes individual $i$ indifferent between P and the status quo.[7]

This idea of money equivalents under uncertainty can be illustrated with the example of a risk-reduction policy, and indeed is the basis for the so-called "value of statistical life" (VSL). Assume that, in the status quo, individual $i$ has a probability $\pi_i$ of surviving the current year, and probability $(1 - \pi_i)$ of dying. If she survives, her income this year will be $c_i$. Policy P reduces the risk of death, for example by removing environmental toxins. Policy P is not costless; for example, polluters will need to incur compliance costs to reduce toxins, which may in turn lower shareholder profits, reduce workers' wages, or increase the prices of marketed goods. Imagine that, were the policy to be adopted, individual $i$'s probability of surviving the current year would be greater ($\pi_i^*$, which is greater than $\pi_i$). However, her income this year with the policy in place, were she to survive, would be less ($c_i^*$, which is less than $c_i$). The policy makes her better off on the risk dimension, but worse off on the income dimension.

Assume, for the sake of simplicity, that the policy does not change anything else (the individual's non-income attributes, the price level, or her future income stream conditional on surviving the current year). The status quo then means a probability $\pi_i$ of her surviving the current year and, if so, enjoying income $c_i$. The policy P means a probability $\pi_i^*$ of her surviving the current year and, if so, enjoying income $c_i^*$. In all other respects the status quo and policy are identical. Then individual $i$'s *money equivalent* for the policy is the amount $(\Delta c_i)$ that makes her indifferent, ceteris paribus, between the combination of survival probability $\pi_i$ and income $c_i + \Delta c_i$, and the combination of survival probability $\pi_i^*$ and income $c_i^*$.

If we make the reasonably plausible assumption that individuals have a standing preference for more income, money equivalents will be correlated with well-being changes. In the case of policy choice under conditions of certainty: if an individual is better off with a policy as compared to the status quo, her money equivalent will be positive; if she is worse off, her money equivalent will be negative; if she is indifferent, it will be zero. If she is better off with one policy than a second, her money equivalent for the first policy will be larger; if she is indifferent between the two policies, her money equivalents will be the same. Similarly, under conditions of uncertainty: if an individual's *expected well-being* is greater with a policy as compared to the status quo, her money equivalent will be positive; if her expected well-being is less with the policy as compared to the status quo, her money equivalent will be negative; if the policy does not change her expected well-being, her money equivalent will be zero. If her expected well-being is greater with one policy than a second, her money equivalent for the first policy will be greater; and the two money equivalents will be the same if the two policies produce the same expected well-being for her.

CBA—that is, *unweighted* CBA, without distributional weights—evaluates policies by summing money equivalents across the affected population. Policy P is ranked better (worse) than the status quo, iff it has a positive (negative) sum of money equivalents. Similarly, Policy P$^+$ is ranked better (worse) than Policy P iff the sum of money equivalents for P$^+$ is larger (smaller) than the sum of money equivalents for P.

CBA lacks a firm ethical justification. Indeed, in theoretical welfare economics, the arguments against CBA are well known (e.g., Blackorby & Donaldson, 1990).[8] There is, however, a weird disjunction between this theoretical literature, and the world of applied economics and governmental practice, where CBA is dominant.

Consider the following arguments for CBA. I use quotation marks to indicate each possible argument: a defense of CBA that a proponent of CBA might voice. A criticism of the argument then follows.

## (1) Kaldor-Hicks Efficiency

"If a policy is chosen by CBA over the status quo, the sum total of the money equivalents of the 'winners' (those better off with the policy) is greater, in magnitude, than the sum total of the money equivalents of the 'losers.' Thus, there exists a scheme of transfer payments, from winners to losers, that if coupled with the policy would make everyone better off than the status quo. Although the policy is not Pareto superior to the status quo,[9] it is 'Kaldor-Hicks' efficient." However, the scheme of transfer payments just mentioned may not be administratively feasible, given the costs of taxation, the difficulty of identifying winners and losers, the indirect effects of the transfer payments, etc. Moreover, even if the scheme *is* feasible, the *possibility* of such payments does not itself make the policy *actually* better than the status quo. Ignoring the feasibility considerations just mentioned, assume that whenever P is chosen by CBA over the status quo, there exists a transfer scheme T such that everyone's expected well-being is greater with P + T as compared to the status quo. This itself is hardly grounds for choosing P; it is grounds for choosing P only if, in addition, the decision maker predicts that T will likely be adopted along with P. In actual regulatory practice, CBA is used without any such prediction.

## (2) Long-Run Benefits

"In the long run, virtually everyone will benefit if government uses CBA in deciding which policies to adopt." This argument is sometimes voiced—although rarely rigorously defended—by proponents of CBA. In assessing the argument, we need to keep in mind the question "compared to what?" There is indeed some plausibility in thinking that virtually everyone's expected welfare is greater if the government uses CBA in selecting policies, as compared to complete inaction—whereby government enacts no policies at all, beyond what is required to keep in place a minimal baseline of the "night watchman" state. But there is *no* plausibility at all in thinking that virtually everyone's expected welfare is greater if government uses CBA, as compared to every other defensible policy-analysis procedure that it might use. For example, those whose expected well-being is low, relative to most of the population, might expect to be benefitted—as compared to CBA—if government uses a policy-analysis procedure designed to help the worse off.

## (3) Rough Proxy for Utilitarianism

"CBA is a rough proxy for utilitarianism." The difficulty with this defense of CBA is that the marginal utility of income declines. The welfare gain from the incremental dollar, for a rich person, is less than the welfare gain from the incremental dollar, for a poorer person. Utilitarianism (as we shall see momentarily) evaluates policies by summing utilities: $u_i(P)$ is the utility of person $i$ with policy P; $u_i(S)$ is her utility with the status quo. If the ratio $(u_i(P) - u_i(S))/\Delta c_i$ were constant (if dollars converted into utility at a constant rate) then CBA would be a perfect proxy for utilitarianism. But in fact this ratio tends to decline as individual $i$ becomes richer. What this means is that CBA is a good proxy for utilitarianism only in contexts where the distribution of income among the winners and losers is roughly the same. In other contexts, CBA might well approve a policy even though it reduces total welfare (the sum of utilities) compared to the status quo. CBA with utilitarian distributional weights is, in general, a better proxy for utilitarianism than unweighted CBA: because the former procedure better mimics utilitarianism in the latter contexts, and does so equally well in the former.

## Utilitarianism and Prioritarianism

Utilitarian and prioritarian methodologies for policy evaluation are specific versions of the so-called "social welfare function" (SWF) framework

—a framework backed by much scholarly work (although not reflected in governmental practice, certainly not in the United States). On the SWF framework, see generally Adler (2012).

The utilitarian and prioritarian methodologies, and every other approach within the SWF framework, require an *interpersonally comparable utility function*. This utility function, denoted $u(.)$, is supposed to reflect well-being levels and differences. For example, under certainty: $u_i(P) > u_j(P)$ iff individual $i$ is better off with P than individual $j$. Similarly, $u_i(P) - u_j(P) > u_k(P) - u_l(P)$ iff the difference between individual $i$'s well-being and individual $j$'s well-being (were P to be adopted) is greater than the difference between individual $k$'s well-being and individual $l$'s (were P to be adopted). Under uncertainty: $u_i(P) > u_j(P)$ if the expected well-being of individual $i$ with P is greater than the expected well-being of individual $j$. And similarly for differences in expected well-being.

Where does $u(.)$ come from? This is a difficult but, I believe, answerable question for proponents of the SWF framework. If individuals have the same preferences, the answer is relatively straightforward. Utility theory shows how a given preference structure can be represented by a utility function; $u(.)$ is just a utility function representing these common preferences.

In reality, however, there is surely some degree of preference heterogeneity among the population affected by policy choice. What this means is that individual $i$'s ranking of bundles of income, non-income attributes, and market prices may be different from individual $j$'s ranking. For plausible proposals about the construction of $u(.)$ in such cases, see Marc Fleurbaey's extensive scholarship on "equivalent incomes" (e.g., Fleurbaey and Blanchet, 2013), or my own work on "extended preferences" (Adler, 2012, Ch. 3; Adler, in press). The latter approach, in effect, says this. Assume $i$ and $j$ have different preferences over bundles; $f(.)$ represents the preferences of individual $i$; $h(.)$ represents the preferences of individual $j$. The difficulty is that neither function is unique. For example, if $f^*(.)$ is a rescaled version of $f(.)$, such that $f^*(.) = af(.) + b_i$, with $a_i$ positive, $f^*(.)$ *also* represents $i$'s preferences.

However, we can get around this difficulty by making a few judgments to the effect that individual $j$ with a particular bundle is equally well off as individual $i$ with a particular bundle. This will allow us to determine unique scaling factors for $f(.)$ and $h(.)$, and thereby nail down function $u(.)$. $u_i(P)$ is just $f(P)$ scaled up or down by the appropriate factors; and $u_j(P)$ is just $h(P)$ scaled up or down by the appropriate factors.

Assume, henceforth, that an interpersonally comparable utility function $u(.)$ can indeed be constructed. Utilitarianism and prioritarianism both use this function, but in different ways.

Consider, first, conditions of certainty. Assume there are $N$ individuals in the population of interest. Utilitarianism, as mentioned, sums utilities.

It says: policy P is better than the status quo iff $u_1(P) + u_2(P) + \ldots + u_N(P)$ $> u_1(S) + u_2(S) + \ldots + u_N(S)$. Similarly, policy P* is better than policy P iff $u_1(P^*) + u_2(P^*) + \ldots + u_N(P^*) > u_1(P) + u_2(P) + \ldots + u_N(P)$.

Prioritarianism gives greater weight (priority) to well-being changes affecting worse off individuals. It does so by summing "transformed" utilities: utilities adjusted via a concave transformation function, which I'll denote as $g(.)$, and which is illustrated in Figure 2.1. Under certainty, the prioritarian methodology is as follows: policy P is better than the status quo S iff $g(u_1(P)) + g(u_2(P)) + \ldots + g(u_N(P)) > g(u_1(S)) + g(u_2(S)) + \ldots + g(u_N(S))$. Similarly, policy P* is better than policy P iff $g(u_1(P^*)) + \ldots + g(u_N(P^*)) > g(u_1(P)) + \ldots + g(u_N(P))$.

The difference between utilitarianism and prioritarianism — between a methodology that simply sums utilities, and one that gives priority to the worse off—is captured by the so-called Pigou-Dalton principle. Let $\Delta u$ denote a positive change in well-being. Assume that Policy P effects a pure transfer of well-being from someone who is better off to someone who is worse off, leaving everyone else unaffected. (Of course this is an unrealistic case, but in ethical debate it is often simplified and hypothetical cases that allow us to sharpen our understanding of the differences between competing approaches). That is to say, one individual in the status quo is at level $u_{Higher}$, while another is at level $u_{Lower} < u_{Higher}$. Were the policy to be enacted, the first individual would lose $\Delta u$ in well-being, while the second individual would gain exactly that, such that the first ends up with $u_{Higher} - \Delta u$, the second with $u_{Lower} + \Delta u$, and is still no better off than the first (either strictly worse off, or equally well off).

The Pigou-Dalton principle stipulates that, in such a case of a pure welfare transfer, the policy is better than the status quo. Utilitarianism does not conform to the Pigou-Dalton principle: note that utilitarianism will rank the policy and the status quo as equally good, since the total sum of utilities is unchanged. By contrast, by virtue of the concave shape of the transformation function $g(.)$, prioritarianism *will* conform to the Pigou-Dalton principle, as shown in Figure 2.1.

Why embrace the Pigou-Dalton principle? Why might it be seen as ethically attractive? One way to see its force is through the lens of individual "claims" (Adler, 2012, Ch. 5). Each person, we might say, has a standing ethical claim to be made better off. If we can improve one person's welfare, and leave everyone else unaffected, then we should do so.[10] Often, however, claims will conflict. Some will be made better off by a policy choice, some worse off. The Pigou-Dalton principle expresses a plausible basic principle for handling conflicting claims. Consider the case described two paragraphs above: The first individual (the one who would be at $u_{Higher}$ with the status quo, and $u_{higher} - \Delta u$ with the policy) has a claim in favor of the status quo, since she is better off (by Δ*u*) with the status quo. The second individual has a claim in favor of the policy. Since everyone else (by hypothesis)

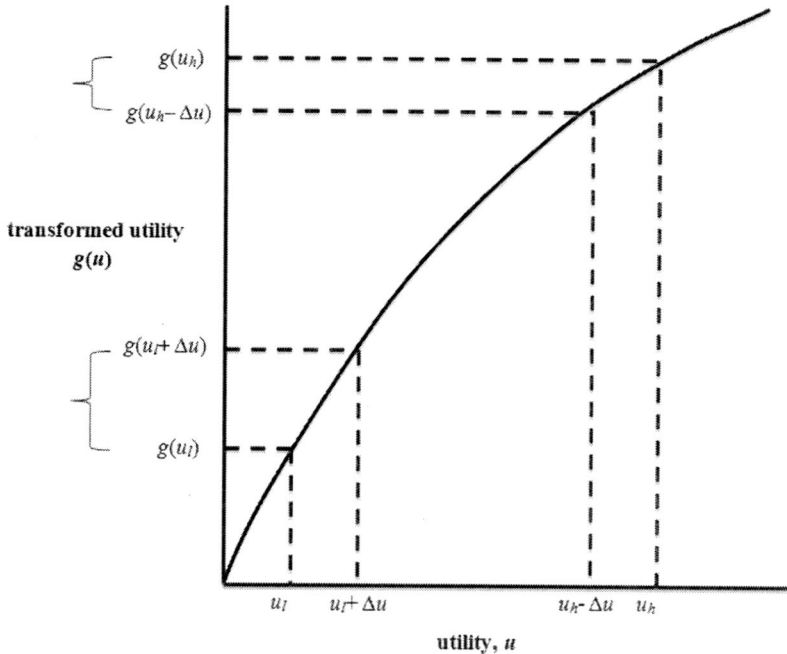

*Note:* A Pigou-Dalton transfer moves $u_h$ to $(u_h - \Delta u)$, and moves $u_l$ to $(u_l + \Delta u)$. Note that this yields a net increase in the sum of transformed utilities, since $g(u_l + \Delta u) - g(u_l) > g(u_h) - g(u_h - \Delta u)$.

*Source:* This figure was originally published as Figure 2.2 in Adler, Matthew (2012) *Well-Being and Fair Distribution: Beyond Cost-Benefit Analysis*, New York, NY: Oxford University Press, USA, p.79. Reprinted here by permission of Oxford University Press, USA, http://www.oup.com.

**Figure 2.1.**   The weight given by prioritarianism to well-being changes affecting worse off through "transformed" utilities.

is unaffected, they all have zero claims, and the ranking of the policy versus status quo comes down to deciding whether the first individual or the second has the stronger claim. But (very plausibly) the second individual does. The second individual can reasonably say to the first: "What I would gain, were the policy to be enacted, is exactly what you would lose. Insofar as the magnitude of well-being *changes* is *one* factor determinative of claim strength, our claims are equally strong. Moreover, I am worse off than you in the status quo, and would remain no better off even if the policy were adopted. Insofar as well-being *levels* are *another* factor determinative of claim strength, my claim is stronger. On balance, don't I have the stronger claim?"

Whether justified via the language of "claims," or in some other way, the Pigou-Dalton principle seems very plausible. Complexities emerge, however, when we shift to the context of policy choice under uncertainty (Adler 2012, Ch. 7). Let an outcome be a possible allocation of bundles (income, non-income attributes, market prices, etc.) to each person in the population. The status quo corresponds to a probability distribution across outcomes; a given regulatory policy is a different such distribution. Each individual has an expected well-being number (her expected utility) associated with the status quo, and with each regulatory option. We can distinguish three rules for evaluating policies. I describe them informally; precise formulas are given in a footnote.[11]

## (1) Utilitarianism

The status quo and each policy option are assigned a number equaling the expected sum of individual utilities (which in turn is mathematically equal to the sum of individuals' expected utilities).

## (2) Ex Ante Prioritarianism (EAP)

The idea, here, is to apply the transformation function $g(.)$ to each individual's expected utility. The status quo and each policy are assigned a number equaling the sum of transformed expected utility.

## (3) Ex Post Prioritarianism (EPP)

While the structure of assessment for EAP is individual-by-individual (assigning each an expected well-being number, and only then bringing the $g(.)$ function into play), EPP proceeds in a different fashion. It first assigns an overall ethical value to each possible outcome, namely the sum of transformed utilities. It then calculates the probabilistic expectation of these ethical values, that is, the expected value of the sum of transformed individual utility.[12]

Table 2.1 illustrates the difference between utilitarianism, EAP, and EPP. Utilitarianism is indifferent between the status quo and the Policy. The sum of expected utilities (or the expected sum of individual utilities) is 100 in the status quo, and 100 for the policy.

**Table 2.1.   The Difference Between Utilitarianism, EAP, and EPP Regarding the Status Quo and the Policy**

|  | Status Quo | | | Policy | | |
|---|---|---|---|---|---|---|
|  | *Outcome x, Prob. = 1/2* | *Outcome y, Prob. = 1/2* | *Expected Utility* | *Outcome z, Prob. = 1/2* | *Outcome w, Prob. = 1/2* | *Expected Utility* |
| Jim | 70 | 30 | **50** | 50 | 60 | **55** |
| June | 30 | 70 | **50** | 50 | 40 | **45** |

*Note:* The numbers that are not bold are individual utilities, while the bold numbers are expected utilities. For example, the status quo yields outcome x with probability ½; in outcome x, Jim has utility 70 and June utility 30. These utilities are switched in outcome y. Jim's expected utility from the gamble between x and y is 50, as is June's.

EAP prefers the status quo. This is because (relative to the Policy) the status quo effects a pure transfer in *expected well-being* from Jim to June. With the policy, Jim's expected well-being would be 55, while June's would be 45. If the status quo is left in place, Jim's expected well-being decreases by 5 units, and June's increases by the same amount.

Finally, EPP prefers the Policy. This is because each of the two possible policy outcomes (each person getting 50 units of realized utility, or one getting 60 and the other 40) is preferred by the Pigou-Dalton principle to each of the two possible status quo outcomes (Jim getting 70 and June 30, or vice versa). Thus the sum of transformed utilities for each of the latter outcomes is less than the sum of transformed utilities for each of the former; and therefore the expected value of the sum of transformed utilities (the EPP formula) is greater for the Policy as compared to the status quo.

To see more fully what's at stake between Utilitarianism, EAP and EPP, consider two new axioms: (1) *the ex ante Pareto principle*, namely that if each person's expected well-being is greater with one policy as compared to a second, the first is better; and (2) *stochastic dominance*, namely that if every possible outcome of one policy is better than every possible outcome of a second, the first policy is better. As Table 2.2 shows, utilitarianism has the virtue of satisfying both of these. EAP conforms to the ex ante Pareto principle, but violates stochastic dominance; EPP conforms to stochastic dominance, but violates the ex ante Pareto principle.

The choice between utilitarianism, EAP, and EPP thus poses something of a trilemma. Stochastic dominance seems to be a very basic principle of (consequentialist) rationality. If one policy is sure to yield a better outcome than a second, how can choosing the second be rational? Ex ante Pareto seems to embody one aspect of (welfarist) respect for persons: if well-being is the ultimate grounds for ethically justified choice, how can it be better

**Table 2.2.   Utilitarianism, EAP and EPP With Regard to the Ex-Ante Pareto Principle and Stochastic Ddominance**

|  | Status Quo | | | Policy | | |
|---|---|---|---|---|---|---|
|  | Outcome x, Prob. = 1/2 | Outcome y, Prob. = 1/2 | Expected Utility | Outcome z, Prob. = 1/2 | Outcome w, Prob. = 1/2 | Expected Utility |
| Pam | 90 | 10 | **50** | $50 - \varepsilon$ | $50 - \varepsilon$ | **$50 - \varepsilon$** |
| Sarah | 10 | 90 | **50** | $50 - \varepsilon$ | $50 - \varepsilon$ | **$50 - \varepsilon$** |

*Note.* The table follows the same format as Table 2.1. The number $\varepsilon$ is positive. Utilitarianism chooses the status quo. EAP also does, since the prioritarian transformation function $g(.)$ always has a positive slope, as can be seen from Figure 2.1. The value $g(50 - \varepsilon)$ is less than the value $g(50)$. Finally, for any given transformation function, there is some $\varepsilon$ sufficiently small such that the sum of $g(90)$ and $g(10)$ is less than the sum of $g(50 - \varepsilon)$ and $g(50 - \varepsilon)$. Thus, if $\varepsilon$ is small enough, the outcome in which Pam gets utility 90 and Sarah 10, or vice versa, is seen as worse (by the prioritarian) than the outcome in which both get $50 - \varepsilon$. And so EPP prefers the Policy.

Note that ex ante Pareto favors the status quo, since each person's expected well-being is greater there. Thus Utilitarianism and EAP conform to that principle, while EPP violates it. Stochastic dominance is more subtle. According to prioritarianism (as just explained), every possible outcome of the status quo is worse than every possible outcome of the Policy, with $\varepsilon$ sufficiently small. Thus EAP violates stochastic dominance, while EPP satisfies it. According to utilitarianism, every possible outcome of the status quo is better than every possible outcome of the Policy. (For the utilitarian, an outcome with total utility 100 is better than an outcome with total utility $100 - 2\varepsilon$.). Thus utilitarianism, given its own scheme for ranking outcomes, satisfies stochastic dominance by choosing the status quo.

to choose the course of action reducing everyone's expected well-being? Finally, the Pigou-Dalton principle, as already discussed, has a powerful justification in the notion of individuals' claims.

However, it turns out to be impossible to satisfy the trio of stochastic dominance, ex ante Pareto, and Pigou-Dalton. Utilitarianism, EAP, and EPP each make different choices about which two of the trio to respect.

My own (ethical) preference is for EPP. But it is beyond the scope of this chapter to make the case for EPP, as against utilitarianism and EAP. Rather, what I wish to stress here is that a plausible ethical defense can be mounted for each—by contrast with unweighted CBA, criticized above. In the case of EPP and EAP, this defense is just the Pigou-Dalton principle, combined with either stochastic dominance or ex ante Pareto. In the case of utilitarianism, this defense is the realization that—however attractive Pigou-Dalton might seem at first blush—it cannot be combined with ex ante Pareto and stochastic dominance.[13]

These three methodologies can each be put into practice via direct implementation, namely characterizing each policy as a probability distribution across outcomes; converting these into utility numbers for individuals in the population of interest; and then applying the utilitarian, EAP, or EPP formula. Indeed, this is how the approaches are sometimes used in academic work.

However, utilitarianism and EAP can also be approximated by CBA with distributional weights (Adler, 2013). The generic form of weighted CBA is to assign each policy the sum of individuals' money equivalents for the policy, multiplied by individual weighting factors (which are determined by each individual's status quo bundle, and do not vary from policy to policy). That is, policy P is assigned the value $w_1\Delta c_i + \ldots + w_N\Delta c_N$. Policy P* is assigned the value $w_1\Delta c_i^* + \ldots + w_N\Delta c_N^*$.

In the case of utilitarianism, the weights adjust for the declining marginal utility of money. An individual with a lower such marginal utility (e.g., a wealthier person) is given a lower weight. In the case of EAP, the weights have a dual role—both to adjust for the declining marginal utility of money, *and* to give greater weight to well-being changes affecting the worse off. EPP (it turns out) is more difficult to approximate with weights, and is thus probably better implemented directly.

## Risk Regulation

This section will review some key results regarding the application of the four methodologies discussed previously (CBA without distributional weights [again, "CBA"], utilitarianism, EAP, and EPP) to a particular policy domain, fatality risk regulation. Much regulatory policy, certainly in the United States, is concerned with reducing fatality risks from pollutants, automobiles, workplace hazards, or consumer products. Benefits attributed to fatality risk reduction, via the "value of statistical life" (VSL), are central to the cost-benefit analyses that regulatory bodies submit to OIRA (Cropper, Hammitt, & Robinson, 2011; on governmental practices with respect to the VSL, see generally Robinson, 2007). Moreover, this domain nicely illustrates similarities and differences among the four methodologies.

What follows is an informal summary of the detailed, formal analysis undertaken in Adler, Hammitt, and Treich (2014).[14] We can model the four methodologies in a tractable manner by thinking of individuals as differentiated by income and by the risk of dying in the current period (e.g., year). To be sure, individuals have many other attributes, but to keep the model simple these are assumed to be identical.[15]

Thus the status quo is a list of income amounts and survival probabilities for each person in the population. A given policy is a different such list—for example, increasing the survival probability for some, at some cost in income, which they or others incur.

Each of the four methodologies uses some formula for assigning an overall number to a given policy option (i.e., the status quo and each policy alternative). We might call this number the "social value" or "ethical value" of the policy option. It seeks to encapsulate the overall goodness of each option, and to do so in a way that is impartial between everyone in the population.[16] In the case of CBA, the social/ethical value of a given option is just the sum of money equivalents; in the case of utilitarianism, it is the sum of expected utilities; for prioritarianism, it is either the expected sum of transformed utilities (EPP), or the sum of each individual's transformed expected utility (EAP).

We now think about the *change* in social value that occurs with a small increase in a given person's status quo survival probability. (Small changes allow us to deploy powerful techniques from calculus in comparing the four methodologies. Moreover, regulatory policies in the United States typically do produce only small changes in fatality risk, for example, a 1 in 100,000 reduction in someone's annual risk.). If we reduce a given person's chance of dying during the next year by 1 in 100,000, for example, what is the change in social value according to CBA? According to utilitarianism, EAP, or EPP?

Let us use $SVRR^{CBA}$ to mean the change in social value according to CBA (the change in the sum of money equivalents) per unit of risk reduction. $SVRR^{U}$, $SVRR^{EAP}$, and $SVRR^{EPP}$ are the parallel values for the other methodologies. SVRR stands for "social value of risk reduction."

$SVRR^{CBA}$ is just what economists call VSL. That latter term means the amount of money that someone is willing to pay or accept in exchange for a small change in her risk, divided by the risk change. And it's not hard to see that this is exactly the same as $SVRR^{CBA}$.

To be clear, SVRR (for each of the methodologies) is an individual-specific value. It quantifies the social/ethical gain to be had from reducing a particular person's fatality risk, given *his or her* attributes. As already mentioned, the simple model being used here characterizes individuals in terms of income and baseline (status quo) survival probability. Thus, in this modeling context, SVRR can depend upon someone's income and/or her baseline survival probability.

SVRR is an indicator of the social priority given to reducing various individuals' risks. Assume that SVRR for one person, Alice, is greater than SVRR for a second, Bob. This means that a unit of risk reduction, delivered to Alice, yields a greater social gain than a unit of risk reduction, delivered to Bob. A methodology with an SVRR greater for Alice than Bob will prefer a policy that reduces Alice's risks, to a policy that reduces Bob's by the same amount, ceteris paribus. Relatedly, this methodology will be willing to incur greater costs (in lost income) for a given reduction in Alice's risks, than for the same reduction in Bob's risks.

SVRR is "positively income-sensitive" if this number increases with income, ceteris paribus. This means that if Gregory has greater income than Hugh, and both have the same baseline survival probability, SVRR for Gregory is greater than for Hugh. Similarly, to say that SVRR is "positively sensitive to baseline risk" means: if Xavier has a lower baseline survival probability (greater baseline fatality risk) than Yolanda, and the same income, Xavier's SVRR is greater. SVRR has the property of "equal value of risk reduction" if everyone has the same SVRR, regardless of income or baseline risk.

The key contribution of Adler, Hammitt, and Treich (2014) is to *compare* SVRR$^{CBA}$, SVRR$^{U}$, SVRR$^{EAP}$, and SVRR$^{EPP}$ with respect to income sensitivity and sensitivity to baseline risk. Table 2.3 summarizes our results.

**Table 2.3.  The Social Value of Risk Reduction (SVRR) for Four Policy Methodologies**

|  | *Positively Income-Sensitive?* | *Positively Sensitive to Baseline Risk?* | *Equal Value of Risk Reduction?* |
|---|---|---|---|
| CBA | Yes | Yes | No |
| Utilitarianism | Yes | No | No |
| EPP | Under some parameter assumptions | No | Under restrictive parameter assumptions |
| EAP | Under some parameter assumptions | Yes | No |

As Table 2.3 suggests, and as the underlying analysis shows in great detail, each of the three SWF methodologies differs in important ways from the other two. But let's train our attention here on the comparison between CBA, on the one hand, and the three alternatives, on the other.

Note that SVRR$^{CBA}$ is positively income-sensitive. The reason, it turns out, is twofold. First, income increases well-being; a unit of risk reduction for a higher-income person translates into a bigger change in expected well-being than for a lower-income person, ceteris paribus. Second, for a given change in expected well-being, someone with a lower expected marginal utility of money—for example, a richer person—will have a larger money equivalent.

SVRR$^{CBA}$ is also positively sensitive to baseline risk. Intuitively, if someone has a lower baseline survival probability, a dollar of income is less useful for him or her—because it is less likely that the individual will survive to spend that income—and thus that person's willingness to use that income in paying for risk reduction is greater.

Note that the utilitarian SVRR, as with CBA, *is* positively income-sensitive. However, SVRR$^{U}$ is not sensitive to baseline risk. Neither is SVRR$^{EPP}$, although SVRR$^{EAP}$ is. Surprisingly, perhaps, each of these prioritarian

SVRRs *can* be positively income-sensitive. This depends upon the degree of ethical preference for the worse off (the shape of the transformation function in Figure 2.1 shown previously), and also on the specific utility function that translates wealth into well-being. Channeling risk reduction to a higher-income person can be expected to yield a greater increase in well-being, but this benefit is conferred upon someone who is better off (by virtue of having higher income) and thus the benefit is ethically down-weighted.

Note that the combination of properties characteristic of SVRR^CBA—positive income-sensitivity and positive sensitivity to baseline risk—does not hold true of utilitarianism or EPP, and only of EAP under certain parameter assumptions. This shows that welfarist critiques of CBA are *not* moot. The proponent of CBA cannot respond to criticism by utilitarians or prioritarians by saying: "In practice, all of our methodologies can be expected to achieve basically the same ranking of policies."[17] Rather, as Table 2.3 shows, CBA differs importantly from the others in how it channels risk reduction. (See also Adler [2013], illustrating the difference between CBA and weighted CBA with respect to risk regulation.). To be sure, in a specific policy choice situation, CBA and one or another of the SWFs might end up with the same ordering of the options. (That could of course also be true of CBA and a non-welfarist methodology.) But its general tendencies in distributing risk reduction, as summarized in the two properties of "positive income sensitivity" and "positive sensitivity to baseline risk," are different from utilitarianism, EPP, and EAP (except with certain parameter assumptions).

A further result (not stated in Adler, Hammitt, & Treich, 2014) can be shown. In an important sense, CBA has a greater *degree* of income sensitivity than all of the other methodologies. Assume that Rich has more income than Poor, but the two have the same survival probabilities. For a given risk reduction $\Delta p$ that a policy might produce for Poor, let $\Delta p^*$ be the risk reduction for Rich with the same social value. It turns out that $\Delta p^*$ according to CBA is *smaller* than $\Delta p^*$ according to utilitarianism, EAP and EPP.[18]

While CBA and the other methodologies differ in *whose* risk reductions they prioritize, they have in common the feature of according *some* such priority. CBA and the other methodologies are similar in that they all violate "equal value of risk reduction" (with the exception of EPP under restrictive parameter assumptions). Equal value of risk reduction demands social indifference between giving one person, Sara, a unit of risk reduction, and giving that unit to Trish, regardless of how Sara and Trish may differ—in this model, regardless of differences in their incomes or baseline risks. But such differences could well mean that the size of the change in Sara's well-being from the unit of risk reduction is different from the size of the change in Trish's. It is therefore not to be expected that welfarist methodologies will satisfy equal value of risk reduction; and indeed the methodologies discussed here generally do not.

I mentioned earlier that the academic version of CBA (the version described in this chapter) differs in one critical respect from the methodology employed in governmental practice. We now come to that difference. U.S. regulators generally assign a unit of risk reduction the same money value regardless of the beneficiary. In other words, VSL (the willingness to pay per unit of risk reduction, i.e., SVRR$^{CBA}$) is not differentiated by an individual's income, baseline risk, or other characteristics such as age, gender, education, health state, etc. The VSL that one sees in U.S. regulatory practice is, instead (some estimate of) the population-average willingness to pay per unit of risk reduction. In an infamous episode, the EPA considered differentiating VSL by age; but this generated a political firestorm, and U.S. regulators have since used population-average values (Robinson 2007).

Table 2.3 calls this practice into question, just as it calls into question academic (unweighted) CBA. Perhaps non-welfarists have good grounds for assigning equal ethical value to each unit of risk reduction (regardless of the beneficiary) but welfarists do not.


## Conclusion

The use of cost-benefit analysis (CBA) for environmental and risk regulation has been vigorously criticized by non-welfarists (Ackerman & Heinzerling, 2004). This chapter offers a less familiar critique: CBA is problematic even from the perspective of welfarism.

Welfarists believe that the ethical status of policy options is wholly determined by their impacts on individual well-being, not by deontological constraints or other such non-welfare considerations (Adler, 2012, Ch. 1). Some welfarists (utilitarians) focus solely on the sum total of well-being. Others ("prioritarians") give greater weight to well-being changes affecting worse-off individuals, and thereby assign ethical significance both to aggregate welfare and to its distribution. Prioritarianism under conditions of uncertainty bifurcates into "ex ante" (EAP) and "ex post" (EPP) versions. A plausible ethical case can be made for each of the trio of utilitarianism, EAP, and EPP.

CBA in its traditional, textbook version evaluates policies by summing money equivalents, without distributional weights. Money equivalents for individuals' risk reductions are specifically calculated using the construct of the "value of statistical life" (VSL). CBA *is* a version of welfarism (Adler, 2012, pp. 88–114), but not an ethically attractive one, for reasons summarized above.

Moreover, the difference between CBA and more plausible specifications of welfarism is not trivial. *Each* of the trio of utilitarianism, EPP, and EAP differs from CBA, in deciding whose risks to reduce when risk reduction is not costless. CBA (in its textbook version, not actual governmental practice) gives priority to individuals with more income and to individuals at higher baseline risk of dying. This combination of properties is not true of utilitarianism or EPP, and only of EAP under certain parameter assumptions. Moreover, CBA turns out to give *greater* priority to those with higher incomes than any of the other approaches.

CBA in governmental practice treats everyone equally when it comes to risk reduction. The money equivalent of reducing someone's fatality risk is calculated using a population-average VSL, so that this amount is identical regardless of the beneficiary's income, baseline risk, or other characteristics such as age or health state. This too is problematic from the perspective of welfarism. The well-being benefit from reducing someone's risk will generally not be constant across the population. Whatever the features that make for a better life (income, health, leisure, friends, pleasure), someone who is better situated with respect to those features gains a greater amount in expected well-being from a given reduction in her fatality risk, than someone who is less well situated. For utilitarians, this gain in expected well-being just *is* the ethical benefit of risk reduction. For prioritarians, the ethical benefit from a unit of risk reduction depends not only on the expected gain to well-being/gain to expected well-being, but also upon distributional considerations, namely whether the recipient can expect to be worse off than others (EPP) or is worse off than others in term of her expected well-being (EAP). But here, too, we should not anticipate that this ethical benefit will turn out to be the same regardless of the features of the person whose risk is reduced.

What is the lesson in all this for risk management? The lesson is methodological, namely that we need to move beyond CBA (both the textbook and governmental versions) as tools for evaluating risk-reduction policies. One way to do so is via CBA with distributional weights (Adler, 2013). Another is via direct application of utilitarian or prioritarian social welfare functions (Adler, 2012). Both are feasible, and would constitute ethical progress. Non-welfarists may well object, arguing that an ethically justified framework for risk regulation would look very different from CBA, utilitarianism, EAP, or EPP. The broader debate between welfarists and non-welfarists cannot be engaged here. Still, welfarists and non-welfarists can at least concur that CBA in either of the forms discussed in this chapter —summing distributionally unweighted money equivalents, or assigning a constant money value for each unit of risk reduction—is a flawed basis for risk management.

## NOTES

1. It is, of course, impossible to provide a full treatment of these topics in a brief and non-formal chapter. I have addressed them at much greater length elsewhere (Adler, 2012; Adler, 2013; Adler, Hammitt, & Treich, 2014; Adler, 2015; Adler, in press).

2. A fuller treatment of the topics covered in this section is provided by Adler (2012, pp. 88–114, 554–571); citations to the academic literature on CBA are given there.

3. "Policy" is a very general term, meant to indicate some course of action that government might undertake. Enacting a regulatory measure is a policy. So is, for example, building infrastructure.

4. The status quo is some baseline. By contrast with utilitarianism, EAP, and EPP, the procedure of CBA requires such a baseline—relative to which money equivalents are defined. Typically, the baseline is *inaction*: what would occur, were government to leave existing laws in place rather than changing the law by enacting some new regulatory measure or other type of policy. I therefore label the baseline as the "status quo." However, the reader should understand that the methodology of CBA does not depend upon which baseline is chosen. To be sure, the ranking of policies by CBA in any given policy choice situation may well change, depending upon the choice of baseline; but the general methodology about to be described does not.

5. The definition of money equivalent just offered equates it with an individual's "equivalent variation" rather than her "compensating variation." On the reason for doing this see (Adler, 2012, pp. 92–98; Adler, 2013).

6. The term "iff," used often in this chapter, is an abbreviation for "if and only if." "A iff B" states an equivalence between A and B: A is the case whenever B is the case, and only when B is the case.

7. Let $(c_i,\ \mathbf{p},\ a_i)$ denote a possible bundle of income, market prices, and non-income attributes that individual $i$ might have. Let $\pi_S(c_i,\ \mathbf{p},\ a_i)$ be the status quo probability of bundle $(c_i,\ \mathbf{p}, \mathbf{a}_i)$, and $\pi_P(c_i,\ \mathbf{p},\ \mathbf{a}_i)$ the probability of that bundle given policy P. Let $\mathbf{B}$ be the set of all possible bundles, and $f_i(.)$ an expected utility function—such that the ranking of probability distributions in terms of their expected $f_i(.)$ values corresponds to individual $i$'s preference ranking of the distributions. Then $\Delta c_i$ is the amount of money such that:

$$\sum_{(c_i,\mathbf{p},\mathbf{a}_i)\in\mathbf{B}} \pi_S\left(c_i,\mathbf{p},\mathbf{a}_i\right) f_i\left(c_i+\Delta_i, \mathbf{p}, a_i\right)= \sum_{(c_i,\mathbf{p},\mathbf{a}_i)\in\mathbf{B}} \pi_p\left(c_i, \mathbf{p}, a_i\right) f_i\left(c_i, \mathbf{p}, a_i\right)$$

8. Adler and Posner (2006) argues against CBA as a criterion of moral rightness, and suggests that CBA should instead be seen as a rough proxy for overall well-being. The correlation between CBA and overall well-being in choosing among a given group of policies depends on the extent of income differences among those affected by this choice; distributional weights adjust for such differences.

9. The Pareto principle (strictly, "weak" Pareto) says that if everyone has greater well-being with one policy than a second (the first policy is "Pareto superior"), the first policy is better. For a "stronger" version of the principle, also accepted by economists, see below note 10.

10. This is what the "strong" Pareto principle says: if one or more individuals are better off with one outcome as compared to a second, and everyone else is indifferent, then the first outcome is better.

11. Let $b_i$ be individual $i$'s bundle of income, market prices, and non-income attributes. That is, $b_i = (c_i, \mathbf{p}, \mathbf{a}_i)$. Outcome $x = (b_1^x, b_2^x, ..., b_N^x)$, with $b_i^x$ denoting the bundle of individual $i$ in outcome $x$. Let $\pi_S(x)$ denote the probability of $x$ given the status quo; and $\pi_P(x)$ the probability of $x$ given policy P. Let $\mathbf{O}$ be the set of all outcomes. Let $u_i(x)$ denote the utility assigned by $u(.)$, our interpersonally comparable utility function, to individual $i$ in outcome $x$ (given his bundle there, $b_i^x$). Then utilitarianism, EAP, and EPP employ the following formulas for assigning a value to a given option, which are then ranked in the order of these values. (I give the formula for an arbitrary policy P; the formula for the status quo option of inaction is produced by substituting "S" for "P."). (1) Utilitarianism.

$$\sum_{x \in o} \pi_p(x)\left(\sum_{i=1}^{N} u_i(x)\right) = \sum_{i=1}^{N}\sum_{x \in o} \pi_p(x) u_i(x). \quad (2) \text{ EAP. } \sum_{i=1}^{N} g\left(\sum_{x \in o} \pi_P(x) u_i(x)\right) \quad (3) \text{ EPP.}$$

$$\sum_{x \in o} \pi_P(x)\left(\sum_{i=1}^{N} g\left(u_i(x)\right)\right) = \sum_{i=1}^{N}\sum_{x \in o} \pi_P(x) g\left(u_i(x)\right).$$

12. To be sure, as the formula for EPP in the footnote above shows, the expected value of the sum of transformed utilities is equal to the sum of each individual's expected transformed utility. Neither is the same, mathematically, as EAP: the sum of each individual's transformed expected utility.

13. To be sure, a case *against* Pigou-Dalton (against either EAP or EPP) is not yet a case *for* utilitarianism. John Harsanyi's so-called "aggregation theorem" seeks to make that affirmative case (see Adler 2012, pp. 526–527, n. 89); Mongin and Pivato (in press).

14. See also the related discussion in Adler (2013), illustrating the difference between CBA and weighted CBA with respect to risk regulation.

15. In the Adler, Hammitt, and Treich (2014) model, $c_i$ is wealth, not current income; but the two are the same if resources held in previous periods have not been saved. Because the discussion in the chapter until now has been pitched in terms of income, not wealth, I describe the Adler, Hammitt, and Treich (2014) results in those terms.

16. Such impartiality is characteristic of CBA and the three methodologies, whatever their other differences.

17. Indeed, even if CBA and the three others *were* the same with respect to positive income-sensitivity and sensitivity to baseline risk, this *gross* similarity would not mean that the four methodologies would converge in their ranking of policies in any given choice situation. Income and baseline-risk sensitivity are simply first-cut indicators of the degree of similarity between the methodologies.

18. In terms of the model of Adler, Hammitt, and Treich (2014), this result assumes that $v'(.)$ is zero.

## REFERENCES

Abellan-Perpinan, J. M., Herrero-Blanco, C., & Pinto-Prades, J. L. (in press). QALY-based cost-effectiveness analysis. In M. D. Adler and M. Fleurbaey (Eds.), *Oxford Handbook of Well-Being and Public Policy*. New York, NY: Oxford University Press.

Ackerman, F., & Heinzerling, L. (2004). *Priceless: On knowing the price of everything and the value of nothing*. New York, NY: New Press.

Adler, M. D. (2012). *Well-being and fair distribution: Beyond cost-benefit analysis*. New York, NY: Oxford University Press.

Adler, M. D. (2013). Cost-benefit analysis and distributional weights: An overview. [Unpublished manuscript]. Retrieved November 19, 2014, from http://papers/ssrn.com/sol3/papers.cfm?abstract_id=2313388

Adler, M. D. (in press). Extended preferences. In M. D. Adler and M. Fleurbaey (Eds.), *Oxford handbook of well-being and public policy*. New York, NY: Oxford University Press.

Adler, M. D., Hammitt, J. K., & Treich, N. (2014). The social value of mortality risk reduction: VSL versus the social welfare function approach. *Journal of Health Economics*, *35*, 82–93.

Adler, M. D., & Posner, E. (2006). *New foundations of cost-benefit analysis*. Cambridge, MA: Harvard University Press.

Alkire, S. (in press). The capabilities approach. In M. D. Adler & M. Fleurbaey (Eds.), *Oxford handbook of well-being and public policy*. New York, NY: Oxford University Press.

Blackorby, C., & Donaldson, D. (1990). A review article: The case against the use of the sum of compensating variations in cost-benefit analysis. *The Canadian Journal of Economics*, *23*, 471–494.

Adler, M. D. (2015). Welfarism, equity, and the choice between statistical and identified victims. In I. G. Cohen, N. Daniels, & N. Eyal (Eds.), *Identified versus Statistical Lives*. New York, NY: Oxford University Press.

Cropper, M., Hammitt, J. K., & Robinson, L.A. (2011). Valuing mortality risk reductions: Progress and challenges. *Annual Review of Resource Economics*, *3*, 313–336.

Fleurbaey, M., & Blanchet, D. (2013). *Beyond GDP: Measuring welfare and assessing sustainability*. New York, NY: Oxford University Press.

Fujiwara, D., & Dolan, P. (in press). Happiness-based policy analysis. In M. D. Adler & M. Fleurbaey (Eds.), *Oxford handbook of well-being and public policy*. New York, NY: Oxford University Press.

Mongin, P., & Pivato, M. (in press). Social evaluation under risk and uncertainty. In M. D. Adler & M. Fleurbaey (Eds.), *Oxford handbook of well-being and public policy*. New York, NY: Oxford University Press.

Renda, A. (2011). *Law and economics in the RIA world*. Cambridge, England: Intersentia.

Robinson, L. A. (2007). How U.S. government agencies value mortality risk reductions. *Review of Environmental Economics and Policy*, *1*, 283–299.

Sen, A., & Williams, B. (Eds.). (1982). *Utilitarianism and beyond*. Cambridge, England: Cambridge University Press.

CHAPTER 3

# THE ETHICS OF RISK MANAGEMENT IN THE EUROPEAN UNION AND THE UNITED STATES

## A Comparative Perspective

**David J. Vogel**

### INTRODUCTION

This chapter will examine the ethical dimensions of risk management through a comparative historical study of regulatory policies and politics in the United States and the European Union. It will begin by contrasting the contemporary approaches to managing health, safety, and environmental risks in the United States and the European Union. It then will place the contemporary period in historical perspective, seeking to describe and explain how and why American and European approaches to risk management have shifted over time. Both sets of comparisons reveal the very different values that can and do underlie risk management policies

*Ethics and Risk Management*, pp. 31–43
Copyright © 2015 by Information Age Publishing
All rights of reproduction in any form reserved.

across the Atlantic. These differences, in turn, have had important policy consequences.

Risk management policies are not ethically neutral: they invariably privilege some values—and interests—over others. Policies that lead to more stringent regulations may make it more likely that potentially dangerous risks or hazards will be addressed and that those who are subject to these risks will be appropriately protected. But at the same time, they may also harm public welfare by leading to the misallocation of both public and private resources, and may make it more difficult for firms to develop and market new welfare-enhancing technologies. Alternatively, policies that result in less stringent regulations may expose vulnerable populations (as well as society as a whole) to hazards that could have been prevented if appropriate regulations had been in effect. This in turn may reduce public trust in the regulatory policy process.

## BACKGROUND

The United States and the European Union (EU) are both Western, democratic, advanced, and industrial societies. This means both sets of governments have a broad and similar commitment to protect the health, welfare, and physical environment of their citizens, and they have the administrative, scientific, and technological capacity to do so. As democracies (or in the case of the EU, a group of democratic governments), public officials in both the EU and the United States are broadly accountable to the public. Citizens and a wide range of business and non-business interest groups all have ways of participating in the policy process.

In addition to these similarities, there has also been considerable interaction between the United States and Europe. These transatlantic links have several dimensions. One of them is economic: Many American and European based multinationals have extensive investments in each other's markets and there is a substantial amount of transatlantic trade; each is the other's second most important trading partner. Moreover, a quarter of all transatlantic trade consists of transactions within the same firm that has investments on the other side of the Atlantic (Baldwin, Peterson, & Stokes, 2003). Second, there is substantial interaction among European and American environmental and consumer activists. Some environmental organizations (such as Greenpeace) have chapters on both sides of the Atlantic. Third, health, safety, or environmental risks that emerge on one side of the Atlantic are likely to receive media attention (and thus surface on the political agenda) on the other side. Fourth, there is extensive interaction among scientists and scientific advisory bodies and institutions across the Atlantic. This means that policymakers have access to much of the same research on the many risks that confront citizens and nature in advanced industrial societies. The level of scientific expertise and the access of scientists to the policy process are also broadly similar.

Moreover, the scope and extent of transatlantic interaction on each of these dimensions has steadily grown. Accordingly, this should logically have led the United States and the European Union to adopt regulatory approaches that reflected and prioritized similar values. This in turn should have resulted in similar regulatory policies with respect to the wide range of health, safety, and environmental risks faced by their citizens, especially as many of these risks are similar, if not identical on both sides of the Atlantic. This, however, has not been the case.

For regardless of these similarities, the European and American approaches to risk management differ substantially in many important ways and these differences show no sign of diminishing. Consequently, many similar risks have been regulated rather differently in the United States and the European Union. During the last quarter-century, risk regulations adopted in Europe have tended to be more stringent, risk averse, innovative, and comprehensive than those adopted by the American federal government. These divergent policies, in part, reflect important differences in the politics and ethics of risk management.

## The Legitimate Role of Public Opinion

One important difference has to do with the weight or deference policymakers have recently chosen to accord to public opinion. To what extent should the public's concerns, values, perceptions, and fears affect regulatory decisions? Many influential critics of American risk-management decisions such as Cass Sunstein (2002), John Graham and Jonathan Wiener (1995), Aaron Wildavsky (1998), Stephen Breyer (1993), and Robert Hahn (1996), have argued that the public is too often misinformed: it has a poor understanding of what risks it actually faces. There is a pervasive gap between the risks about which the public worries most and those to which it is actually exposed—misinformation that is often exacerbated by the media. Moreover, the public's perception of particular risks is often influenced by other risks about which it has heard, even though these risks may be unrelated to one another. Such serial panics can produce an "informational cascade" (Sunstein, 2005). According to Cass Sunstein, an influential critic of American risk regulation who served as director of the Office of Information and Regulatory Affairs in the Obama White House, "[i]nsofar as people lack their own means for judging a claim's validity, there is a danger that the beliefs generated by a cascade will be factually incorrect" (Sunstein, 2002, p. 86).

This skepticism of the validity of the public's risk perceptions has played an influential role in enabling American policymakers to act independently of public opinion. For example, in the early 1980s four firms applied to the U.S. Food and Drug Administration (FDA) for permission to market the genetically modified growth hormone BST (Vogel, 2012, pp. 66–70). When a dairy cow is given additional doses of this naturally occurring hormone, her milk-yield increases and she produces less waste. The federal government conducted extensive testing on the safety of milk produced by cows to which the growth hormones had been administered. The FDA's conclusion, backed by the National Institutes of Health (NIH) and the Congressional Office of Technology Assessment (COTA), was that this milk was indistinguishable in every important respect from conventionally produced milk.

There was, however, considerable public opposition to the approval of BST. An editorial in the *Washington Post* raised a number of ethically related public health issues. It argued:

> The word [milk] is synonymous with the best and purist we have, things like babies and white teeth. If our milk, which is supposed to be nourishing and comforting, is riddled with still more drugs—pumped out of sick and diseased cows—what is left? ... What person is their right mind would chose to ingest a bioengineered hormone—whose long-term effects have not been studied—so cows can produce more milk that we don't need? (Mason, 1994)

Various surveys reported that between 20% and 50% of consumers had reservations about drinking milk from BST-treated cows, and that 60% considered this milk to be unsafe (Brody, 1993). Nonetheless in November, 1993, the FDA gave regulatory approval to BST. According to FDA Commissioner David Kessler, "[t]his has been one of the most extensively studied animal drug products ... the public can be confident that ... milk from BST-treated ... cows is safe" (Gunset, 1993). In short, the advice of the regulatory body's scientific experts proved more influential than the public's risk perceptions and ethical concerns.

## The Ethics of Mandatory Labeling

Adding to the gap between public opinion and the scientific expertise on which the FDA relied, was the agency's subsequent decision not to require milk or other dairy products produced from BST-treated cows to be so labeled. Again, the regulatory agency's decision was scientifically based: it argued that there was no basis for requiring that this milk be labeled since it was identical, in every essential way, to the milk produced by cows that had not been given BST. Such a labeling requirement, the FDA reasoned, would not only provide consumers with no relevant information, but it might well mislead them into believing that there was a substantive difference between milk produced with and without the application of BST.

This latter decision especially outraged critics of the dairy growth hormone: even if the government deemed it to be safe, should they not be able to decide for themselves if they wanted to consume it or feed it to their children? Ethically, the FDA's decision not to require labeling privileged the interests of those milk producers who planned to use BST—who feared a labeling requirement would reduce their sales—over the freedom of choice of those risk-averse consumers who preferred to consume milk from cows that had not received BST.

A similar but even more heated and prolonged battle was waged in the United States about whether food produced from genetically modified seeds should be labeled. (Vogel, 2012, pp. 83–84). While the health risks of genetically modified organisms (GMOs) have not been highly salient in the United States—most Americans are unaware that virtually all the processed agricultural products they consume contain genetically modified ingredients—there has been considerable support for a labeling requirement. When the FDA asked for public input on product labeling, the majority of the 50,000 submissions it received supported regulations requiring that food containing genetically modified ingredients be so labeled. For many advocates of labeling, this was an ethical issue of transparency and freedom of choice: they wanted to know if they were consuming food that had been derived from GM seeds so they could avoid it. Yet the FDA declined to issue such a requirement: because GM foods are "substantially equivalent" to conventionally produced foods there is no sound reason for a labeling requirement.

Both these labeling controversies reflected conflicts between the risk perceptions of the public and those of the government. Yet in each case regulatory, decision makers chose to act paternalistically: in their roles as regulatory risk managers, they privileged the values that they held important, namely scientific advice, over those of a more risk-averse public whose preferences, fears, and values they considered ill informed.

## European Responsiveness to Public Risk Preferences

By contrast, European regulatory authorities have typically been much more responsive to the public's risk preferences. The regulation of genetically modified organisms (GMOs) is an important example. While public opposition to GMOs in Europe has many sources, including a deeply rooted distrust of new agricultural technologies and fears of American business domination of European food production, the perceived health risks of consuming GM ingredients have been the most influential. The scientific advice given to European officials has been the same as that given to their American counterparts, namely that numerous studies have been unable to find any health risks associated with the consumption of GM food.

In contrast to Americans, who have been largely indifferent to the safety risks of GM foods, their safety risks have been highly salient in Europe. Either Europeans do not trust the scientific advice given to the EU, or they have other reasons for opposing GM products. In any event, as a German government official put it, "Europeans do not want genetically modified food—period. It does not matter what the research shows; they just don't want it" (Jordan & O'Riordan, 1995, p. 61). Significantly, EU regulations have been broadly consistent with the public's risk preferences and perceptions. Virtually no GM crops are grown in Europe and, due to the EU's highly stringent labeling requirements, few food products that contain GM ingredients are available for sale in Europe.

There are other examples that illustrate how European officials have often made policy decision that privileged or deferred to the public's risk perceptions—even when these perceptions run counter to or are not supported by the scientific advice European officials have received. For example, during the 1980s, widespread fears emerged about the health risks of consuming meat from cattle that had been treated with growth-promoting hormones. These fears, which led to a substantial boycott of veal in several countries, were initially prompted by newspaper articles in Italy that had reported cases of babies becoming deformed after their expectant mothers had eaten veal treated with hormones. While it turned out that these deformities were unrelated to the use of beef hormones (rather, they were linked to a growth supplement given to dairy cows that was rapidly banned), they quickly escalated public anxieties about the health risks of *all* hormones given to cattle.

The EU's scientific advisory body carefully reviewed the five hormones that were still being widely administered to cattle in Europe and concluded that when properly used, they posed no risks to human health. Nevertheless, public concerns about the safety of the hormones persisted —encouraged by European consumer and environmental groups that opposed all hormone use. After prolonged deliberations in 1985, the EU decided to ban the use of the five disputed hormones. In justifying this decision, the EU's agricultural commissioner explained: "[S]cientific advice is important, but it is not decisive," adding that "not all political decisions are based on science" (Peterson, 1989, p. 461).

## The Role of Risk Assessment

The contrasting rationales of European and American public officials for the risk management decisions cited above are closely linked to another important transatlantic difference in the ethics of risk management. It has to do with the role that scientific risk assessments, scientific advice, and expertise in general should play in regulatory policymaking. In recent decades, "[q]uantitative risk assessment has emerged as the dominant paradigm in the U.S. for including science in regulatory decision making as the best way to manage threats to the environment" (Charnley & Elliott, 2002, p. 10363). "The risk-based approach is now the central element in environmental and public health decision making in the U.S." (Trickner & Raffersperger, 2001, p. 199).

This reliance on scientific expertise, which typically involves quantitative risk assessments that assess the likelihood and magnitude of particular risks, has been strongly supported by the American Congress, administrative rule making and the courts. It effectively raises the evidentiary threshold required to support policy interventions that either prevent new products or technologies from being introduced, or bans or restricts existing ones. As a result, regulators cannot impose restrictions on products or production processes without being able to provide convincing scientific evidence of harm. The intention of this approach is to prevent both public and private resources from being misused by imposing "unnecessary" regulations that do little or nothing to protect public health and welfare.

The increasing influence of the precautionary principle in Europe represents a very different ethical approach to risk management. One of the earliest introductions was featured in a 1984 German government report on the regulation of air quality: it stated that precaution "means acting when conclusive evidence ascertained by science is not yet available" (Morag-Levine, 2003: 11). Similarly, the 1990 Ministerial Declaration on the North Sea urged signatory governments to "apply the precautionary principle, that is to take action to avoid potentially damaging impacts ... even when there is no scientific evidence to prove a causal link between emissions and effects" (Soule, 2000, p. 318).

According to Principle 15 of the 1992 Rio Declaration on Environment and Development, "where there are threats of irreversible damage, lack of full scientific certainty shall not be used as a reason for postponing cost-effective measures to prevent environmental degradation" (Jordan & O'Riordan, 1995, p. 69). This approach to making risk-management decisions was explicitly endorsed by the EU in the 1992 Maastricht Treaty on the European Union and its application was clarified in a 2000 memo from the European Commission. Its goal was to enable regulatory officials to be proactive and in doing so, reduce potential harms and avoid "unnecessary" risks. It privileged the values of public health and safety and environmental protection on the grounds that it was "better to be safe than sorry."

Compared to a reliance on risk assessments, the precautionary principle reduces the threshold required to trigger regulatory intervention. In practice, it has enhanced the ability of European officials to deny approval

to potentially hazardous or harmful new technologies, and it has facilitated their ability to remove existing ones from the market. Its application
has played a critical role in many of the recent differences between European and American regulatory policies. These include the EU's refusal to
authorize the approval of BST, its restrictions on antibiotics in animal feed,
chemicals in cosmetics, the much earlier ban on phthalates in children's
products, and its extensive restrictions on GMOs.

REACH (Regulation on Registration, Evaluation, Authorization and
Restriction of Chemicals), the 2006 legislation that reformed and significantly strengthened EU's approach to the regulation of chemicals, was
strongly influenced by a White Paper that argued the dangers of *not* adopting restrictions on chemicals until there was conclusive scientific evidence
that they were harmful. It explicitly stated: "whenever scientific evidence
is available, but there is still uncertainty, decision-making must be based
on precaution" (Heyvaert, 2006, p. 51). More broadly, the principle's
application has provided European officials with broad discretion to issue
relatively stringent risk regulations when there is strong public demand for
them, even when the scientific justification for them is unclear or contested.

## Transatlantic Value Differences

The American and European approaches to risk management uphold
and prioritize different values. The American reliance on risk management
assumes a confidence in the ability of scientists or other technical experts
to accurately distinguish between those risks that do, or will, pose an unacceptable threat to public health, safety or environmental quality, and those
that do not or are unlikely to do so. It presumes that the existing state of
scientific research is sufficient to both measure the risks we face and to
calculate cost-effective and appropriate responses to them: "Risk is actu-
arial in spirit.... When used in environmental decision making, risk retains
the connotation of something that can be clearly defined, and quantified,
hence measured" (Jasanoff, 2000, p. 72).

This confidence in science's ability to assess, measure, and predict health,
safety, and environmental risks, however, is precisely what the precautionary
principle challenges. The precautionary principle assumes that there are
important limits to the scope and accuracy of existing scientific knowledge.
What a reliance on scientific risk assessments fails to recognize is that there
is much we still do not know or understand about the causes and consequences of the risks to both humans and the physical environment posed
by modern technologies. A reliance on risk assessment is flawed because
it is incapable of acknowledging the importance of uncertainty or what we
still do not know. It does not sufficiently appreciate the possibility that we

are likely to be surprised. In short, what importantly distinguishes recent European and American approaches to risk regulation is not the scientific evidence on which they were based but rather how much confidence policymakers—and the public—place in scientific expertise.

## The Historical Development of Two Risk Paradigms

These differences in European and American risk regulations are not deeply rooted; rather they are politically contingent. In fact, beginning in the 1960s and persisting through around 1990, the risk regulations adopted in the United States were typically more stringent than those adopted on the other side of the Atlantic. For example, through the late 1980s, it was much more difficult for a drug to be approved in the United States than in Germany or Great Britain; Several pesticides and food additives were more restricted in the United States than in Europe. The United States recognized and responded to the health risks posed by ozone-depleting chemicals much earlier than the European Union, and it was the first country to regulate automotive emissions—including imposing a ban on leaded gasoline.

What then subsequently happened on both sides of the Atlantic? What made the United States become more reluctant to adopt new risk-averse regulations and the European Union become more willing to do so? In brief, both sets of new policy approaches can be said to represent a reaction or response to the perceived "failed" policies of the past. In the case of the United States, this involved a broad intellectual, legal, and political backlash against American regulatory stringency. It was rooted in the influential claim that in too many cases, the United States had regulated too much.

For example, in 1995, the political scientist Aaron Wildavsky published a study with the rhetorical title: *But Is it True?* (Wildavsky, 1993). It carefully reviewed the scientific evidence behind a number of widely publicized health, safety, or environmental "scares," many of which had led to additional government regulation. These included dieldrin, saccharin, DDT, PCBs, Dioxin, Alar, arsenic in drinking water, abandoned hazardous waste sites, and asbestos in schools. The book's conclusion was that in each of these cases policymakers and the public had either been misled by activists or misinformed by the media.

The implication of this study, along with numerous others, many of which were published by conservative research organizations, was that regulators had devoted considerable resources to protecting the public and the environment from many risks that turned out to be non-existent or trivial. Many of the "alarm bells" so loudly rung by activists and widely publicized in the media were "false alarms." In short, many regulations were based on "phantom risks." Scarce resources had been squandered because the costs that they imposed on business had not actually resulted in any improvements in safety, health, or environmental quality. To prevent this from reoccurring, regulators needed to be more careful: the best way to do so, it was concluded, would be to subject each claim of harm to careful and scientifically sophisticated risk assessments.

Europeans had a very different perception of the shortcomings of their previous regulatory policies. In their case, the most influential claim was that they had been *insufficiently* rather than excessively stringent. Too often, regulators had failed to appreciate early warning signs, insisting on more conclusive scientific evidence of harm before they were willing to impose restrictions. The most important such case involved "mad cow" disease (BSE) in Great Britain. After this disease had broken out among cows (by the early 1990s more than 7,000 British cattle had become affected and were put to death), there was considerable public anxiety as to whether this horrible disease could also affect humans who had consumed beef. British regulatory officials and their scientific advisors assured the public that this was not possible: a position that they maintained for 8 years, notwithstanding some studies suggesting that transmission of the disease from animals to humans might be possible. Their messages were consistent: "British beef is 100% safe" and "there is no scientific evidence of a causal link between BSE in cattle and Creutzfeldt-Jacob Disease in humans" (Fisher, 2004, p. 82). Yet the risk assessments that these assuring messages were based on turned out to be misinformed.

The lesson Europeans learned from this and other cases of flawed risk assessments, was that regulators should act in a precautionary manner: they should be anticipatory and proactive and not wait until there was conclusive evidence of harm before imposing restrictions on business activities that might have adverse impacts. In short, they should be more skeptical of the ability of regulatory science to accurately assess and predict risk. A report published by the European Environmental Agency in 2013 represents a useful counterpoint to the Wildavsky volume. It identified a long list of risks that either had been too laxly regulated in the past, or were not now being taken sufficiently seriously. These included tobacco, vinyl chloride, Bisphenol A, seed dressing insecticides, mobile phones and nanotechnology (European Environmental Agency, 2013). In each case, the costs of inaction were described as excessive and capable of being avoided if regulators had been willing to heed plausible, but not yet proven, "early warnings."

## Assessment

The American and European approaches to risk management each focus on reducing one kind of policy error. The American reliance on risk assessments is intended to reduce the number of false positives; that is, risks that were initially viewed as harmful, but turned out to be safe. By contrast, the precautionary principle in the European Union is designed to reduce the number of false negatives; that is, risks that were not initially considered serious, but turned out to be so. Each approach privileges some values over others. American risk assessments are likely to reduce the misallocation of both private and public resources, minimize public anxieties and promote innovation; while the precautionary principle in Europe is likely to minimize the likelihood of significant, but avoidable, threats to public health, safety or the physical environment.

Furthermore, the American reliance on risk assessments makes it more likely that some dangerous risks will fail to be adequately regulated while the European precautionary principle makes it more likely that potentially welfare-enhancing innovations will be unnecessarily delayed or prevented. These differences raise a number of critical ethical questions with regard to risk. Are we better off by promoting or retarding the pace of new technological innovations? Will the introduction of new technologies, such as nanotechnology or agricultural biotechnology, improve public welfare, or create new hazards? Are we becoming more or less vulnerable to threats on our health, safety, and the environment caused by human activity? Most fundamentally, are the products and processes of advanced industrial capitalism actually safer than we now believe, or are they more hazardous than we can now imagine? In short, is what we do not now know likely to make us anxious, or complacent?

These important queries suggest that there are no easy answers to the question of which approach to risk management is more welfare-enhancing (Adler, 2001). Much depends on one's perceptions and beliefs. If one believes that false positives represent the most important cause of regulatory policy failures, then developing a more stringent screen for imposing new regulations makes sense. Alternatively, if one holds that false negative policy errors represent the most common and significant cause of regulatory policy failure, then the most responsible policy approach is to develop a less stringent screen for imposing new regulations. Such debates are likely to continue on both sides of the Atlantic.

## CONCLUSION

While each approach has important value and policy implications, it is difficult to conclude that one is more or less ethical: each has both strengths and weaknesses.

This should not be surprising, as both approaches may well be too extreme. That is to say, sometimes a reliance on risk assessments may represent the more ethical approach to addressing risks, while at other times it may be too rigid or inflexible. Likewise, the precautionary principle can easily be misused (after all it is often impossible to prove beyond all reasonable doubt that something is safe), while at other times, a more proactive approach to recognizing potential, though not-yet-proven risks may be more responsible. There is no "one size fits all": each risk must be assessed on its own terms, with the recognition that any decision may be prone to error.

Ultimately risk regulation is a political choice, made by the public, the media, activist groups, business firms and associations, and government officials. In the final analysis, it is also an ethical decision, based on our values, judgments, beliefs, fears, and hopes.

## REFERENCES

Adler, M. (2001). *Well-being and distribution: Beyond cost-benefit analysis.* London, England: Oxford University Press.

Baldwin, M., Peterson, J., & Stokes, B. (2003). Trade and economic relations. In J. Peterson & M. Pollack (Eds.), *Europe, America: Transatlantic relations in the twenty-first century* (pp. 29–31). London, England: Routledge.

Breyer, S. (1993). *Breaking the vicious circle: Toward effective risk regulation.* Cambridge, MA: Harvard University Press.

Brody, J. (1993, November 17). Of luddites, cows, and biotechnology miracles, *New York Times.* Retrieved September 11, 2014, from www.nytimes.com/1993/11/17/health/personal-health-395493.html?module=Search&mabReward=relbias%3As%2C%7b%222%22%22%3A%22RI%3A14%2

Charnley, G., & Elliott, E. D. (2002). Risk versus precaution: Environmental law and public health protection. *Environmental Law Reporter News and Analysis,* 32(3), 10363–10366.

European Environmental Agency. (2013). Late lessons from early warnings: Science, precaution, innovation. Copenhagen, Denmark: European Environmental Agency.

Fisher, E. (2004). *Risk: Regulation and administrative constitutionalism.* Oxford, England: Hart.

Graham, J., & Wiener, J. (Eds.) (1995). *Risk vs. Risk: Tradeoffs in Protecting Health and the Environment.* Cambridge, MA: Harvard University Press.

Gunset, G. (1993, November 6). FDA clears use of milk hormone, *Chicago Tribune.* Retrieved September 11, 2014, from http://articles.chicagotribune.com/1993-11-06/business/9311060066_1_recombinant-bovine-somatotropin-bst-milk-production

Hahn, R. (1996). Preface. In R. Hahn (Ed.), *Risks, costs and lives saved: Getting better result from regulation* (pp. vii–ix). New York, NY: Oxford University Press.

Heyvaert, V. (2006). *Guidance without constraint: Assessing the impact of the precautionary principle on the European Community's chemicals policy* (No. 6, pp. 27–60). New York, NY: Oxford University Press.

Jasanoff, S. (2000). *Technological risk and cultures of rationality.* Washington, DC: National Academies Press.

Jordan, A., & O'Riordan, T. (1995). The precautionary principle in UK environmental law and policy. In T. Gray (Ed.), *UK Environmental Policy in the 1990s* (pp. 57–84). London, England: Macmillan.

Mason, M. (1994, March 7). Milk? It may not do a body good: A furor over hormones, labeling & health, *The Washington Post*, p. C5.

Morag-Levine, N. (2003). *Chasing the wind: Regulating air pollution in the common law state*. Princeton, NJ: Princeton University Press.

Peterson, J. (1989). Hormones, heifers and high politics—biotechnology and the Common Agricultural Policy. *Public Administration*, *67*(4), 455–471.

Soule, E. (2000). Assessing the precautionary principle. *Public Affairs Quarterly*, 309–328.

Sunstein, C. (2002). *Risk and reason: Safety, law and the environment*. Cambridge, England: Cambridge University Press.

Sunstein, C (2005). *Laws of fear: Beyond the precautionary principle*. Cambridge, England: Cambridge University Press.

Trickner, J., & Raffersperger, C. (2001). The American view of the precautionary principle. In T. O'Riordan, J. Camerson, & A. Jordan (Eds.), *Reinterpreting the precautionary principle* (pp. 183–202). London, England: Cameron.

Wildavsky, A. (1988). *Searching for safety*. New Brunswick, NJ: Transaction Books.

Wildavsky, A. (1993). *But is it true? A citizen's guide to environmental health and safety issues*. Cambridge, MA: Harvard University Press.

Vogel, D. (2012). *The politics of precaution: Regulating health, safety, and environmental risks in Europe and the United States*. Princeton, NJ: Princeton University Press.

# CHAPTER 4

# RISK MANAGEMENT AND CONFLICTS OF INTEREST

**Leslie Francis**

## ABSTRACT

Risk management aims to reduce the costs of adverse events. In entities such as hospitals, risk managers do this in two ways: by reducing the likelihood or seriousness of adverse events, and by reducing the costs of these events when they do happen. Activities aimed at the latter present direct conflicts of interest between protecting the institution and respecting the interests of the clients served by the institution—so-called institutional conflicts of interest. Activities aimed at the former would appear to benefit all parties (and thus escape problems of conflicts): those at risk of accidents (because the risk is reduced) and the institution (because reducing risks also reduces the costs of adverse events). However, this appearance may also be misleading if efforts to reduce risks to agents of the institution (such as hospital staff) conflict indirectly with efforts to reduce risks to clients (such as patients). Here, too, institutional conflicts of interest may arise for the risk manager.

This chapter will discuss the role of the risk manager in handling institutional conflicts of interest in health-care organizations. When risk managers attempt to reduce the costs of adverse events to the institution, conflicts of interest are likely to arise and to present ethical issues for the risk manager.

*Ethics and Risk Management*, pp. 45–66

Copyright © 2015 by Information Age Publishing

These conflicts are institutional ones that are built into the risk manager's role: the risk manager's goal is to settle potentially expensive claims on terms that are favorable to the institution rather than on the terms that might be most beneficial to the patient. These conflicts must be identified and managed ethically.

## INTRODUCTION

In the play, *An Enemy of the People*, Ibsen's character Dr. Thomas Stockmann informs local officials that their town's well-known and highly lucrative baths are contaminated by runoff from a local tannery. Stockmann is the chief medical officer for the baths, which are much sought after for their healing capabilities. After observing unusual episodes of illness in some of the baths' visitors, Stockmann sends water samples off for analysis to a major university. When the results indicate contamination, he urges closure of the baths to protect the health of visitors—a judgment based on his assessment of the risks and benefits of leaving the baths open.

Ibsen's play is a classic drama of honesty and self-righteousness against community spirit and greed—with all the subtle strengths and weaknesses of each of these. But it is also a prescient drama about the role of a public-health risk manager, and the individual and social conflicts attending that role. As an individual, Stockmann prides himself on being a scientist and is careful to voice his concerns to the community until he has confirmed the test results. Yet there is also a ring of "I told you so" in how he conveys the news to the town officials; Stockmann had argued for a more expensive piping system that would have avoided the risk of contamination of the baths. Although Stockmann expects to be a town hero for what he has learned, it comes as no surprise to the audience that he is disbelieved, dismissed from his position, evicted from his home, and declared an "enemy of the people."

In the play, Ibsen draws a masterful portrait of conflicts of interest: Stockmann has interests in his scientific reputation, his family, his position as medical director, and his medical practice. The town has financial interests in the success of the baths and in its reputation. The town leaders have interests in their positions with the town as well as their own economic interests. But there is more. At the end of the play, Stockmann is confronted with perhaps the most traditional form of conflict of interest: he learns that the owner of the tannery, his wife's adoptive father, was planning to leave a sizeable inheritance to Stockmann's wife and children. To pressure Stockmann to clear the tannery of responsibility for the pollution, his adoptive father-in-law has invested his fortune in the baths and tells Stockmann that unless the baths are cleared, he will leave the fortune to a charity. Deprived of income with which to support his family, Stockmann faces a "horribly painful dilemma," which is deepened by the recognition that some believe that he has criticized the baths so that his adoptive father in law could profit from investing in the baths on highly favorable terms. Yet Stockmann remains pure: he refuses the inheritance and plans to provide medical care for the poor in the town. Ibsen's play was written over 100 years ago, but today's health-care risk managers face many of these same conflicts of interest.

This chapter will begin with a discussion of conflicts of interest, both individual and institutional. It then will consider the role of the health-care risk manager and explains how that role may incorporate institutional conflicts of interest. The chapter then will apply this analysis to the role of the risk manager in disclosure or apology programs designed to reduce malpractice costs. It will conclude with three suggestions for alleviating these conflicts of interest: limitations on confidentiality requirements in settlement agreements; a requirement that patients receive independent advice before entering these agreements; and development of the capability for independent review of settlements.

## UNDERSTANDING CONFLICTS OF INTEREST

Understood most broadly, conflicts of interest in the professional context occur when judgments about the exercise of professional obligations are, or might be, affected unduly by interests extrinsic to professional relationships. One influential characterization of this situation, is that "secondary" interests adversely affect "primary" professional interests. (Thompson, 1993). Identifying such conflicts thus requires a determination of professional obligations as primary interests; an understanding of what interests are extrinsic to the professional relationship, and thus secondary; and judgments about when such secondary interests affect, or might affect, professionals in ways they should not.

Some professions, such as law, have developed highly formalized statements of professional obligations and how various conflicts of interest may affect them; disciplinary mechanisms may be invoked when actions violate these obligations. Other professions have far less elaborate professional codes. Unlike law or medicine, many professions—including health-care risk management in most states—do not require licensure, which is a common method for the enforcement of professional obligations. In many fields, moreover, contractual obligations to employers (such as confidentiality, non-compete clauses, or agreements to limit services), may lie in uneasy tension with primary profession obligations or other secondary interests.

As will be discussed more fully below, there also may be no clear delineation of which interests are considered secondary to the professional relationship. Personal financial interests and interests of family members are standardly identified as such interests. (Lo & Fried, 2009, p. 32) General ideological orientations or political affiliations are frequently not judged to be conflictual interests, even though they may affect decision making; unless they can be linked directly to some form of personal advantage. Interests in reputation, public recognition, or career advancement may be as influential on decision making; but far more difficult to identify than financial interests (Thompson, 1993). They thus may be considered secondary interests, although they are often not addressed directly in professional codes of conduct or conflicts of interest policies.

Secondary interests are not problematic per se. They may become problematic when they divert judgment in the context of professional relationships. Thompson (1993) writes:

> The secondary interest is usually not illegitimate in itself, and indeed it may even be a necessary and desirable part of professional practice. Only its relative weight in professional decisions is problematic. The aim is not to eliminate or necessarily to reduce financial gain or other secondary interests (such as preference for family and friends or the desire for prestige and power). It is rather to prevent these secondary factors from dominating or appearing to dominate the relevant primary interest in the making of professional decisions.

In health care, observational research has addressed correlations between individual economic interests of physicians and treatment recommendations (Lo & Fried, 2009, Ch. 6). Such research also has revealed correlations between relationships with pharmaceutical companies (and other commercial enterprises) and published research findings (Lo & Fried, 2009, Ch. 4). When the interests of patients or human subjects are compromised, the influence of conflicts of interest can clearly be problematic. A well-known illustration is the death of Jesse Gelsinger, a research participant who died in a trial of gene therapy at the University of Pennsylvania. The study's lead researcher had substantial financial interests in the company that would profit if the trials were successful—interests that were valued at approximately $13.5 million and perhaps much more (Wilson, 2010). The university also had equity interests in the company and financial interests in continuing to receive research support from the company. Indeed, the researcher was permitted to have such large financial interests in an agreement that supposedly shielded him from making scientific decisions and provided the university with the relationship with the company. Neither Jesse Gelsinger nor his family were informed of the extent of the financial ties; nor of the study's potential risks, which had become apparent in earlier trials using animals as well as with earlier patients in the study (Wilson, 2010). The firestorm of criticism that followed Gelsinger's death focused primarily on these financial ties; but reputational, career, and institutional interests may also have played important roles in the tragedy, so much so that Wilson (2010) has argued that prohibition of the financial ties might not have been all that was necessary.

Discussions of conflicts of interest in health care increasingly recognize that institutional conflicts may exist in addition to individual conflicts (Rose, 2013; Friedman & McKinney, 2013; Lo & Field, 2009; Emanuel & Steiner, 1995) According to the Institute of Medicine, "Institutional conflicts of interest arise when an institution's own interests or those of its senior officials pose risks of undue influence on decisions involving the institution's primary interests" in the sense of obligations to those the institution serves (Lo & Field, 2008, p. 218). Federal regulations regarding government ethics also recognize the reality of institutional conflicts of interest; government employees, even special government employees such as those serving on advisory committees or temporary employees on leave from other positions, must not participate in the development of policies that might have a distinct impact on their institutions other than as members of a general class of institutions (Code of Federal Regulations, Title 18, § 2640.203, 2014). The examples in these regulations cite financial concerns, such as the development of a grants and contracts policy. Federal regulations governing conflicts of interest in federally funded research likewise focus on the financial interests of researchers or persons in institutional positions of authority (Code of Federal Regulations, Title 42, Part 50, 2014; Code of Federal Regulations, Title 45, Part 94, 2014; Friedman & McKinney, 2013).

Particularly as federal funding for biomedical research has become more limited, academic medical institutions have pursued ties with industry. Concerns about maintaining the loyalty of commercial donors may impact decisions about faculty members, and threaten the freedom to publish information critical of donors (Shafer, 2003). Competition to retain well-funded faculty members and to pursue grant opportunities has intensified as well. These are institutional—not individual—conflicts of interest and may require policies to address them (Friedman & McKinney, 2013) or perhaps even restrict them (Shafer, 2003). Arguably, they may be as serious as individual conflicts of interest that are diverting judgments away from the institution's obligations to the individuals they serve (Lo & Fried, 2009, p. 216). However, regulations and institutional policies currently in place typically address institutional conflicts only as they are reflected in individual conflicts. There are some exceptions: for example, Stanford University's institutional conflict of interest policy states explicitly that if investigators at the university are engaged in research that may affect the university's intellectual property rights or equity holdings, these properties will be sequestered in an account held by an independent third party (Stanford University, 2014).

Conflict of interest rules seek to preserve the integrity of professional judgment and to maintain confidence in them (Thompson, 1993). Both individual and institutional conflicts of interest may result in a lack of trustworthiness and concomitantly inappropriately placed trust when those served by the institution do not realize that the institution's interests are being placed first (Rose, 2013).

## THE ROLES OF HEALTH-CARE RISK MANAGERS

Risk management in health care addresses the frequency, severity, and costs of adverse events. It is still a relatively new and still evolving professional field. Emerging in the 1970s in response to perceptions of a "malpractice crisis" of increased costs, the field originally sought to confront loss reduction directly by prevention and mitigation (Core Risk Services 2014). The American Society for Healthcare Risk Management (ASHRM) was founded in 1980 as the American Society for Hospital Risk Managers, and it reflects these dual goals of increased safety and reduced institutional costs from errors or accidents.

One major way in which health-care risk management has been evolving as a field, is its relation to (and interconnection with) quality improvement. For the most part, the fields have developed along separate paths and employ different goals and methods. If the goal of risk management is reduction of losses due to malpractice claims, and the goal of quality improvement is patient safety and care quality, the two are distinct enterprises each with unique ethical concerns. For example, the argument that it is appropriate to use patient data without consent for quality improvement activities as that might benefit their ongoing care or the care of patients like them, cannot be applied as easily to the use of patient information to reduce liability costs (Jennings et al., 2007, Baily, Bottrell, Lynn, & Jennings, 2006). Data analyses devoted to patient safety may prioritize identifying events that may affect many people, but that are unlikely to result in high-cost litigation; whereas analyses devoted to loss prevention may prioritize efforts to prevent events that give rise to such litigation. On the other hand, to the extent that improved patient safety and care quality reduce malpractice costs—as they surely do at least to some extent—the goals of the two fields align. Indeed, in many small health-care facilities, the same staff may perform both functions.

As concerns about patient safety and care quality have drawn increased attention, the need for connections between risk management and quality improvement activities has increasingly been emphasized. The publication of research about the frequency of medical errors (e.g., Leape, 1994) has highlighted problems of patient safety (IOM, 1999) as well as the possibility that improved patient safety would reduce the costs of malpractice. The subsequent growth of the patient safety movement, has led to recognition that risk management and care quality functions must work together (ASHRM, 2007). A primary example of the disclosure, apology, and offer programs follows (that of the University of Michigan): it incorporates risk-manager analysis of whether care was reasonable, with how unreasonable forms of care can be avoided. The program assigns risk managers to particular clinical areas in order to carry out these patient-safety activities (Boothman et al., 2009). Such efforts of health-care risk managers that are directed to reducing the frequency or severity of adverse events, or to improving care quality, would appear to be aligned with the interests of patients. To the extent that this alignment exists, the interests of the health-care facility and its patients are not in conflict.

In many other ways, however, the interests of health-care facilities and risk managers who work in them may be in conflict with the interests of patients. These conflicts, and the ethical issues they create, will be the focus of the remainder of this chapter. The next section outlines the ethical principles that have been developed for public and private risk managers; and then considers how they might function in the context of conflicts of interest between institutions and the patients they serve. The chapter continues with an in-depth discussion of an institutional conflict of interest that is arguably endemic in the role of the risk manager: development of disclosure, apology, and offer programs designed to encourage early settlements in situations in which patients were harmed by medical errors. A concluding section explores three possibilities for addressing this conflict: limitations on confidentiality requirements in settlement agreements; a requirement that patients receive independent advice before entering these agreements; and development of the capability for independent review of settlements.

## Ethics for Healthcare Risk Managers

The ASHRM Code of Professional Conduct (2012) divides risk-manager responsibilities into two groups: responsibilities to the profession, and responsibilities to those they serve. In the framework for conflict of interest analysis given above, these responsibilities would be the primary interests of the risk manager.

Among responsibilities to the profession, the ASHRM Code lists: identifying, acknowledging, and disclosing potential conflicts of interest.

Responsibilities to those served include: respect by practicing in a non-discriminatory manner; recognizing that patients and their families are entitled to fair treatment; communicating honestly and factually; and sharing confidential information only where appropriate and permitted by law. This set of responsibilities also emphasizes patient safety: the responsibilities of the risk manager include investigating and analyzing events to reduce the likelihood of similar injury to others; promoting cultural change that encourages reporting events that might result in injury; and advocating for patient safety.

In a third section, the ASHRM Code discusses individual conflicts of interest in further detail. This section singles out as conflicts of interest for risk managers: transactions with former employers or business associates; business transactions inuring to personal benefit or benefit of family members; and investments or activities that conflict or appear to conflict with the interests of employer or client. The code judges that business transactions inuring to personal benefit are unacceptable even with disclosure; other potential conflicts require full disclosure, but may be permissible.

The ASHRM code's treatment of conflicts of interest thus focuses on individual economic benefit or other individual benefits; not the possibility that the role of the risk manager may itself involve a conflict of interest between the interests of the health-care institution and the interests of the patients it serves. For the risk manager, the primary professional interests of providing patients and their families with fair treatment and communicating factually and honestly, could be deflected by the secondary interests of the institution in reducing costs and the secondary interests of the risk manager him or herself in professional reputation, job security, and advancement. In this individual focus, the ASHRM code is not alone; official ethics statements for public risk managers take a similar stance. The Public Risk Management Association, the association of risk managers in the public sector, has a Code of Ethics (2014) that gives these illustrations of prohibited conflicts of interest: misuse of public resources, improper outside employment, acceptance of gifts or nepotism, and engagement in activities that will create a hostile work environment. Yet contemporary discussions of institutional conflicts of interest note that the analysis applied to conflicts in research and patient treatment may also be relevant to other aspects of the health-care enterprise (Lo & Field, 2009, p. 32).

## DISCLOSURE PROGRAMS AND INSTITUTIONAL CONFLICTS OF INTEREST

A recent, highly praised strategy for health-care institutions to reduce costs of malpractice litigation, has been to encourage early settlement through disclosure, apology, and an offer to patients. This strategy is often proposed as a replacement for a "deny-and-defend" strategy in seeking to win malpractice lawsuits. It has resulted in multiple state laws that shield disclosures or apologies from litigation in a wide variety of ways (Boothman, et al., 2009). Important differences among such programs include whether they are disclosure only, whether they include apologies, and what kinds of disclosures are made. For example, some programs merely acknowledge to the patient that an adverse event occurred that was related to their care, without in any way apologizing or admitting responsibility for the event. Others will say they were sorry for what occurred, but take care not to link such expressions of sympathy with admissions of fault that might give rise to liability claims.

The contemporary apology movement began with a report of "humanistic" risk management policies at a Veterans Affairs medical center that reported reduced liability payments (Kramen & Hamm, 1999). Although the study reported only a small case series and policymakers recognized that Veterans Affairs institutions might not be representative of health-care institutions more generally, the reported findings generated great interest. In 2010, the Agency for Healthcare Research and Quality (AHRQ) funded a series of demonstration projects that tested the concept that early disclosure of errors might reduce litigation costs (Mello, Studdert, & Kachalia, 2014). One larger hospital system with a disclosure program (that also received grants under the AHRQ program—the University of Michigan) has reported reduced claims frequency, transaction costs, incidence of litigation, and time to dispute resolution (Boothman et al., 2009). In addition, the Michigan experience has reported a cultural shift to patient safety after inception of the disclosure program (Boothman, Imhoff, & Campbell, 2012).

Some published studies have indicated reductions in litigation and settlement amounts after institution of a program of disclosure (Adams, Elmunzer, & Scheiman, 2014). Other studies have suggested that the changes were more likely to occur with cultural changes within institutions rather than being associated with state law innovations (Perez & DiDona, 2010). These studies reported data that might suggest changes that were in both the interests of patients and the interests of institutions, if institutions shifted to a culture of patient safety that resulted in reduced frequency of costly errors. On the other hand, reports of reduced costs may reflect reduced litigation costs and lower settlement offers to patients rather than concerns that were reflecting the interests of patients. The impact of institutional conflicts of interests thus remains unclear from these studies.

To consider the extent to which institutional conflicts of interest may have been recognized or acknowledged in studies of apology or disclosure programs, or in reports of the programs themselves, I conducted a *pubmed* search for "apology and malpractice and date after 2000."[1] This search yielded a total of 42 articles. Many of these cited other articles discussing apology and disclosure programs, and I included these as well in my database. After excluding all articles reporting activities outside of the United States and articles about which no information was available (primarily trade publications or local bar journals), I then reviewed 35 articles for the following factors: (1) did the article express a view about whether disclosure or apology was ethically desirable?; (2) did the article express a view about whether disclosure or apology was likely to create an improved climate of patient safety or otherwise improve care?; (3) did the article express a view about whether apology or disclosure was likely to reduce the costs of litigation?; and (4) did the article raise any questions about whether the patient's interests were adequately represented in the process of settlement after apology or disclosure? Full results of my analysis are presented in the table in Appendix A.

Some of the articles were discussions of the apology and disclosure movement presented as information to particular medical specialties (e.g., Vercler, Buchman, & Chung, 2015, plastic surgeons; Sohn & Bal, 2012, orthopedists; Surbone, 2012, oncologists; and Baker, Lauro, & Sintim-Damoa, 2008, radiologists). Some articles focused on physician reluctance to disclosure and how this might be overcome (e.g. Surbone, 2012; Pelt & Faldmo, 2008; Saxton & Finkelstein, 2008); and Wei, 2007). Many were articles in law reviews describing or assessing the impact of the different types of state apology and disclosure laws (e.g. Mello, Studdert & Kachalia, 2014; Raper, 2011; Hyman, 2010; Mastroianni et al., 2010; Perez & DiDona, 2009; Robbennolt, 2009; and McDonnell & Guenther, 2008). Three reported on the success of their institutional apology and disclosure programs (Boothman, Imhoff, & Campbell, 2012, University of Michigan; Quinn & Eichler, 2008, Colorado COPIC program; Kraman et al., 2002, Lexington VA).

Ten articles raised questions about fair compensation for patients, several in ways that suggested sensitivity to the possibility of institutional conflicts of interest. Articles portraying the University of Michigan program, for example, cited cost reductions as only an incidental advantage of an effort to create an environment of fairness and openness (Boothman, Imhoff, & Campbel, 2012; and Chung et al., 2011). Hyman (2010), cited data to the effect that patients had reported satisfaction with disclosure programs and did not report feeling pressured unfairly into settlements. Several articles pointed out that physicians might have had fiduciary responsibilities to their patients that were not shared by risk managers (Loren et al., 2010; Quinn & Eichner, 2008; and Mello, Studdert & Kachalia, 2014) noted that compensation may be difficult to calculate fairly. Chung et al. (2011) cautioned against the possibility that physicians and hospitals that were independent actors (and not covered under a single self-insured malpractice umbrella) may behave strategically in order to shift liability costs to others involved in care.

Two articles stood out in raising questions about the possible impact of disclosure programs on fairness to patients. In a 2014 critical analysis of the impact of tort reform on liability costs, Mello, Studdert & Kachalia argued that tort reforms did not account for a significant percentage of the reduction in liability costs over the preceding decade. Instead, they argued that initial reports from the AHRQ demonstration projects suggested that programs communicating about injury with patients had had promising results. These authors noted, however, that the proactive compensation component of these programs "may be more difficult for institutions to consistently execute" than communication, because insurers calculated compensation offers based on the likelihood of suit rather than on a principled analysis of whether substandard care caused harm. In their study of disclosure, apology, and offer programs, Bell and coauthors (Bell et al., 2010) conducted key informant interviews and found increased transparency, improved patient safety, reduced liability costs, and rapid and fair compensation as goals of these programs. Informants also feared that these programs would be perceived as "anti-consumer" efforts to settle cases quickly, for limited amounts, and without the benefit of independent advice for patients. In the judgment of this study's authors, "Making whole those patients who have been harmed through medical negligence as quickly and fairly as possible after a harmful error, diminishes any conflicts of interest on the part of the physician or the institution to help the patient while avoiding litigation and helps preserve therapeutic relationships between patients and caregivers" (Bell et al., 2010, pp. 694–695).

Despite raising the issue of compensation fairness, none of these articles conceptualized the possibility of institutional conflict of interest directly. Importantly, none raised the possibility that risk managers might face this conflict in dealing with the disclosure process, making recommendations about settlement offers, or discussing compensation with patients.

## CONCLUSION: SOME RECOMMENDATIONS FOR CHANGE

Despite their clear benefits, disclosure programs present possibilities of institutional conflicts of interest. They might encourage patients to settle claims of injury for settlement amounts that are unfair. Many discussions of these programs in the literature did not recognize these fairness concerns. Others, while recognizing the possibility of unfairness, did not conceptualize it in terms of a conflict of interest. In this conclusion, I suggest three additions to the disclosure process that might help to mitigate conflict of interest risks.

### (1) Reminding the Patient That They Have An Opportunity to Seek Outside Counsel and That Doing So Might Be Beneficial to Them

When attorneys representing health-care clients consider entering into transactions with patients, this is an attorney-client conflict of interest. In such cases, ethical rules require attorneys to tell their clients that they have an opportunity to seek outside counsel (ABA, 2013). The institutional conflicts of interest faced by the risk manager or others representing the health care provider are similar in structure. Affording the opportunity for independent representation might thus be seen as an appropriate conflict-mitigation measure.

### (2) Reconsidering the Confidentiality of Settlement Agreements

When settlements are reached during the course of litigation, a condition of the settlement is typically that the settlement amount will be kept secret. This makes it difficult for patients and their representatives to know what others in similar circumstances may have received. It also makes it difficult for researchers to scrutinize the fairness of settlement patterns (Knutsen 2010). Publication of settlement amounts in particular cases can present significant risks to patient privacy. It also risks misleading others, as publication of settlement amounts will not reveal the unique features of individual cases. On the other hand, publication of aggregate numbers (such as how many settlements have been reached by the provider in a given year, in what categories of cases, and for what amounts), might increase transparency in a manner that supports public interests in improved care and fairness to patients.

### (3) Establishing a Mechanism for Impartial Review of Disclosure, Apology, and Offer Programs

In her review of the Jesse Gelsinger case, Wilson (2010) argued that banning institutional conflicts of interest would not have solved the problem of risks to patients that these pose. Instead, she argued for an ongoing external review of these conflicts; much as data safety monitoring boards assess the risks to patients of clinical trials on an ongoing basis. Along these lines, the University of Michigan's disclosure, apology, and offer program featured an internal review committee, which assessed the risk manager's determinations of whether the error in care was an unreasonable one before a settlement offer was made. This committee was designed to have a range of experts to counter the tendency to "protect ones own" (Boothman et al., 2009). As an internal committee, however, it did not fully mitigate the risks of institutional conflicts.

Apology, disclosure, and offer programs have growing appeal. Yet they present clear institutional conflicts of interest for risk managers. These conflicts have been under appreciated in published assessments of these programs. Efforts to mitigate these conflicts should be further explored by risk managers.

## NOTE

1. Other search strategies, such as "(apology or disclosure) and (malpractice or liability)" yielded thousands of articles, most dealing with malpractice risks.

## REFERENCES

Adams, M. A., Elmunzer, J. B., & Scheiman, J. M. (2014). Effect of a health system's medical error disclosure program on gastroenterology-related claims rates and costs. *American Journal of Gastroenterology* 109: 460–464.

American Bar Association (ABA). (2013). *Model rules of professional conduct* 1.8(a) (2). Retrieved November 9, 2014, from www.americanbar.org/groups/professional_responsibility/publications/model_rules_of_professional_conduct/rule_1_8_current_clients_specific_rules.html

American Society for Healthcare Risk Management (ASHRM). (2007). "Different roles, same goal: Risk and quality management partnering for patient safety." Retrieved November 9, 2014, from www.ashrm.org/ashrm/education/development/monographs/Monograph.07RiskQuality.pdf

American Society for Healthcare Risk Management (ASHRM). (2012). "Healthcare risk management code of professional conduct." Retrieved November 9, 2014, from www.ashrm.org/ashrm/about/governance/files/codeconduct.pdf

American Society for Healthcare Risk Management (ASHRM). (2014). "Celebrating 30 years, A brief history of ASHRM: 1980–2010." Retrieved November 9, 2014, from www.ashrm.org/ashrm/about/history/a_brief_history_of_ashrm/

Baker, S., Lauro, C., & Sintim-Damoa, A. (2008). Malpractice allegations and apology laws: Benefits and risks for radiologists. *Journal of the American College of Radiology* 5(12); 1186–1190.

Baily, M. A., Bottrell, M., Lynn, J., & Jennings, B. (2006). *The ethics of using qi methods to improve quality and safety of care.* Garrison, NY: The Hastings Center.

Bell, Sigall K., Smulowitz P. B., Woodwardm A C,, Mello, M.M., Duva, A.M., &Boothman, R. C. (2012). Disclosure, apology, and offer programs: stakeholders' views of barriers to and strategies for broad implementation. *Milbank Quarterly, 90*(4), 682–705.

Boothman, R, C., Blackwell, A. C., Campbell, D. A., Jr., Commiskey, E., & Anderson S. (2009). A better approach to medical malpractice claims? The University of Michigan Experience. *Journal of Health & Life Sciences Law, 2*(2), 125–159.

Boothman, R. C., Imhoff, S. J., & Campbell, D. A. Jr. (2012). Nurturing a culture of patient safety and achieving lower malpractice risk through disclosure:

Lessons learned and future directions. *Frontiers of Health Services Management* *28*(3), 13–28.

Chung, E., Horowitz, J. R., Pottow, J. A. E., & Jagsi, & Reshma, J. (2011). Malpractice suits and physician apologies in cancer care. *Journal of Oncological Practice, 7*(6), 389–393.

Core Risk Services. (2014). History of health care risk management programs. Retrieved from November 9, 2014, from www.coreriskservicesinc.com/history.php

Dresser, R. (2008). The limits of apology laws. *Hastings Center Report, 38*(3), 6–7.

Emanuel, E. J., & Steiner, D. (1995). Institutional conflicts of interest. *New England Journal of Medicine, 332*, 262–268.

Foucar, E., & Wick, M. R. (2007). Tort reform: The pathologists' perspective. *Seminars in Diagnostic Pathology, 24*(2), 131–147.

Fredricks, T. R. (2012). Efficacy of a physician's words of empathy: An overview of state apology laws. *Journal of the American Osteopathic Association, 112*(7), 405–406.

Friedman, R. S., & McKinney, R. Jr. (2013). Is conflict of interest becoming a challenge for institution-based institutional review boards? *Clinical Cancer Research, 19*, 4034.

Hyman, C. S., Liebman C. B., Schechter, C. B., & Sage, W. M. (2010). Interest-based mediation of medical malpractice lawsuits: A route to improved patient safety? *Journal of Health Politics, Policy and Law, 35*(5), 797–828.

Ibsen, H. (1882). An enemy of the people [R. Farquharson Sharp, Trans.]. Retrieved November 9, 2014, from www.gutenberg.org/files/2446/2446-h/2446-h.htm

Institute of Medicine. (1999). *To err is human: Building a safer health system.* Washington, DC: National Academies Press.

Jennings, B., Baily, M. A., Bottrell, M., & Lynn, J. (2007) (Eds.). *Health care quality improvement: Ethical and regulatory issues.* Garrison, NY: The Hastings Center.

Kachalia, A., &. Bates, D. W. (2014). Disclosing medical errors: The view from the USA. *The Surgeon, 12*, 64–67.

Kachalia, A., & Mello, M. M. (2011). New directions in medical liability reform. *New England Journal of Medicine, 364*(16), 1564–1572.

Knutsen, E. (2010, Summer). Keeping settlements secret. *Florida State University Law Review 37*: 945–979.

Kramen, S. S., Cranfill L., Hamm, G., & Woodard, T. (2002). John M Eisenberg patient safety awards advocacy: The Lexington Veterans Affairs Medical Center. *Joint Commission Journal of Quality Improvement, 28*(12), 646–670.

Kramen, S. S., & Hamm, G. (1999). Risk management: Extreme honesty may be the best policy. *Annals of Internal Medicine, 131*(12), 963–967.

Leape, L. L. (1994). Error in medicine. *Journal of the American Medical Association, 272*, 1851–1857.

Lo, B., & Field, M. J. (Eds.). (2009). *Conflict of interest in medical research, education, and practice.* Washington, DC: Institute of Medicine.

Loren, D.J. et al.(2010). Risk managers, physicians, and disclosure of harmful medical errors. *Joint Commission Journal of Quality & Patient Safety, 36*(3), 101–108.

Mastroianni, A. C., Mello, M. M., Sommer, S, Hardy, M., & Gallagher, T. H. (2010). The flaws in state "apology" and "disclosure" laws dilute their intended impact on malpractice suits. *Health Affairs, 29*(9), 1611–1619.

McDonnell, W. M., & Guenther, E. (2008). Narrative review: Do state laws make it easier to say 'I'm sorry?' *Annals of Internal Medicine, 149*(11), 811–815.

Mello, M. M., Studdert, D. M., & Kachalia, A. (2014, October 30). The medical liability climate and prospects for reform. *Journal of the American Medical Association*. doi:10.1001/jama.2014.10705.

Pelt, J. L., & Faldmo, L. P. (2008). Physician error and disclosure. *Clinical Obstetrics & Gynecology, 51*(4), 700–708.

Perez, B., & DiDona, T. (2009). Assessing legislative potential to institute error transparency: A state comparison of malpractice claims rates. *Journal for Healthcare Quality, 32*(3), 36–41.

Public Risk Management Association. (2014). "Code of ethics." Retrieved November 9, 2014, from www.primacentral.org/resources/codeofethics.pdf

Quinn, R. E., & Eichler, M. C. (2008). The 3Rs program: The Colorado experience. *Clinical Obstetrics and Gynecology, 51*(4), 709–718.

Raper, S. E. (2011). No role for apology: Remedial work and the problem of medical injury. *Yale Journal of Health Policy, Law & Ethics, 11*, 267–327.

Regis, C., & Poitras, J. (2010). Healthcare mediation and the need for apologies. *Health Law Journal, 18*, 31–49.

Robbennolt, J. (2009). Apologies and medical error. *Clinical Orthopedics and Related Research, 467*(2), 376–382.

Rose, S. L. (2013). Patient advocacy organizations: Institutional conflicts of interest, trust, and trustworthiness. *Journal of Law, Medicine & Ethics, 41*(3), 680–687.

Saitta, N., & Hodge, S. D. Jr. (2012). Efficacy of a physician's words of empathy: An overview of state apology laws. *Journal of the American Osteopathic Association, 112*(5), 302–306.

Saxton, J. W., & Finkelstein, M. M. (2008). Adverse event management: Your evidence to decrease professional liability risk. *Journal of Medical Practice Management, 24*(1), 5–8.

Shafer, A. (2004). Biomedical conflicts of interest: A defense of the sequestration thesis—learning from the cases of Nancy Olivieri and David Healy. *Journal of Medical Ethics, 30*, 8–24.

Sohn, D. H., & Bal, S. B. (2012). Medical malpractice reform: The role of alternative dispute resolution. *Clinical Orthopaedics and Related Research, 470*(5), 1370–1378

Stanford University. (2014). Rule 4.7. Institutional conflict of interest in research involving human subjects. Retrieved November 9, 2014, from http://doresearch.stanford.edu/policies/research-policy-handbook/conflicts-commitment-and-interest/institutional-conflict-interest-research-involving-human-subjects

Surbone, A. (2012). Oncologists' difficulties in facing and disclosing medical errors: Suggestions for the clinic. *American Society of Clinical Oncology Education Book.* e24–27.

Taft, L. (2005). Apology and medical mistake: Opportunity or foil? *Annals of Health Law. 1*, 55–94.

Thompson, D. (1993). Understanding financial conflicts of interest. *New England Journal of Medicine, 329*, 573–576.

Vercler, C. J., Buchman, S. R., & Chung, K. C. (2015). Discussing harm-causing errors with patients: An ethical primer for plastic surgeons. *Ann Plast Surg., 74*, 140–144.

Wei, M. (2007). Doctors, apologies, and the law: An analysis and critique of apology laws. *Journal of Health Law. 40*(1), 107–159.

Wilson, R. T. (2010). The death of Jesse Gelsinger: New evidence of the influence of money and prestige in human research. *American Journal of Law & Medicine, 36*(2–3), 295–325.

Zimmerman, R. (2004). Doctors' new tool to fight lawsuits: Saying "I'm sorry." *Journal of the Oklahoma State Medical Association, 97*(6), 245–247.

**Appendix A: Table of Articles Surveyed**

| Study | Date | Disclosure Ethical? | Quality Improvement? | Reduced Costs? | Institutional Conflict? | Notes |
|---|---|---|---|---|---|---|
| Mello, Studdert & Kachalia | 2014 | Y* | Y | Y | Article notes that compensation associated with disclosure may be difficult for insurers used to assessing compensation by the likelihood of litigation | Discussion of reforms and effect on liability claims |
| Vercler, Buchman & Chung | 2015 | Y | Y | Y | | |
| Kachalia & Bates | 2014 | Y | Y | Y | | |
| Petronio | 2013 | Y | | Y | | |
| Bell et al. | 2012 | Y | Y | Y | Y | |
| Murtagh et al. | 2012 | | | Y (arguing more patients might sue and costs rise) | | |
| Fredricks | 2012 | Y | | | | |
| Saitta & Hodge | 2012 | Y | | Y | | |
| Surbone | 2012 | Y | | | | |
| Sohn & Bal | 2012 | | | Y | | |

(Appendix continues on next page)

## Appendix A: (Continued)

| Study | Date | Disclosure Ethical? | Quality Improvement? | Reduced Costs? | Institutional Conflict? | Notes |
|---|---|---|---|---|---|---|
| Boothman, Imhoff & Campbell | 2012 | Y | Y | Y | Goal of Michigan program to compensate patients quickly and fairly; recognizes the difficulties in valuing claims economically. States that one way to value claims would be what they might bring in litigation; failing to heed this might lead patients to think they are being made cheap offers and treated unfairly. | |
| Raper | 2011 | Y | Y | | | |
| Kachalia & Mello | 2011 | | Y | Y | | Analysis of tort reforms |
| Conway et al. | 2011 | | | | | |

*(Appendix continues on next page)*

**Appendix A: (Continued)**

| Study | Date | Disclosure Ethical? | Quality Improvement? | Reduced Costs? | Institutional Conflict? | Notes |
|---|---|---|---|---|---|---|
| Chung et al. | 2011 | Y | Y | Y | Describes Michigan program as creating environment of fairness and openness; cost savings an incidental advantage | Notes that the Michigan approach may not work in systems that don't self insure their physicians under an umbrella, because of the possibility of strategic behavior to shift costs |
| Hyman | 2010 | | Y | | No, but does consider whether patients felt pushed into settlements and whether they reported satisfaction with the process | |
| Mastroianni | 2010 | Y | | Y (arguing that state apology laws are inadequate to reduce provider fears of litigation; suggests adopting "best practices" for disclosures | | |

(Appendix continues on next page)

## Appendix A: (Continued)

| Study | Date | Disclosure Ethical? | Quality Improvement? | Reduced Costs? | Institutional Conflict? | Notes |
|---|---|---|---|---|---|---|
| Perez & DiDona | 2009 | | Y (arguing that there is no significant difference in paid malpractice claims between states with and states without disclosure or apology laws) | Y | | |
| Loren et al. | 2010 | Y | | | Compares fiduciary role of physicians to risk-manager role in protecting institution from financial harm | |
| Regis & Poitras | 2010 | Y | | Y | | |
| Robbinnelt | 2009 | Y | | Y | | |
| Boothman et al. | 2009 | | | | | |
| McDonnell & Guenther | 2008 | Y | Y | Y | Citations to the possibility that patients may receive inadequate compensation | |

(Appendix continues on next page)

**Appendix A: (Continued)**

| Study | Date | Disclosure Ethical? | Quality Improvement? | Reduced Costs? | Institutional Conflict? | Notes |
|---|---|---|---|---|---|---|
| Baker, Lauro & Sintim-Damoa | 2008 | Y | Y | Y (also noting that disclosure may increase risks to radiologists, given their separation from patients) | | |
| Quinn & Eichler | 2008 | Y | Y | Y | Reports importance of bearing in mind fiduciary responsibilities to patients | |
| Pelt & Faldmo | 2008 | Y | | Y | | |
| Saxton & Finkelstein | 2008 | | | Y | | |
| Dresser | 2008 | | | | Overview of the limits of apology laws; mentions the need for patient compensation | |
| Foucar & Wick | 2007 | | | General overview of tort reform | | |
| Wei | 2007 | Discussion of barriers to apologies and how to overcome them | | | | |

(Appendix continues on next page)

**Appendix A: (Continued)**

| Study | Date | Disclosure Ethical? | Quality Improvement? | Reduced Costs? | Institutional Conflict? | Notes |
|-------|------|---------------------|----------------------|----------------|-------------------------|-------|
| Wagner | 2006 | Y | | | | |
| Taft | 2005 | Y (healing power of apology) | Y | Y | Discusses how liability shields for expressions of sympathy, but not for admissions of wrongdoing that corrupt the moral power of apology. | |
| Zimmerman | 2004 | | | Y | | |
| Kraman et al. | 2002 | Y | Y | Y | | |

CHAPTER 5

# THE SOCIAL AND ENVIRONMENTAL COSTS OF ENERGY DEVELOPMENT

## Risks and Ethical Considerations

**Christopher A. Simon**

## ABSTRACT

The chapter will discuss social and environmental costs associated with the recent surge in fossil-fuel extraction, nuclear, and renewable energy development. More specifically, I will examine shale gas and oil hydraulic fracturing, uranium mining, and renewable energy development in the United States and Canada. The externalities of fossil energy development—its impact on rural communities and local ecology—are significant. In the case of renewable energy, the impacts long-term on public lands, water, and wildlife are often undervalued compared to the positive impact (both short term and long term) of green energy development. Canadian uranium development in northern Saskatchewan has, similarly, been viewed as a net positive compared to the negative externalities this production generates. I will argue that undervaluing the risks associated, not only with fossil fuel and uranium

*Ethics and Risk Management*, pp. 67–89
Copyright © 2015 by Information Age Publishing

extraction but also with green energy development, has ethical implications for key public concerns such as energy security, sustainability, and meaningful commitment to future generations.

## INTRODUCTION

The world is thirsty for energy, but the thirst has grown exponentially and without a clear conscience. For millennia, petroleum and natural gas were "alternative" sources of energy in particular regions of the world and were used for limited purposes: for instance, the use of flammable natural gas in ancient China (Ogden & Baron, 1976) and the burning of lamp oil in 14th century Persia (Sorkhabi, 2005). A solid form of petroleum known as bitumen was used in ancient times as a sealing material as well as for mummification of human bodies (Schwartz & Hollander, 2000). Coal in various forms has been burned primarily for heat (warmth and cooking fuel) for thousands of years, but also had been a key part of the development of tool making (Mattsusch, 2008).

Energy use in the premodern society has been limited. While there were markets in bitumen and other easily transportable energy materials, liquid petroleum and natural gas was primarily used *in situ*. With the dawn of the modern energy era in the 1870s and 1880s, the demand for petroleum, natural gas, and electricity increased dramatically. In the early 19th century, coal became a more prominent form of energy as it was used in steam engines for transportation and the operation of other forms of equipment; this was due particularly to the fact that coal became a cheaper energy source when compared to charcoal. The same was true of the growing popularity of natural gas in lighting as whale oil became less price-competitive. Fossil energy had limited uses until market demand for reasonably priced and readily available energy alternatives led to widespread adoption.

That said, while markets played a key role, government policy has made fossil energy extraction more feasible (and often at a low cost) as a result of public-land policies, generous royalty rates, and relaxed or non-existent environmental standards. In the case of the United States and Canada, vast public lands containing a plethora of plant, mineral, and animal resources—and varying water supplies—were quickly seen as sources of wealth generation and the basic materials needed in the creation of the modern industrial society.

The 1940s and 1950s saw a rise in the capability and supply of nuclear energy. Nuclear energy was not the result of a market shift in resource preferences, per se, but rather a direct result of a government policy that promoted the "peaceful" use of atomic energy following its devastating and highly controversial military use in the Second World War. With the development of nuclear energy, came the need for nuclear fuel in the form of uranium oxide; a mineral found throughout the world, but important to this study—a mineral found in sizeable quantities in the United States and Canada.

With the growing awareness about climate change (and with the growing sense of risk associated with fossil energy use), the nuclear-energy plant operations safety and waste issues, federal, state, provincial, and local government policies in the United States and Canada increasingly promoted and subsidized the development and use of green energy. Since the 1970s, but more particularly in the last 20 years, biofuels, geothermal, solar, tidal, and wind technologies in the production of clean low or zero carbon fuels were being developed to meet the energy needs of an energy-hungry society. While still in the early stages of development, the progress in renewable green energy development has been exponential, with energy prices beginning to close in on the prices of fossil energy; in some cases, emerging as price-competitive.

Markets and governments have grown in tandem to create a modern world with high-energy demands. Government has facilitated market growth in areas where growth was already occurring due to technological advancements, as in the case of fossil energy and electrification. In the case of nuclear energy, the government created markets to "civilianize" the use of a potent military weapon technology. Finally, alternative energy policies have created a demand for clean energy sources; a response to the growing scientific evidence of climate change, and the need and demand for a sustainable energy future that promotes environmental and public health, as well as the responsible use of natural resources.

Working closely to meet energy demand in a general sense, government and markets have had their own unique priorities and often remained blind to a more general concern for morally-responsible development. Government often responded to a narrow range of interests: business, environmental, and public interest groups, along with sub-national government, scientific experts, and bureaucracies. In order to meet the energy demands of a growing society, it became necessary to consider energy policy alternatives in light of their ability to meet energy demands at a reasonable cost (price, as well as risk); but it was one that also limited marginal social costs, and took into serious consideration moral dilemmas posed by its development and use. This chapter will reflect on the development of fossil, nuclear, and renewable energy in the United States and Canada.

## POLICY ANALYSIS AND ENERGY DEVELOPMENT

Policy analysis has and will continue to play a big role in energy source development. The end of petroleum has been proclaimed many times, and yet the resource is being developed at a greater and greater rate in North America. Nuclear-energy development has been sluggish over the last several decades, due to concerns about health risks associated with power plants and spent fuel. Renewable energy has made great leaps forward, but has significant room to grow before it reaches parity with fossil, nuclear, and hydropower. For several decades to come, there is no clear sense that our choices will be under duress due to supply shortfall. In other words, we have real alternatives and we can make choices about our energy future.

Weimer and Vining (1992) have outlined a policy-analysis framework that can be used here to consider energy-source development. First and foremost in their framework is the role of philosophy of governance, which has a significant impact on how energy development is conceived in terms of costs and benefits. Philosophy of governance shapes how certain types of energy development occur; are shaped by public policy, and by the marketplace, or by some combination of public and private forces. While philosophy of governance may not play a direct role in formal policy analysis, it does shape the way policy analysis has been received and incorporated into policymaking. Among the most central goals of policy analysis, particularly in the case of energy development policy, has been the identification of negative policy externalities. Negative externalities constrain individual rights. Policy analysis goes further to identify Pareto optimal policy choices, which maximize social benefit while minimizing social costs (MC = MB).

In considering the role of government, it is necessary to consider energy as developed from the standpoint of an economic "good." In other words, energy development contributes to needed energy supply, which maximizes affordability and availability. The analysis of energy development is not just about minimizing negative externalities; it is also about feeding an existing infrastructure and, to put it in simple terms: keeping the lights on. That said, despite differences in philosophy of governance, modern society, and socio-economic relationships have required that government play some role in energy development due to the important goal of protecting the social welfare of its citizens, as well as managing the legal transfer of ownership from sovereign to private firms, which develop energy resources that are often located subsurface on publically-owned lands, and/or which may impact ecosystems. Private-property rights disputes may also arise due to energy-development innovations, which again demand the attention of the sovereign acting as arbiter, which is prioritizing or managing public and private goals.

The philosophy of governance has been shaped, to a significant degree, by social values. Social values have evolved in recent decades, reshaping the ways in which negative externalities are conceptualized, defined, and prioritized. In the book *Culture Shift in Advanced Industrial Society*, Inglehart (1990) has demonstrated that post-Second World War generational cohorts placed greater policy emphasis on the quality of life and the reduction of environmental risks. These younger generational cohorts were referred to by Inglehart as "post-materialist"—generations for whom economic benefit plays a diminished role in relation to social and environmental benefit. Focusing on environmental management, a policy area that is closely related to energy development issues, Pierce and his colleagues at Oregon and Washington state universities conducted a cross-border Canada-United States comparison studying the impact of postmaterialist values and political culture (Pierce, Lovrich, Steel, Steger, & Tennert, 2000). The authors found further confirmation of Inglehart's theory, as well as support for the cross-national institutional comparisons completed by Seymour Martin Lipset (1989) in his classic account: *Continental Divide: The Values and Institutions of the United States and Canada*.

Public goods are defined broadly by post materialists: Examples of public goods include the quality and availability of water and clean air. Environmental degradation in the pursuit of energy development has been viewed unfavorably by those individuals holding post-materialist values. Post materialists have tended to be highly sensitive to the issue of environmental risk; so evidential damage or not, the threat of environmental degradation has oftentimes been sufficient cause to oppose energy development through political and social action. As Lipset (1989) and Pierce et al. (2000) point out, however, that Canadian and U.S. political cultural traditions have impacted the level and types of political and social reaction that have arisen in response to perceived or real negative impacts on public goods.

Policy analysis involves a delicate balancing act. On the one hand, energy resource development reduces energy costs to consumers and maximizes economic and social benefits. Reasonably-priced fuel means that transportation is more affordable, thus allowing for work and pleasure commuting. Economically affordable electricity and natural gas translate into affordable cooling costs for homes in the arid southwestern United States, and affordable heating costs in the northern latitudes of Canada and the United States. Conversely, an increased energy supply can produce steep marginal social costs: that is, negative externalities that may impact the quality of public goods.

The information in Figure 5.1 helps us consider the delicate balance between consumer surplus and marginal social costs. By way of example, consumer surplus (P1acP2) is created by the increased supply of petroleum resulting from oil and gas leases on public lands. Producer surplus (P1aeP2) is greater than the MPC (ecd) associated with the increased quantity supplied. From the consumer and producer standpoint, the increased production of the marketable private good maximizes one dimension of energy security—namely, affordability (a lower price for energy). Conversely, increased supply is associated with higher marginal social costs (abc). The increased marginal social costs might be increased air pollution, greater urban sprawl in metropolitan areas, and the related social equity and health problems associated with the increased supply of fossil energy, which is needed to provide infrastructure and maintain the flow of social and business enterprise.

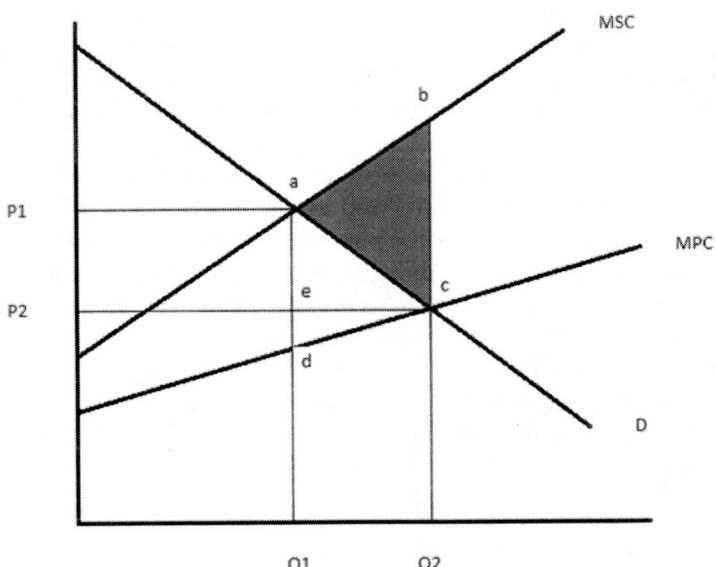

**Figure 5.1.**   The delicate balance between consumer surplus, producer surplus and marginal social costs.

It is important to note that the direct negative impacts of energy development on public lands, in the form of the degradation of soils, loss of native vegetation and indigenous species could just as easily occur on private lands developed for energy extraction. Contamination or depletion of aquifers as a result of oil and gas-well drilling and the long-distance transport of their products by pipeline or rail, is a serious concern; and it has potential negative externalities that bring large social costs no matter if the drilling and/or transport occurs on public or private lands.

Additionally, the age-old precedent in resource extraction known as the "rule of capture," likely invites the systematic overdevelopment of natural resources. Long term, sustainable development can invite resource depletion, which will produce additional marginal social costs as resource scarcity becomes increasingly evident, despite technological innovations designed to overcome petroleum and other mineral scarcities. Resource overuse and development occurs at a rate greater than substitute goods innovations can reach marketable status; and, at a rate greater than social-behavioral change can occur.

Infrastructure adaptations, needed to make innovative substitute energy goods feasible, frequently occur at a slow pace. Established public infrastructure projects are often the beneficiaries of intergovernmental resource transfers, which are made possible by powerful elected officials in state and federal legislatures. Intergovernmentalism often involves closely knit policy networks composed of elected and appointed officials; science and technology experts; private-sector entrepreneurs, seeking long-term resource supplies; friendly (or at least stable) regulatory and taxation policy environments; and long-term public or private contractual relationships. For example, fossil energy resource development has relied heavily on the knowledge that interstate (and even international) transportation (via roads/highways, rail, pipeline, or through port facilities) will be available and with stable and quantifiable costs. Infrastructure of this type requires that elected and appointed officials from the local level up to the national level who are accessible and can act as stakeholders in the energy development process over the long term. Stable intergovernmental policy networks play an important role in energy development.

Public-works projects and public-private partnerships to establish energy infrastructure are built on political and economic relationships that play a role in long term economic decisions; electoral politics and legislator power-bases; and citizen and community social, political, and economic patterns of life. The fairly rapid changes required for energy innovation implementation that tout lower or marginal social costs, might (paradoxically) produce new and even more damaging marginal social costs. They also might lead to serious uncertainty about shifts in electoral politics and significant economic change at the community, state, and national level. For example, decisions to close nuclear power plants in California and Washington would have long-term economic and social impacts that might reduce marginal social costs, as promised at the time; but they might impose long-term economic and social costs in the future. Reversing such decisions would require significant time and resources, particularly if the infrastructure in question was dismantled or moth-balled. It would also require substantial and long-term reversals in terms of political powerbases; large-scale turnover of key career administrators in administrative agencies; and a view change in the role of government in energy development.

Such reversals are possible; and they have occurred in the past, with significant consequences on energy development. The election of a large freshman class into Congress in the 1972 general election brought with it a substantial and new powerbase supportive of green energy; this played a significant role in passing key environmental and public utility reforms. President Barack Obama benefitted from the economic reversal in 2008 and the election of Democratic majorities in both chambers of Congress; this helped him gain support for the American Recovery and Reinvestment Act, which led to heavy public investment in renewable energy. As a two-term U.S. president, Obama has also been able to develop key environmental and energy regulations that have led to a weakened role for coal-fired electricity generation and have promoted clean renewable energy. That said, the promotion of renewable energy and coal regulations did not prevent the development of shale oil and natural-gas technology and development on private lands; it only stunted its eventual development on public lands by slowing down permitting processes and placing limits on pipeline development.

The previous discussion illustrates how government and the private sector have been faced with significant dilemmas due to the sunk costs (and related benefits) that make attractive the status quo. Economic theory postulates that markets will change in response to price signals. As prices for a particular energy good rise, lower-cost substitutes will become more attractive to energy consumers. From an energy consumer perspective, the marginal social costs of energy production and use—such as climate change, fossil energy depletion, and health risks—have been less likely to shape energy choices; rather it is supply, demand, prices, opportunity costs, and availability of substitute goods that are more likely to shape choice.

In the case of government, however, a whole myriad of issues must be considered in terms of policies associated with energy production. Market concentration poses a significant dilemma for governments seeking to promote market choice and fair prices. For instance, the petroleum market in the early to mid-20th century was controlled almost entirely by seven major oil companies. Until the passage of the Public Utilities Regulatory Policy Act of 1978 and subsequent landmark energy laws at the state and national levels, local electrical utilities were vertically organized, controlling nearly all aspects of electricity production and distribution within their region. Highly concentrated energy markets frequently have offered energy producers enormous political and economic power, and they have reduced the likelihood that consumers could make economic choices about energy that reflected their economic and social value preferences.

Government policy, in addition to regulating and broadening concentrated markets, might help consumers make better and more informed choices about the true costs and benefits associated with different energy sources. In other words, government policy may result in more informed individual choices that could result in lower demand for energy sources seen as having high marginal social costs (such as energy sources associated with the production of greenhouse gases, elevated human health risks, and damaging to native ecosystems), and a greater demand for low MSC alternatives (Grubb, 1992). As mentioned earlier, consumers can make choices based on costs and benefits readily seen and understood. It follows that informing consumers about the true costs of fossil energy use might shape their preferences in perhaps marginal, but nevertheless societally significant, ways.

Government policy could be used to regulate markets and open markets to new suppliers; and to inform citizens of the true costs and marginal social costs associated with the development and use of various energy sources. As mentioned previously, citizen respondents have expressed concern about the aesthetic qualities of life, and displayed concern for the impact of climate change, and about the equitable and sustainable use of resources. In these opinion responses, there has been a movement away from pure economic interests and greater emphasis on the moral dimension; in other words, post materialists want to live well, but they want to know that they are making good choices in the broadest sense of the word. Despite this stated preference, despite growing alternatives, a disconnect has remained between the day-to-day energy choices (based largely on price) and the larger focus on "good" or moral choices in energy development and use.

In the book, *But Will the Planet Notice? How Smart Economics Can Save the* World, Gernot Wagner (2011, p. 8), has stated that the vast majority of people, on a daily basis, focus on meeting their material needs rather than actively considering the moral basis of their choices or how they are related to sustainability and the planet's future. Perhaps even more importantly, Wagner argued that most people have little interest in altering their choice behavior.

The facts are brutally clear. The collective will and drive of billions voids most if not all feel-good efforts of freelance environmental heroism. It's the tremendous power of channeling those billions of individual decisions through markets that has provided Americans, Europeans, and a few lucky others with unprecedented levels of personal wealth. It has pulled hundreds of millions of Chinese out of poverty, and it is increasingly doing so for millions of others. They open up the playing field for innovators and entrepreneurs to create comforts that most of us can't imagine living without. (Wagner, 2011, p. 8)

Wagner tends to accept that market-driven choice is largely immutable, but he argues that individual and collective choices must be more carefully guided by moral principles, as well. He concluded that new efforts to politically shape market forces in such areas as energy development, have the potential of integrating the moral principles of environmental stewardship and intergenerational justice into markets.

Along these same lines, Michael Sandel in his book *What Money Can't Buy*, argued that commercialization of nearly every aspect of human society has had significant moral and ethical implications (Sandel, 2012). With regards to energy development, Sandel was highly critical of pollution tax credits as a method of bypassing regulator impacts on fossil energy development. As Sandel (2012) argued, pollution tax credits were, in effect, licenses to pollute. The moral dimension is critical to the development of energy that promotes sustainability, and protects the environment, as well as overall planetary health and existence. However, as noted earlier, corporations and too many consumers have made decisions on the basis of short term economic gain or on the minimization of personal expense. The BP-well blowout and its impact on the Gulf of Mexico is a good example of corporations that focused on short-term economic gain rather than the potentially marginal social and environmental costs of a tragedy in the making (Ladd, 2012).

Just as the 2008 economic crisis developed as a result of corporate and political decision making, as well as individual incentive for short-term financial gain; there is an impending energy-development crisis that will be attributed to the same malformed institutional and individual incentives and choices. In the case of the 2008 crisis, institutions and individuals were quick to respond in the aftermath, saving the world economy from what could have been a long and dark economic depression. With the exception of cries against "corporate greed" and the "richest one percent," there was little to no discussion of the moral dimension of the economic crisis; in the sense that a very broad and deep swath of individuals made choices that reflected short-term gain rather than a long-term and meaningful interest in advancing economic, environmental conditions, and social stability and sustainability. The same may be true of what is now occurring in energy development. To illustrate the points made above, the chapter will now move on to a discussion of developments in shale oil/gas mining in the United States, uranium mining in Canada, and renewable energy developments in the United States.

## OIL AND GAS SHALE IN THE UNITED STATES, TAR SANDS IN CANADA

In the late 20th century, petroleum and gas production in the United States were declining at a steady pace. The decline in U.S. petroleum production in the lower-48 states had been declining since the 1950s. The decline was reversed for several years in the 1980s by the opening of the North Slope in Alaska to increase petroleum production. The North-Slope policy shift was initiated by the Reagan Administration, which placed less emphasis on energy conservation and environmental protection, and greater emphasis on increased energy supply as a way of driving down fossil energy prices and jump-starting the U.S. economy.

The Reagan policies proved to have a short term effect on domestic energy supplies. With maturing oil fields in Alaska and the lower-48 states, the U.S. production continued to decline through the 1990s raising significant concerns about U.S. foreign petroleum dependency. North Slope oil has declined significantly, with calls from energy companies and so-called Tea Party conservatives for the opening the Artic National Wildlife Refuge (ANWR) to petroleum and gas development. In a comprehensive study commissioned in 2003 by U.S. Secretary of Energy Spencer Abraham, the National Petroleum Council found that there was a "fundamental shift in the supply and demand balance" of natural gas. The study noted that natural-gas supplies were becoming tighter while demand was rising, which led to foreboding price spikes in the early 2000s (Shackhouls, 2003). The period brought together three serious concerns about the future path of domestic energy in the United States: (1) dwindling domestic supply meant increased reliance on foreign suppliers, with energy sources often originating in regions with elevated levels of political and social turmoil; (2) growing concerns about the impact of terrorism on the "way-of-life" in the United States and other developed nations; and (3) growing concerns and evidence about the impact of fossil energy on the concentration of greenhouse gases in the upper atmosphere and subsequent climate change.

With the aforementioned concerns actively in the minds of policymakers and voters, along with fresh memories of the tragedy of September 11, 2001, the Energy Policy Act of 2005 (EPAct, 2005), and a whole host of state green-energy and sustainability initiatives (for example, renewable energy portfolio standards) became the foundation of a new green-energy policy agenda. Unlike the post-1973 energy crisis, however, the focus in this green-energy policy renaissance focused on environmental stewardship, clean energy, and sustainability.

Around the same time, however, there was a reversal of fortunes for domestic petroleum and natural-gas production. Hydraulic fracking, a technology that had been in research and development for decades, was widely commercialized in the early 2000s and produced an upsurge in shale oil and gas production in the United States. Fracking involves the injection of fluids—a mixture of fracking chemicals and specific forms of sand—into oil exploration wells to loosen oil and gas products from rock formations deep beneath the surface. The fracking fluids and oil/gas products are then pumped out and separated.

The Marcellus shale region that lies beneath portions of Ohio, New York, Pennsylvania, and West Virginia has witnessed tremendous growth in shale-energy production. In North Dakota and eastern Montana (and extending into southern Alberta, Canada), the Bakken formation has led to enormous growth in shale oil and gas production. A large portion of the gas produced, however, is flared off due to a lack of pipeline capacity to transport the gas to retail markets. Similar shale energy booms have occurred in several other states, such as Utah and Colorado, albeit on a far smaller scale.

The energy production boom has led to enormous growth in local revenue for many individuals. The economic boom has also led to enormous growth in job opportunities for construction firms, drilling platform operators, and petroleum engineers, hydrologists, and production operations crews. Much like the days of the California Gold Rush in the 1850s or the oil-catting days in Oklahoma's oil boom in the 1920s and 1930s, huge man-camps have formed in these oil and gas-boom regions.

In Canada, a similar boom has been occurring for some time. The tar sands in Alberta are composed of bitumen, a thick often semi-hardened petroleum formation not dissimilar from the asphalt slurries seen on road surfaces. In fact, an early use of the Alberta tar sands was, in fact, to pave roads. The Canadian tar sands were known to the First Nations peoples, and later came to the attention of Europeans in the 18th century. In the 1920s Canadian researchers began to explore the commercial techniques of separating the petroleum value of the tar sands from the sand and other impurities. While Canadian tar sand petroleum production has been steadily growing for the last four decades, the rate of growth has increased substantially since the late-1990s. In 1999, Canada was producing approximately 600,000 barrels per day. As of 2013, Canadian tar sand production is approximately 1 million barrels per day. According to the Canadian Association of Petroleum Producers, the tar sands contain 33 billion barrels of recoverable petroleum reserves (Capp, 2014). Canada has been ranked the third largest producer of natural gas globally, and is the fifth largest energy producer. Nearly all of the petroleum exported by Canada (approximately 2.6 million barrels per day) is sold to its neighbor to the south, the United States (CAPP, 2014; Energy Trends Insider, 2014).

The development of difficult-to-access shale oil and gas in the United States and bitumen in Alberta, Canada's tar sands is an energy and water intensive process. The energy return on investment (EROI) for the production of shale oil and gas is approximately four. In other words, it takes the energy of one barrel of oil to produce four barrels of oil for sale. By comparison to the early days of petroleum production, EROI stood at approximately 100 (Leeb 2014). In addition to the low EROI for shale oil and tar sands production, water usage is very high. According to Anu Mittal, director of the Natural Resources and Environment Team in the U.S. Government Accountability Office (GAO), the average water use to produce one barrel of shale oil is 4.8 barrels of water (Mittal, 2011, p. 8). The GAO report and testimony goes on to note that while water availability for shale oil and gas development, at least in initial stages of development, is likely to be available; if development of shale gas and oil is expanded, it will come into conflict with other demands on water resources (Mittal, 2011, p. 9).

In order to not be caught without needed water, shale oil operators have purchased water rights to more than a billion gallons of water in the western United States (Simon, 2009). Water has always been at a premium in the arid West, but water has become more precious as climate change and drought have parched the most populous state, California. The marginal social impact of using 97 billion gallons of water for energy production, as opposed to food production and domestic use, is a serious challenge for policymakers (Galbraith, 2013; Goldenberg, 2014). In California, recent legislation has been sent to Governor Jerry Brown that could potentially allow state and local policymakers to set restrictions for groundwater use, despite the fact that the water rights are privately held (Marois, 2014). Similar water restrictions could be imposed in other Western states if drought conditions persist. Deep aquifers are currently being pumped to support crops and domestic water use at non-sustainable rates.

> Groundwater comes from aquifers—sponge-like gravel and sand-filled underground reservoirs—and we see this water only when it flows from springs and wells. In the United States, we rely on this hidden—and shrinking—water supply to meet half our needs, and as drought shrinks surface water in lakes, rivers, and reservoirs, we rely on groundwater from aquifers even more. Some shallow aquifers recharge from surface water, but deeper aquifers contain ancient water locked in the earth by changes in geology thousands or millions of years ago. These aquifers typically cannot recharge, and once this "fossil" water is gone, it is gone forever—potentially changing how and where we can live and grow food, among other things. (Dimick, 2014; Nicot & Scanlon, 2012)

According to a report published in *Environment 360*, nearly 98 billion gallons of water is pumped per year from the Athabasca River in Alberta, Canada, for use in tar sands oil production. "That quantity of water exceeds the amount of water that the city of Toronto, with a population of 2.8 million people, uses annually ... a growing number of scientists and economists ... contend that the timing and magnitude of these diversions are drying up wetlands, disrupting water flows, and potentially threatening riparian habitats thousands of miles downstream along the Mackenzie River basin, which drains 20% of Canada" (Struzik, 2013).

Canada's tar-sand development has required enormous energy inputs. The electricity demand for Alberta's tar sand production has required 5% of all electricity used in Canada. There is an additional thermal-energy demand (steam) to separate the oil from the tar sands. While Alberta produces electricity using biomass, coal, hydropower, and natural gas, there is a large carbon footprint from at least two of the energy sources listed, which poses additional social and environmental cost concerns (Doluweera, Jordaan, Moore, Keith, & Bergerson, 2011). Co-generation of thermal energy and electricity *in situ* is one way of reducing social (e.g., health) and environmental risks associated with carbon emissions. Shale oil and gas development also has been energy intensive, as noted in the EROI statistic cited previously; a great deal of energy is employed in the refining process as well as the electricity and fuels needed in the drilling and extraction process.

Both tar-sand and shale oil/gas development cause a great deal of water and soil pollution. Pro-industry advocates of these alternative and highly-lucrative, fossil-fuel sources claim that environmental damage is comparably less damaging than other daily activities in which society engages (Engelder, 2011). There is, however, clear evidence that tar sands and shale/oil gas development have been contributing in some ways to water and land pollution. Osborn and his colleagues found methane contaminating drinking water, but no evidence of fracking fluid contamination, as a result of shale oil/gas fracking in the Marcellus (Osborn, Vengosh, Warner, & Jackson, 2011; Rozell & Reaven, 2012; Popkin, Duke, Borchers, & Ilvento, 2013). In the case of the tar sands, environmental damage in a fragile ecosystem could be difficult to reverse (Pasqualetti, 2009). The delayed, but anticipated, completion of the Keystone XL pipeline would likely increase the flow of oil from Alberta into the United States, leading to accelerated production rates.

Of particular concern with shale oil/gas development and oil (or tar) sand development has been the difficulty of controlling non-point source pollution and subsequent marginal social and environmental costs. The regulation of the control point source pollution by industries has proven to be much more feasible for government regulatory agencies. Energy development companies are, therefore, not forced through regulation to factor in marginal social costs into the "true cost" of energy produced (Holahan & Arnold, 2013).

Arguably, the delayed decision to approve Keystone XL by the Obama Administration has been related to the polluting nature of oil/tar sand energy development (Mufson, 2014). A pipeline from Alberta to Hardisty, Texas, would increase the supply of oil/tar sand energy and lead to higher social and environmental costs. The Keystone XL delay has not thwarted Canada's enthusiasm for a pipeline to increase production rates. The approved Northern Gateway pipeline will carry petroleum from Alberta through British Columbia to Pacific Ocean ports for shipment to Asian markets. Unlike a more politically conservative climate in Alberta and Saskatchewan, British Columbia tends to be more progressive and ecologically sensitive. The Northern Gateway approval has been greeted with environmental protests related to the social and environmental costs that the pipeline might produce (Viera, 2014).

## URANIUM ISSUES IN THE UNITED STATES AND CANADA

While several new plants are scheduled for completion within the next five years, the United States continues to operate 100 commercial nuclear reactors for the generation of electricity (World Nuclear Association, 2014a). The new construction prospects follow a 30-year drought on nuclear-power plant construction following the 1979 nuclear accident at Three Mile Island. While the accident was largely contained, the social/health and environmental costs of nuclear power were seen as significant; in part, due to greater sensitivity to environmental risk. Canada operates 19 nuclear power plants with a combined 19-gigawatt production capacity. There is a great deal of interest in the use of nuclear power to meet the electrical energy needs of Alberta's oil sand development. Saskatchewan has a similar interest in nuclear power, particularly due to the location of massive deposits of uranium ore in its province near Cigar Lake. Uranium mining, processing, and use can be viewed as an opportunity for significant economic development (World Nuclear Association, 2014b).

In both the United States and Canada, uranium mining has been a growth industry despite the sluggish efforts to construct next generation commercial nuclear reactors. In 2012, uranium mines in the United States, which are located primarily in Colorado, New Mexico, Utah, and Wyoming, produced 4.6 million pounds of uranium oxide ($U_3O_8$). This was the highest production level in the previous nine years (Energy Information Agency, 2014a). By contrast, Canada produced nearly 18 million pounds of uranium oxide. "All of Canadian [uranium] production comes from four mines in northern Saskatchewan," which contains two of the worlds' largest uranium production facilities (Nuclear Energy Agency, 2014).

Uranium producer Cameco operates the biggest uranium mining and processing plants in northern Saskatchewan; it has among the biggest uranium processing facilities in the world. Cameco, which is the largest publicly traded uranium producer in the world, is based in Saskatoon, Saskatchewan. It has proven difficult to fully understand the impact of uranium mining operations in northern Saskatchewan because much of the operational data about mining operations (data that serves as the basis for criticism (or praise) of mining operations) has apparently been collected and made available by Cameco (Jamasmie, 2013). There are, however, scientific and anecdotal studies of uranium tailings' impact on human and (more generally) environmental health and water quality. The studies have indicated that the use of arsenic and other toxic chemicals in uranium mining and processing have been harmful to human and animal health, acting as poisons that alter ecosystems in significant ways.

Additionally, anecdotal reports indicate that abandoned mines—particularly mines from the 1950s and 1960s— have not always been cleaned up in ways that reduce environment and health risks. New technologies in mining operations have made things a bit safer, thanks to *in situ* preprocessing of uranium ore, as opposed to open pit operations of old where ore was re-located for preprocessing activities that led to a higher risk of water, air, and soil contamination. Critics of uranium mining in the United States and Canada point to health and ecosystem impacts in mining regions. Mine dewatering issues are also of concern, although mining companies point out that the impact on water is more limited due to the fact that uranium ore is fairly stable prior to processing. Naturally occurring radioactivity is present in water in areas not adjacent to uranium processing facilities—in other words, health risks exist independent of mining operations. Political debate aside, there is evidence that supports the contention that uranium mining has in the past and may continue to create marginal social and environmental costs.

While this chapter does not deal with nuclear-waste issues, it is important to note that in addition to energy production issues, nuclear energy production has a waste problem. In the United States, nuclear waste is stored on site in cooling ponds or dry storage facilities at nuclear-power facilities. A central repository for nuclear waste remains a politically contentious issue. A waste depository was constructed at Yucca Mountain in Nevada, but the facility approval and use as a waste depository was put on hold for the foreseeable future due to concerns about the stability of the geological formations beneath the facility and other possible environmental impacts over the long term (Brumfiel, 2013). In Canada, nuclear waste is stored on site for several years (in cooling ponds), and then dried and shipped to one of the six dry storage facilities in Canada (Nuclear Waste Management Organization, 2014).

## RENEWABLE ENERGY AND MARGINAL SOCIAL COSTS

Both Canada and the United States are significantly invested in renewable energy, albeit the levels of commitment and types of energy developments differ. Nearly 60% of Canada's electricity needs are met by hydroelectric dams, whereas conventional hydroelectric dams produce approximately 6.8% of electricity generated in the United States. Both Canada and the United States have made significant investments in wind power. While Canada has approximately 5.7 gigawatts of installed wind generation capacity, the United States has 59 gigawatts installed capacity. Canada's solar capacity is minimal, which reflects the nation's climate—cold, dark winters that would reduce the efficiency of solar photovoltaic and solar thermal energy development. Biomass capacity in the United States is approximately 5.5 gigawatts of installed capacity compared with Canada which has approximately 1.7 gigawatts installed capacity. Geothermal energy in the United States (installed capacity of 3.7 gigawatts) is more developed than Canada primarily because of geological conditions—the geothermal resources of the United States are simply greater than those of Canada; but Canada does use heat pumps in commercial buildings and residences to access the available heat resources of the earth.

Marginal social and environmental costs of renewable energy are highly contestable: renewable energy advocates and detractors each claim the high ground in the debate. Highly respected energy-policy scholars such as Benjamin Sovacool, who has done yeoman's labor comparing the social and environmental costs of renewable energy in comparison to conventional fossil energy power plants, has faced hostile and unwarranted criticism from energy industry leaders and analysts over his meta-analysis of peer-reviewed studies related to avian mortality rates associated with energy production across multiple sectors (Atomic Insights, 2013).[1]

## Canadian and United States Hydropower in the Pacific Northwest

Canada's significant use of hydropower in comparison to the United States' hydropower capacity and generation, illustrates well the need to address issues surrounding environmental and social costs on both national and international levels. The Columbia River system is a resource that brings into close proximity Canadian and United States hydropower. The controversial Columbia River Treaty (1964) brought Canadian and the United States' governing bodies and hydropower operators into closer collaboration on planning the use of the river and protecting riverine and ancillary ecosystems. Historically, the development of the river for hydropower in the late 19th and 20th centuries has displaced both First People and Native Americans (as well as wildlife) from their traditional lands, often with devastating effects (Price, 1999). A prominent example of wildlife displacement has been the impact of hydropower dams on native salmon and steelhead populations. With native fish numbers rapidly dwindling, the U.S. Environmental Protection agency listed six species of salmon and four species of steelhead on the Endangered Species list. The federal government responded with salmon recovery efforts and a 1995 revisiting of the hydropower generation process on the Columbia River system.

Canadian efforts have reflected similar policy concern for the preservation of salmon runs, but policy responses have not always been easily coordinated in this complex river ecosystem that has multiple international, provincial, state, and federal political, economic, and social stakeholders. According to researchers Barbara Cosens and Mark Williams, the issue of identifying and reducing social and environmental costs in this cross-border example might best managed using an adaptive governance model; this would include multiple governmental and non-governmental stakeholders from the local, provincial, state and federal level. Adaptive governance would emphasize the need to respond to changing conditions, social values, and interests, as well as the need to coordinate policy efforts (Cosens & Williams, 2012).

## Wind and Solar Energy

In the last decade, Canada and the United States have made tremendous strides in developing wind and solar energy. In 2002, Canadian solar-power generation was 0.002 billion kilowatt hours. By 2012, Canadian solar power generation had grown to 0.506 billion kWh, representing a 25,200% increase in solar-power generation. By comparison, the United States generated 0.6 billion kWh of solar power in 2002 that grew to 4.3 billion kWh of solar power in 2012: a 617% increase in generation. In terms of wind-power generation, Canada generated 0.408 billion kWh in 2002 and 140.8 billion kWh in 2012: a 5,555% increase in wind generation. The United States generated 10.4 billion kWh of wind energy in 2002 and 140.8 billion kWh in 2012: a 1,254% increase over the decade (Energy Information Agency, 2014b).

Wind and solar-energy facilities have the potential to pose some social and environmental costs, but proponents of wind and solar energy argue that the social and environmental costs are minimal in relation to the net benefit of developing non-fossil energy sources. Frequently mentioned social and environmental costs of wind energy include visual and noise pollution, and avian mortality. A noise pollution study conducted in Ontario, Canada, found that the distance from wind turbines was related to the level of annoyance expressed by local residences surveyed. Approximately 30% of the individuals surveyed who lived within 550 meters of a wind turbine, reported being annoyed by the noise of the operating turbine; whereas less than 5% of individuals living 2 kilometers or greater distance from the wind turbine reported being annoyed by turbine noises. The study also found that those individuals who reported that they economically benefitted from wind-energy operations, were significantly less likely to report being annoyed by the sound of turbines (Whitfield, Aslund, Ollson & Knopper, 2013). Similar concerns about noise and visual pollution have been discussed in academic literature and news media reports in the United States. Martin Pasqualetti and his colleagues discussed extensively the issue of perceived noise and visual pollution associated with large-scale wind energy turbines; they concluded that scientific studies aside, it was critically important to gain public acceptance through education and collaborative decision making (Pasqualetti et al., 2002; Williams, 2007).

It is clear that wind turbines strike birds leading to avian mortality. In comparison terms, however, it is less clear that wind turbines are in any way more "deadly" than other forms of energy development and generation. In exploring this issue through meta-analysis, Benjamin Sovacool found that while there was evidence of avian mortality associated with wind energy systems, the number of birds and bats killed by wind turbines was a significantly smaller number when compared with the number of birds and bats killed by fossil energy power plants. Sovacool was, however, not conclusive in his findings; careful to note that the results were preliminary and the basis of further research and dialogue about an important social and environmental cost (Sovacool, 2009).

Solar-energy systems in the United States are often small-scale systems on the roofs of homes and businesses. Many large-scale systems are located on public lands in the southwestern United States. Small-scale residential systems are occasionally viewed as a nuisance by neighbors who see the solar panels on the roofs of their neighbors' homes. Large-scale systems, however, have generated other more serious concerns about social and environmental costs. One concern has been that large-scale solar facilities using concentrated solar collectors generate tremendous heat that kills birds that fly through the magnified solar rays (Sweet, 2014). Concerned environmentalists have also focused attention on the impact on threatened wildlife, such as the desert tortoise in the Mojave Desert. Proponents of renewable energy facilities argue that while there are social and environmental costs associated with renewable energy facilities, these costs are fairly minimal compared with the social and environmental costs imposed on humans, wildlife and vegetation, and the planet as a whole by the use of fossil energy (Union of Concerned Scientists, 2013).

## CONCLUSION

This chapter has discussed the marginal social and environmental costs of non-conventional fossil energy, uranium, and renewable-energy production. While the examples used in the essay have been clearly the choice of the author, the point of the essay was not to definitively identify the least-costly form of energy production in terms of marginal social and environmental costs. The purpose here was to illustrate the various types of costs that have been identified, and to then demonstrate that there is no "zero-cost" alterative when it comes to powering the modern world. The world demands far too much energy for human beings to escape the moral hazards created by their energy demands. In that sense, it would be best to consider again the prescient words of Gernot Wagner and Michael Sandel: The authors argue that it is far too easy to fall prey to the notion that individual choice matters very little in solving the world's energy problems. Rather than focus on an economic model of identifying and discussing marginal social and environmental costs, more lasting solutions to our energy problems could be found in asking ourselves (individually and collectively), about our moral responsibility to the planet and its inhabitants both now and in the future.

## NOTE

1. In this short narrative, there is little need to reproduce detailed meta-analyses of the social and environmental costs associated with renewable energy. The point here is not specifically to impugn any particular form of energy production; rather to simply point out that marginal social and environmental costs exist and should be considered in terms of both economic as well as moral terms.

## REFERENCES

Atomic Insights. (2013, July 11). Benjamin Sovacool takes issue with Lorenzini's criticism of his work. Retrieved August 31, 2014, from http://atomicinsights.com/sovacool-vs-lorenzini/

Brumfiel, G. (2013). America's Nuclear Dumpsters. *Slate*. Retrieved March 24, 2015 from http://www.slate.com/articles/health_and_science/nuclear_power/2013/01/nuclear_waste_storage_why_did_yucca_mountain_fail_and_what_next.html

CAPP. (2014). *Basic Statistics*. Retrieved August 31, 2014, from http://www.capp.ca/library/statistics/basic/Pages/default.aspx

Cosens, B. A., & Williams, M. K. (2012). Resilience and water governance: Adaptive governance in the Columbia River Basin. *Ecology and Society, 17*(4), 3–17.

Dimick, D. (2014, August 19). If you think the water crisis can't get worse, wait until the aquifers are drained: We're pumping irreplaceable groundwater to counter the drought. When it's gone, the real crisis begins. *National Geographic News*. Retrieved August 31, 2014, from http://news.nationalgeographic.com/news/2014/08/140819-groundwater-california-drought-aquifers-hidden-crisis/

Doluweera, G. H., Jordaan, S. M., Moore, M. C., Keith, D. W., & Bergerson, J. A. (2011). Evaluating the role of cogeneration for carbon management in Alberta. *Energy Policy, 39*, 7963–7974.

Engelder, T. (2011, September). Should fracking stop? No, it's too valuable. *Nature, 477*, 271–275.

Energy Information Agency. (2014a). Domestic uranium production report— annual. Retrieved August 31, 2014, from http://www.eia.gov/uranium/production/annual/

Energy Information Agency. (2014b). International energy statistics. Retrieved August 31, 2014, from http://www.eia.gov/cfapps/ipdbproject/IEDIndex3.cfm

Galbraith, K. (2013, March 7). As fracking increases, so do fears about water supply. *New York Times.* Retrieved August 31, 2014, from http://www.nytimes.com/2013/03/08/us/as-fracking-in-texas-increases-so-do-water-supply-fears.html?pagewanted=all&_r=0

Goldenberg, S. (2014, February 5). Fracking is depleting water supplies in America's driest areas, report shows: From Texas to California, drilling for oil and gas is using billions of gallons of water in the country's most drought prone areas. *The Guardian.* Retrieved August 31, 2014, from http://www.theguardian.com/environment/2014/feb/05/fracking-water-america-drought-oil-gas

Grubb, M. (1992). *Emerging energy technologies: Impacts and policy implications.* Farnham, England: Ashgate.

Holahan, R., & Arnold, G. (2013). An institutional theory of hydraulic fracturing policy. *Ecological Economics, 94*, 127–134.

Inglehart, R. (1990). *Culture shift in advanced industrial societies.* Princeton, NJ: Princeton University Press.

Jamasmie, C. (2013, October 1) Canada's Cameco scorns report alleging uranium contamination. *Mining.com.* Retrieved August 31, 2014, from http://www.mining.com/canadas-cameco-scorns-report-alleging-uranium-contamination-89951/

Ladd, A. E. (2012). Pandora's well: Hubris, deregulation, fossil fuels, and BP oil disaster in the Gulf. *American Behavioral Scientist, 56*(1), 104–127.

Leeb, S. (2014). Dangerous times as energy sources get costlier to extract. *Forbes.* Retrieved August 31, 2014, from http://www.forbes.com/sites/greatspeculations/2013/06/05/dangerous-times-as-energy-sources-get-costlier-to-extract/

Lipset, S. M. (1989). *Continental divide: The values and institutions of the United States and Canada.* New York, NY: Routledge.

Marois, M. B. (2014). California sets stage for first groundwater regulations. *Bloomberg.* Retrieved August 30, 2014, from http://www.bloomberg.com/news/2014-08-30/california-sets-stage-for-first-groundwater-regulations.html

Mattusch, C. (2008). Metalworking and tools. In J. P. Oleson (Ed.), *The Oxford handbook of engineering and technology in the classical world* (pp. 418–438). New York, NY: Oxford University Press.

Mittal, A. (2011). Energy development and water use: Impacts of potential oil shale development on water resources. [Testimony before the Subcommittee on Energy and Mineral Resources, Committee on Natural Resources, U.S. House of Representatives.] GAO-11-929T. Washington, DC: GAO.

Mufson, S. (2014, April 18). Obama administration postpones decision on Keystone XL pipeline. *Washington Post*. Retrieved August 31, 2014, from http://www.washingtonpost.com/business/economy/obama-administration-postpones-decision-on-keystone-xl-pipeline/2014/04/18/0c8d9f04-c72a-11e3-8b9a-8e0977a24aeb_story.html

Nicot, J. -P., & Scanlon, B. R. (2012). Water use for shale-gas production in Texas, US. *Environmental Science and Technology, 46*, 3580–3586.

Nuclear Energy Agency. (2014). Country profile: Canada. *Organization for Economic Development*. Retrieved August 31, 2014, from https://www.oecd-nea.org/general/profiles/canada.html

Nuclear Waste Management Organization. (2014). How nuclear waste is managed in Canada. *Nuclear Waste Management Organization*. Retrieved August 31, 2014, from http://www.nwmo.ca/wastemanagement

Ogden H. H., & Baron, R. E. (1976). Synthetic fuels: Prices, prospects, and prior art: Methods for synthetic fuel manufacture are varied and complex. What will be the impact on society if these technologies replace our present supply technologies? *American Scientist, 64*, 407–417.

Osborn, S. G., Vengosh, A., Warner, N. R., & Jackson, R. B. (2011, May 17). Methane contamination of drinking water accompanying gas-well drilling and hydraulic fracturing. [Proceedings of] *National Academy of Sciences, 108*(20), 8172–8176.

Pasqualetti, M. (2009). The Alberta oil sands from both sides of the border. *Geographical Review, 99*(2), 248–267.

Pasqualetti, M., Gipe, P., Righter, R., Brittan, G., Hammarlund, K., Hoppe-Klipper, M., Nielsen, F., Schwahn, C., & Short, L. (2002). *Wind power in view: Wind turbines, aesthetics, and public acceptance, energy landscapes in a crowded world*. San Diego, CA: Academic Press.

Pierce, J. C., Lovrich, N. P., Steel, B. S., Steger, M. A., & Tennert, J. R. (2000). *Political culture and public policy in Canada and the United States: Only a border apart?* New York, NY: Edwin Mellen.

Price, P. (1999). *Keeping the lakes' way: Reburial and the re-creation of a moral world among an invisible people*. Toronto, Canada: University of Toronto Press.

Popkin, J. H., Duke, J. M., Borchers, A. M., & Ilvento, T. Social costs from proximity to hydraulic fracturing in New York state. *Energy Policy, 62*, 62–69.

Rozell, D. J., & Reaven, S. J. (2012). Water pollution risk associated with natural gas extraction from the Marcellus shale. *Risk Analysis, 32*(8), 1382–1393.

Sandel, M. (2012). *What money can't buy: The moral limits of markets*. New York, NY: Farrar, Straus and Giroux.

Simon, S. (2009, March 19). Oil, water are a volatile mix in West. *Wall Street Journal*. Retrieved August 31, 2014, from http://online.wsj.com/news/articles/SB123741925013178161

Shackhouls, B. S. (2003). *Balancing natural gas policy: Fueling the demands of a growing economy*. Washington, DC: National Petroleum Council.

Schwartz, M., & Hollander, D. (2000). Annealing, distilling, reheating and recycling : Bitumen processing in the ancient Near East. *Paléorient, 26*(2), 83–89.

Sorkhabi, R. (2005). Pre-modern history of bitumen, oil and gas in Persia (Iran). *Petroleum History Institute, 6*(1). Retrieved August 23, 2014, from http://petroleumhistory.org/journal/vol_6.html#Sorkhabi

Sovacool, B. K. (2009). Contextualizing avian mortality: A preliminary appraisal of bird and bat fatalities from wind, fossil-fuel, and nuclear electricity. *Energy Policy, 37*(6), 2241–2248.

Struzik, E. (2013, August 5). With tar sands development, growing concern on water use. *Environment 360: Yale University*. Retrieved August 31, 2014, from http://e360.yale.edu/feature/with_tar_sands_development_growing_ concern_on_ water_use/2672/

Sweet, C. (2014, February 12). The $2.2 billion bird-scorching solar project: At California's Ivanpah plant, mirrors produce heat and electricity—and kill wildlife. *Wall Street Journal*. Retrieved August 31, 2014, from http://online.wsj.com/news/articles/SB10001424052702304703804579379230641329484

Union of Concerned Scientists. (2013, March 5). Environmental impacts of solar power. Retrieved August 31, 2014, from http://www.ucsusa.org/clean_energy/our-energy-choices/renewable-energy/environmental-impacts-solar-power.html

Viera, P. (2014, June 18). Canadian officials under fire for Enbridge pipeline approval: Critics say northern gateway project poses too much risk to the environment, British Columbia's economy. *Wall Street Journal*. Retrieved August 31, 2014, from http://online.wsj.com/articles/canadian-officials-under-fire-for-enbridge-northern-gateway-pipeline-approval-1403129299

Wagner, G. (2011). *But will the planet notice? How smart economics can save the world.* New York, NY: Hill and Wang.

Weimer, D. L. & Vining, A. R. (1992). *Policy analysis: Concepts and practice.* New York, NY: Prentice Hall.

Whitfield, M. L., Christoper A., Ollson, A., & Knopper, L. D. (2013). Projected contributions of future wind farm development to community noise and annoyance levels in Ontario, Canada. *Energy Policy, 62*, 44–50.

Williams, W. (2007). *Cape wind: Money, celebrity, class, politics, and the battle for our energy future on Nantucket Sound.* New York, NY: Perseus Books.

World Nuclear Association. (2014a). Nuclear power in the USA. *World Nuclear Association*. Retrieved August 31, 2014, from http://www.world-nuclear.org/info/Country-Profiles/Countries-T-Z/USA--Nuclear-Power/

World Nuclear Association. (2014b). Nuclear power in Canada. *World Nuclear Association*. Retrieved August 31, 2014, from http://www.world-nuclear.org/info/Country-Profiles/Countries-A-F/Canada--Nuclear-Power/

# CHAPTER 6

# MANAGING BIOMASS RISKS

## Flawed Science, Flawed Ethics, and Flawed Regulations

Kristin Shrader-Frechette

### ABSTRACT

Does society manage new, partly uncertain risks in scientifically, ethically, and legally defensible ways? Using the example of biomass incineration for electricity development, this chapter will argue that risk management of biomass energy has largely failed and ought to include three specific strategies: quantitative-human-health risk assessment (QRA); cost-benefit analysis (CBA); and ecological risk assessment (ERA). Without these strategies, communities will be unable to avoid harms. similar to those of fossil fuels; and to provide green electricity. Without them, they will, in fact, face a biomass "perfect storm" of three worrisome trends: massive government subsidies for biomass crop-growing/incineration; dangerous, mostly ultra-fine or nanoparticle, emissions from biomass-incineration plants; and the absence of ultrafine-particulate regulations. Although ultrafine particles have no established dose-response curve, occupational assessments and animal-experiment studies suggest they are more toxic, as a function of mass, than

*Ethics and Risk Management*, pp. 91–103

are fine particles. We estimate that 25 tons of ultrafine-particulate emissions annually from a typical, small, state-of-the-art, biomass-incineration facility could cause roughly 13–40 additional, annual, avoidable fatalities and $95 million–$292 million in health costs, apart from other biomass pollutants and resulting health harms. These costs seem to overwhelm any alleged plant benefits; and urge the immediate evaluation and management of bio-mass-incineration plants through quantitative-human-health risk assessment (QRA), cost-benefit analysis (CBA), and ecological risk assessment (ERA).[1]

## INTRODUCTION[2]

Many communities hope to provide green electricity from in-country fuel sources. They want to avoid dependence on foreign energy suppliers, and they want to avoid the health and climate threats posed by fossil fuels. As a result, many nations are embracing biomass incineration as a source of electricity. In doing so, however, this chapter will show that they often face a biomass "perfect storm" of three worrisome trends: These include massive government subsidies for biomass crop-growing/incineration; dangerous, mostly ultrafine or nanoparticle, emissions from biomass-incineration plants, emissions as bad or worse than those from many fossil-fuel plants; and the absence of ultrafine-particulate regulations.

How can nations provide green energy and yet avoid this perfect storm? After discussing biomass incineration, this chapter will briefly outline three strategies that are needed to provide better management of biomass incin-eration, all of which could have improved the dangerous outcome in the case study assessed in this chapter. All three strategies point to the way that polluters and energy technologists often misuse or ignore the science needed to secure the informed consent of those affected by the technology and paying the bill for it. Using quantitative, human-health risk assessment (QRA) to assess energy technologies, is one strategy that would help inform people about energy-related threats to their health and their rights to life, such as health harms from particulate matter (PM) from fossil fuels and biomass. Using a second strategy—cost-benefit analysis (CBA) to assess energy technologies—would help prevent threats to civil liberties, consent, and due process because of polluters' imposing energy technologies that are alleged to be cost-effective when they are not. Using ecological risk assessment (ERA) in all energy assessment would help prevent threats to the environment, and to environmental ethics that arise from land and resource destruction; as from growing, then incinerating, biomass for energy.

## REGULATORY LOOPHOLES IN BIOMASS INCINERATION

Any time one combusts something—such as oil, gas, or biomass—that combustion generates significant amounts of dangerous particulate-matter (PM), incompletely combusted bits of material that are extremely dangerous to health. PM is so deadly because, once inhaled it can settle in any organ and cause serious harm, ranging from asthma and Alzheimer's disease to strokes and Parkinson's disease.

Although many nations have PM regulations for coarse particles (PMC), those between 10-2.5 micrometers ($\mu$m)—and fine particles (PMF), those between 2.5– 0.1 $\mu$m, no stringent regulations exist anywhere for ultrafine particles (PMUF), those <0.1$\mu$m (100 nanometers) (United States Environmental Protection Agency, 2012). Yet subsequent paragraphs show that the nano-scale PMUF and human-engineered nanoparticles (ENP) are by far the most dangerous of all PM, mainly because of their small size, ability to cross the blood-brain barrier, and slip through skin or any other material.

Although PMUF are not regulated, they appear to be at least 25 times more dangerous than PMF that currently are regulated. Recently the U.S. National Institute for Occupational Safety and Health (NIOSH) recommended airborne exposure limits of 2.4 mg/m$^3$ for the PMF or fine TiO$_2$, and 0.3 mg/m$^3$ for PMUP or ultrafine (including the engineered nanoparticle or ENP) TiO$_2$, as time-weighted average (TWA) concentrations for up to 10 hr/day during a 40-hour work week (NIOSH, 2011a). NIOSH also proposed a recommended exposure limit 1 $\mu$g/m$^3$ elemental carbon as a respirable mass, 8-hour TWA concentration in carbon nanofibers and nanotubes (NIOSH, 2011b).

However, a PMUF-regulatory loophole exists partly because, while scientists all agree that PMUF are far deadlier than PMF or PMC of the same mass, PMUF effects are still being discovered. Thus scientists do not know precisely all the effects that occur as a result of each of the different levels of exposure to PMUF. Also because the toxicology of the nano-sized PMUF and ENP do not behave according to the same mechanisms and modes of action, there can be no common exposure standard for all ENPs and PMUF. Moreover, standards for ENP—like those recommended by NIOSH for TiO2—cannot be used for ambient PMUF because unlike ENP, PMUF include soluble, poorly soluble, and insoluble compounds, each with different toxicological and biokinetic properties. All these differences among PMUF and ENP mean that they are difficult to regulate, despite their deadliness. These differences also mean that polluters can exploit these scientific gaps in understanding; so as to claim that not enough is known, in order to regulate PMUF and ENP. This is a strategy that the tobacco industry followed regarding cigarettes in the United States and a strategy that virtually every environmental polluter follows: demand scientific certainty before allowing regulation, even when enough obviously is known scientifically to know how deadly PMUF and ENP are.

Paradoxically, because 95% of coal-plant particulates appear to be PMF, they receive more attention from health experts than do the deadlier PMF; however, only 4% to 7% of coal-plant particulates are PMUF, and they receive much less attention (Linak, Miller, Seames, Wendt, Ishino-mori, Endo, & Siyamae, 2002). However, biomass/biofuel-plant-particulate releases are mostly PMUF. For example, the number of particles in the size range of 17nm to 300nm, which are emitted from boilers used in three district heating units and which operate on three different biofuels (sawdust, wood pellets, and forest residues), ranged from 6.3 x $10^7$ to 7.7 x $10^7$ particles/cm$^3$, with a particle-size mode ranging between approximately 70nm to 100nm. Interestingly, the concentration of Zn, Cd, Pb, and Cr in the particles depended on the type of fuel, but was generally significantly higher in the smaller particles (Wierzbicka et al., 2005). This means that although all smaller particles are deadlier, these PMUF and ENP (because of their size) are especially deadly because they also adhere to heavy metals such as zinc, cadmium, lead, and chromium. These metals themselves are also very dangerous, independent of size. Degradation of pellets of miscan-thus, a widely used "energy crop," produces $1.0 \times 10^{12}$ particles per gram of sample, where 99% of the particles, by number, have a diameter below 1 $\mu$m and (57% by number are nanoparticles smaller than 0.1 $\mu$m) (Dorge, Mejdi, & Gwenaëlle, 2011). Thus biomass PM appears deadlier, on average, than coal PM, and PM is the major source of fossil-fuel-related deaths.

In essence, given equal masses, PMUF is far more hazardous than PMF/PMC (Brown, Wilson, MacNee, Stone, & Donaldson, 2001). All three PM types can be inhaled, but unlike PMs, PMUF typically cannot easily be released from the body. PMUF can remain in the lungs or migrate, via the blood stream, to other organs like the brain and heart, causing chronic inflammation, cytotoxicity, cellular damage, tissue proliferation, cancer, genetic damage, and neurodegenerative diseases such as Alzheimer's and Parkinson's (Stoeger et al., 2006; Bezemer et al., 2009; Renwick, Brown, Clouter, & Donaldson, 2004; International Agency for Research on Cancer, 2010).

Despite the great risks of PMUF, the fact that biomass/biofuels' aggra-vate global-climate disruption (Le, Jumar, & Drewry, 2011), and the fact that the World Bank, International Monetary Fund, and World Trade Orga-nization all have made food-security-based demands to end biomass-crop subsidies (Brosse, Dufour, Meng, Sun, & Ragauskas, 2012), many nations have not listened: Countries such as Canada, Denmark, England, Germany, Greece, Ireland, Italy, Japan, Portugal, Spain, Sweden, Turkey, and the United States subsidize biomass and biofuels like miscanthus giganteus. Touting energy independence, they offer biomass-crops, biomass-boiler-construction, and biomass-renewable-energy subsidies (Sustainable Energy Authority of Ireland, 2010; Department of Environment, Food, and Rural Affairs, 2007; Sheehan, Chirillo, Schlossberg, Sammons, and Leonard, 2011; Shrader-Frechette & Preisser, 2013). For instance, U.S.-taxpayer biomass subsidies—$3 billion to $5 billion/year (federal), plus $2 billion to

$4 billion-per-plant/year (state)—help explain the 255 existing, and 250 in-progress, biomass-incineration plants in the United States (Monteiller et al., 2007).

## A Biomass-Incineration Proposal

Although one-third of the world's inhabitants face indoor-air pollution from burning biomass (Fullerton, Bruce, & Gordon, 2008; Kunycky & Shrader-Frechette, 2013), many corporations and communities dismiss these health threats from state-of-the-art, electricity-generating-biomass plants, partly because they seek billions of dollars a year in alleged green-energy handouts from the government.

For instance, rural Jasper, Indiana, was facing costly emissions-controls for its outdated, middle-of-town, coal plant. It was one of roughly 250 closing in the United States. Consequently, town leaders accepted a proposal from out-of-state Twisted Oak Corporation (TOC) to convert the old coal boiler to a unit that combusts biomass. TOC's 75-page proposal promised the town lease payments and to inject $200 million in the local economy over 30 years ($6.6 million/year) from the hybrid natural-gas/miscanthus-giganteus-incineration facility (Twisted Oak Corporation, 2010).

In return for TOC's unspecified amounts of lease payments, the town would provide the facility "essential services," including double the water needed by the old coal facility, new electrical lines, and other infrastructure. However, after town leaders saw the proposal, lease-payment amounts were redacted from the public copy of the proposal, as were lease terms, TOC taxes, financing, costs of water/sewer/new electrical lines/contaminated materials, and (TOC-partner) Mendel-Bioenergy information about bio-engineered miscanthus. All redactions by Jasper officials were marked "confidential materials" (Sheehan et al., 2011). Although the facility would sell its electricity on the open market, TOC promised to minimize health and environmental impacts with baghouse filters, biomass-boiler NOX/$CO_2$ best-available-control-technology limits, 560 ppm CO limits, and "voluntary" 0.03 lb./million (MM) Btu limits for PM (Twisted Oak Corporation, 2010; Shaddix, 2011). No quantitative-human-health risk assessment (QRA), no cost-benefit analysis (CBA), and no ecological risk assessment (ERA) were performed, despite massive health risks posed by PM, the unproven economics of miscanthus incineration, local droughts, massive miscanthus water needs, and miscanthus risks of inducing outbreaks of invasive species.

## Biomass-Incineration-Plant Harms

To use QRA to tentatively estimate the possible harms of state-of-the-art, biomass-incineration plant PMUF emissions, we started looking at the well-known PMF (coal-plant) health effects and epidemiological data; this was based largely on using well-known controls for confounders, so as to separate different causal agents. In one-fourth of year 2010, U.S. particulate emissions, of 1.9 million tons (United States Environmental Protection Agency, 2010), were 475,000 tons of coal-combustion PMF (Thurston, Ito, & Ramona, 2011). Harms caused by coal-combustion PMF had been well established by epidemiological science, (summarized in Table 6.1) and of course they were not independent of one another (Schneider, 2004; Schneider, 2000; Shrader-Frechette, 2013). That is, 25 tons PMF would annually cause the following:

**Table 6.1.  Coal PM Harms**

| Harms Caused By Coal-Combustion Pmf in the United States in 2010, that is, 475,000 tons of PMF) |
| --- |
| 30,000 premature deaths |
| 22,000 hospital admissions |
| 26,000 emergency-room visits |
| 38,000 heart attacks |
| 554,000 asthma attacks |
| 3,186,000 lost-work days |

*Sources:* Schneider, 2004; Schneider, 2000; Shrader-Frechette, 2013.

If the Jasper biomass-incineration plant follows its "voluntary" particulate-pollution limit, 0.03 lb/MMBtu-input, and uses a proposed 100,000 tons miscanthus annually (Twisted Oak Corporation, 2010; Shaddix, 2011), it would release 25 tons PMUF: each ton of miscanthus-input provides 16,441,827 Btu (Wang, Dunn, & Wang, 2012), therefore the Jasper-facility 1,644,183 MMBtu-input actually generates 25 tons PMUF emissions. But as preceding paragraphs have shown, 25 tons PMF (not PMUF) would annually cause roughly (25/475,000) of the additional, avoidable harms—across the United States—as 275,000 tons PMF (Schneider, 2000, 2004).

1.6 deaths;

1.2 hospital admissions;

1.4 emergency-room visits;

2 heart attacks;

0.8 bronchitis cases;

29.2 asthma attacks;

167.7 lost-work days.

To roughly estimate a conversion from PMF harms/ton to PMUF harms/ton, despite the absence of a precise, quantitative, dose-response curve (telling what specific pollutant exposure causes what specific health harms), one could use government-recommended-occupational-PMUF data. The U.S. National Institutes for Occupational Safety and Health (NIOSH) recommend occupational-only PMUF standards 8 times stricter than occupational-PMF standards (2.4 mg/m$^3$ for fine $TiO^2$ and 0.3 mg/m$^3$ for ultrafine), to avoid greater-than-1-in-1000, worker-cancer risks (NIOSH, 2011). However, NIOSH warns that these recommendations: (a) are inapplicable to the more-sensitive public—who typically are protected against greater-than-1-in-1-million risks; and (b) cover only a 40-hour-exposure/week, not actual, four-times-longer, 168-hour-exposure/week. Given (a) and (b), perhaps PMUF standards should be, not 8 but, (8)(4) = 32 times more stringent for full-time, not quarter-time, public protection. Of course, given the differences between not all ENP and PMUF, already mentioned, there can be no common regulatory-exposure standard. However, using a NIOSH-multiplier 8 for converting PMF harms/ton to PMUF harms/ton, seems to give a rough approximation (although probably underestimated), of PMUF harms.

But in order to obtain a more precise estimate of PMUF harms/ton, one should recall that PMUF/PMF harms are functions of surface area (Sager & Castranova, 2009; Sager, Kommineni, & Castranova, 2008; Oberdörster, Oberdörster, & Oberdörster, 2005; Renwick et al., 2004; Shrader-Frechette, 2013), and are largest for the smallest PMUF, and smallest for the largest PMUF. Thus, the smallest PMUF/PMF harm— when PMUF=0.1 $\mu$m, PMF = 2.5 $\mu$m—is 25:1 of their surface-area ratio. Animal-experiment data also show PMUF and PMF inflammation and cytotoxicity are roughly equal, given equal surface areas (Sager & Casgtranova, 2009; Sager, Kommineni, & Castranova, 2008; Nyland, Bai, Katz, & Silbergeld, 2009; Fullerton, Bruce, & Gordon, 2008). Thus 25 is a reasonable, tentative, PMF-to-PMUF "harm multiplier." In addition, the calculation of full-time exposure using the NIOSH multiplier it is much closer to 32 times than earlier proposed 8. Therefore the 25 tons/year Jasper-biomass-plant-PMUF pollution can tentatively cause up to 25 times the harms caused by PMF. Estimates of PMUF harms are summarized in Table 6.2; the right-column lower numbers are based on the one-quarter-time, NIOSH conversion factor of 8, and the right-column higher numbers are based on the surface-area-based conversion factor of 25. (Note that an estimated full-time NIOSH conversion factor is 32. Of course, these harm estimates are tentative, given no common mode of action among all PMUFs and ENPs; given the diverse physicochemical properties of PMUFs—as compared to engineered NPs;

and given differences in lung deposition of various inhaled particles. Keep in mind that these harms occur farther away, as well as close to the plant, because the PM can travel for miles before it is inhaled.

### Table 6.2.   PMUF Harms

| Harms Caused by 25 Tons PMF | Harms Caused by 25 Tons PMUF |
| --- | --- |
| 3.6 premature deaths | 13–40 premature deaths |
| 1.2 hospital admissions | 10–30 hospital admissions |
| 1.4 emergency-room visits | 11–35 emergency-room visits |
| 2 heart attacks | 16–75 heart attacks |
| 29.2 asthma attacks | 234–730 asthma attacks |
| 167.7 lost-work days | 1,342–3,355 lost-work days |

If even a small, state-of-the-art biomass-incineration plant causes 13 to 40 avoidable deaths annually across the United States, then at standard value-of-life rates typically used by government and by industry ($7.3 million/life) (Twisted Oak Corporation, 2010), this plant would cause annual harms valued at $95 million to $292 million, just by the deaths caused, apart from other harms. Yet these tentative, annual harms from a small biomass-incineration plant are 14 to 44 times greater than the total annual benefits that supporters attribute to the plant (United States Environmental Protection Agency, 2012). However, if energy assessments required full QRAs, illustrated in part by the preceding data in Tables 6.1 and 6.2, then obviously people could tell how harmful biomass electricity really is to their health, their rights to informed consent, and their rights to due process.

Moreover, because policymakers translate health harms into dollar costs, it is important for every energy assessment to do a CBA. As in the Jasper biomass case, the developers are able to claim the proposed plant will be a moneymaker only because they have done no CBA. Even the partial CBA, done in the previous paragraph, shows that annual biomass health harms outweigh supposed annual energy benefits by factors between 14 and 44. Doing CBA is one way to use polluters' own tools to reveal that frequently their proposals are not genuinely economical; instead they are economical for polluters who ignore the costs to ordinary people.

Finally, if all energy assessments were required to do ERAs, they would capture some of the environmental harms from biomass production, such as depletion of the soil and loss of more lucrative food crops, that impact a region ethically, politically, and economically. ERA is needed, at a minimum, to get a full handle on all the associated costs and benefits of a technology that requires us to use land, water, soil, and so on, so that we can burn crops for electricity.

## Caveats

However, despite no full QRA, CBA, and ERA, additional considerations suggest the preceding, tentative, biomass-incineration plant, annual death and dollar losses are underestimates of the real level of biomass harm. Because state-of-the-art-biomass-incineration plants emit 10–100s of tons of PM/year, most plants' PM/year emissions exceed Jasper's 25-tons PM/year. Consequently, average-biomass-plant-induced-PM deaths are higher than the numbers discussed above (Twisted Oak Corporation, 2010). Also, leading Harvard and NIOSH animal studies have shown that for equal masses, dominant-biomass-pollutant CBPMUF causes more than 65 times inflammation and toxicity than CBPMF; so that even 65 may under predict PMUF harms (Renwick et al., 2004; Le et al., 2011; Shrader-Frechette, 2013). Thus our 8 to 25 (partial NIOSH-based and surface-area based) PHF-multiplier also may under predict PMUF fatalities per plant/year.

Abt Associates—a leading U.S.-government assessor—say average U.S. coal-plant particulates kill 25 people/year (Shaddix, 2011); and average biomass-plant particulates kill far more (Nyland et al., 2009). State-of-the-art biomass facilities can each release 370% more PM than state-of-the-art coal plants, and biomass-PMUF is far more health-damaging (Dorge et al., 2011). Thus our tentative estimate of 13 biomass-PMUF-caused deaths per plant, per year, likely underestimates fatalities. Similarly, given real-world conditions, such as plant owners' not following regulations, 13 may underestimate biomass-plant-PMUF deaths/year, given biomass-plant-induced, ambient-air-regulatory violations (Stoeger et al., 2006). Baghouse filters, planned for the facility, can limit CBPMUF emissions to 50mg/m$^3$ (Wierzbicka et al., 2005), 4,200 times the 12$\mu$/m$^3$ U.S. limit. Without PPMUF regulations and biomass-plant-PPMUF liability, harms may exceed our preceding calculations; this is because biomass-plant-profit incentives and interests are in economic conflict with "voluntary" pollution control. In fact, there is evidence that voluntary regulations very rarely work (United States Environmental Protection Agency, 2010; Thurston et al., 2011). Moreover, virtually all economic data show that biomass-incineration plants are not cost effective; in part this is because it is much more profitable for farmers to grown soybeans for food than miscanthus for biomass incineration (Shrader-Frechette et al., 2013). These economic costs are exacerbated by the fact that miscanthus uses massive amounts of water, more than other crops that can be grown in the same area; and thus it is likely to harm not only local ecosystems, but also the environmental health on which local farming depends (Shrader-Frechette, 2013; Kunycky, & Shrader-Frechettte, 2013).

## CONCLUSION

Even more considerations suggest the preceding biomass-plant's annual death and dollar losses are underestimates. Recall the earlier caveats that suggested higher average-biomass-plant-induced-PM deaths (Booth, 2012), as well as Harvard and NIOSH suggestions that CBPMUF causes > 65 times more inflammation/toxicity than CBPMF (Sager & Castranova, 2009; Sager, Kommineni, & Castranova, 2008). Thus our 8–25 (partial NIOSH-based and surface-area based) PHF-multiplier also may underpredict PMUF fatalities per plant per year.

Similarly, the figure of 13 biomass-plant deaths per year, which was discussed in the previous paragraphs, may underestimate actual biomass-plant-PMUF deaths, as already noted, because Abt Associates say average U.S. coal-plant particulates kill 25 people/year (Schneider & Banks, 2010). Yet average biomass-plant particulates kill far more (Shaddix, 2011) because each plant can release up to 370% more PM than state-of-the-art coal plants; and biomass-PMUF is far more health-damaging, given its small physical size (Brosse et al., 2012).

In addition, biomass-plant-induced, ambient-air-regulatory violations (Sheehan et al., 2011) are likely to be significant, as already mentioned, because the baghouse filters that are planned for the Jasper and other biomass facilities, limit CBPMUF emissions to $50mg/m^3$ (International Agency for Research on Cancer, 2010), 4,200 times the $12\mu/m^3$ U.S. limit, although dilution will likely reduce some of these emissions. Without PPMUF regulations and biomass-plant-PPMUF liability, harms may exceed the preceding calculations because biomass-plant-profit incentives and interests are in economic conflict with "voluntary" pollution control; in fact, voluntary regulations rarely work (Shiell & Chapman, 2000; Spence, 2011).

Public-health protection, sound food policy, and economics all seem to argue against biomass incineration, at least in the case of the heavily subsidized miscanthus giganteus and any other biomass material that could take land away from food crops and crops requiring less water. The one advantage of biomass appears to be the fact that it could reduce reliance on foreign sources of electricity. However, given the abundant coal reserves in the United States, and the climate and health threats posed by coal, it makes little sense to replace coal with biomass incineration, simply because biomass regulations have been lagging.

## NOTES

1. Acknowledgments: Dr. Shrader-Frechette thanks the U.S. National Science Foundation (NSF) for research grant SES-0724781, "Three Methodological Rules in Risk Assessment," during which part of the research for this article was begun. All opinions and errors are those of the authors, not the NSF. The author thanks Philippe Grandjean and EH referees for helpful comments.

2. Abbreviations: CBA, cost-benefit assessment; CBPMF, carbon-black-fine-particulate matter; CBPMUF, carbon-black-ultrafine-particulate matter; CO, carbon monoxide; $CO_2$ carbon dioxide; ERA, ecological risk assessment; $\mu$, micrometers; MM, million; NIOSH, National Institutes for Occupational Safety and Health; NOX, nitrogen oxides; PM, particulate matter; PMC, particulate matter coarse; PMF, particulate matter fine; PMUF, particulate matter ultrafine; QRA, quantitative human-health risk assessment; TiO2, titanium dioxide ; TOC, Twisted Oak Corporation.

## REFERENCES

Bezemer, G. F., Bauer, S. M., Oberdörster, G., Breysse, P. N., Pieters, R. H., Georas, S. N., & Williams, M. A. (2011). Activation of pulmonary dendritic cells and Th2-type inflammatory responses on instillation of engineered, environmental diesel emission source or ambient air pollutant particles in vivo. *Journal of Innate Immunity, 3*(2), 150–166.

Booth, M. S. (2012). *Biomass air pollution*. Springfield, MA: Partnership for Policy Integrity.

Brosse, N., Dufour, A., Meng, X., Sun, Q., & Ragauskas, A. (2012). Miscanthus: A fast-growing crop for biofuels and chemicals production. *Biofuels, Bioproducts and Biorefining, 6*(5), 580–598.

Brown, D. M., Wilson, M. R., MacNee, W., Stone, V., & Donaldson, K. (2001). Size-dependent proinflammatory effects of ultrafine polystyrene particles: A role for surface area and oxidative stress in the enhanced activity of ultrafines. *Toxicology and Applied Pharmacology, 175*(3), 191–199.

Department of Environment, Food, and Rural Affairs (DEFRA). (2007). Planting and growing miscanthus. Retrieved December 12, 2012, from http://www. defra.gov.uk/erdp.

Dorge, S., Mejdi, J., & Gwenaëlle, T. (2011). Thermal degradation of miscanthus pellets: Kinetics and aerosols characterization. *Waste and Biomass Valorization, 2*(2), 149–155.

Fullerton, D. G., Bruce, N., & Gordon, S. B. (2008). Indoor air pollution from biomass fuel smoke is a major health concern in the developing world. *Transactions of the Royal Society of Tropical Medicine and Hygiene, 102*(9), 843–851.

International Agency for Research on Cancer. (2010). *Carbon Black*. Geneva, Switzerland: World Health Organization.

Kunycky, B. N., & Shrader-Frechette, K. S. (2013). Lessons on drought and pollution from the forgotten three billion: An Indiana case study on using biomass crops for generating electricity. *Global Health Perspectives, 1*(1), 55–62.

Le, P. V., Kumar, P., & Drewry, D. T. (2011). Implications for the hydrologic cycle under climate change due to the expansion of bioenergy crops in the Midwestern United States. *Proceedings of the National Academy of Sciences, 108*(37), 15085–15090.

Linak, W. P., Miller, C. A., Seames, W. S., Wendt, J. O. L., Ishinomori, T., Endo, Y., & Siyamae, M. (2002). On trimodal particle size distributions in fly ash from pulverized-coal combustion. *Proceedings of the Combustion Institute, 29*(1), 441–447.

Monteiller, C., Tran, L., MacNee, W., Faux, C., Jones, A., Miller, B., & Donaldson, K. (2007). The pro-inflammatory effects of low-toxicity, low-solubility particles, nanoparticles and fine particles, on epithelial cells in vitro: The role of surface area. *Occupational and Environmental Medicine, 64*(9), 609–615.

National Institutes for Occupational Safety and Health (NIOSH). (2011a). *Current intelligence bulletin 63: Occupational exposure to titanium dioxide.* Atlanta, GA: U.S. Centers for Disease Control and Prevention.

National Institutes for Occupational Safety and Health (NIOSH). (2011b). *Current intelligence bulletin 65: Occupational exposure to carbon nanotubes and nanofibers.* Atlanta, GA: U.S. Centers for Disease Control and Prevention.

Nyland, J. F., Bai, J. J., Katz, H. E., & Silbergeld, E. K. (2009). In vitro interactions between splenocytes and dansylamide dye-embedded nanoparticles detected by flow cytometry. *Nanomedicine, 5*(3), 298–304.

Oberdörster, G., Oberdörster, E., & Oberdörster, J. (2005) Nanotoxicology: An emerging discipline evolving from studies of ultrafine particles. *Environmental Health Perspectives, 113*(7), 823–839.

Renwick, L. C., Brown, D., Clouter, A., & Donaldson, K. (2004). Increased inflammation and altered macrophage chemotactic responses caused by two ultrafine particle types. *Occupational and Environmental Medicine, 61*(5), 442–447.

Sager T. M., & Castranova, V. (2009). Surface area of particle administered versus mass in determining the pulmonary toxicity of ultrafine and fine carbon black: Comparison to ultrafine titanium dioxide. *Particle and Fibre Toxicology, 6*(15). doi:10.1186/1743-8977-6-15.

Sager, T. M., Kommineni, C., & Castranova, V. (2008). Pulmonary response to intratracheal instillation of ultrafine versus fine titanium dioxide: Role of particle surface area. *Particle and Fibre Toxicology, 5*(17).

Schneider, C. G. (2000). *Death, disease, and dirty power.* Boston, MA: Clean Air Task Force/Abt Associates.

Schneider, C. G. (2004). *Dirty air, dirty power.* Boston, MA: Clean Air Task Force/Abt Associates.

Schneider, C. S., & Banks, J. (2010). *The toll from coal: An updated assessment of death and disease from America's dirtiest energy source.* Washington, DC: Abt Associates. Retrieved from http://www.catf.us/resources/publications/files/The_Toll_from_Coal.pdf

Shaddix, C. S. (2011). *Review of Twisted Oak proposal and associated literature.* Jasper, IN: Jasper Utilities Board.

Sheehan, M., Chirillo, S., Schlossberg, J., Sammons, W., & Leonard W. (2011). *Biomass electricity: Clean energy subsidies for a dirty industry.* Cambridge, MA: Biomass Accountability Project.

Shiell, A., & Chapman, S. (2000). The inertia of self-regulation: A game-theoretic approach to reducing passive smoking in restaurants. *Social Science Medicine, 51*(7), 1111–1119.

Shrader-Frechette, K. (2013). Biomass and Effects of Airborne Ultrafine Particulates: Lessons About State Variables in Ecology. *Biological Theory, 8*(1), 44–48.

Shrader-Frechette, K., & Preisser, W. (2013). Renewable technologies and environmental injustice: Subsidizing bioenergy, promoting inequity. *Environmental Justice, 6*(3), 88–93.

Spence, D. (2011). *Self-regulation by firms: A familiar argument returns, Texas enterprise.* Austin, TX: University of Texas McCombs School of Business.

Stoeger, T., Reinhard, C., Takenaka, S., Schroeppel, A., Karg, E., Ritter, B., Heyder, J., & Schulz, H. (2006). Instillation of six different ultrafine carbon particles indicates a surface area threshold dose for acute lung inflammation in mice. *Environmental Health Perspectives, 114*(3), 328–333.

Sustainable Energy Authority of Ireland (SEA). (2010). *Fact sheet miscanthus.* Dublin, Ireland: Renewable Energy Information Office, SEA.

Thurston, G. D., Ito, K., & Ramona, L. (2011). A source of apportionment of U.S. fine particulate matter air pollution. *Atmospheric Environment, 45*(24), 3924–3936.

Twisted Oak Corporation. (2010). *Site lease and repowering proposal: Submitted to City of Jasper Municipal Utility Department.* Sandy Springs, GA: Twisted Oak Corporation.

United States Environmental Protection Agency (EPA). (2010). *Air quality trends, particulate matter.* Washington, DC: EPA.

United States Environmental Protection Agency (EPA). (2012). *Particulate matter.* Retrieved January 2, 2013, from http://www.epa.gov/pm/agriculture.html

Wang, Z., Dunn, J. B., & Wang, M.Q. (2012). *GREET model miscanthus parameter development.* Argonne, IL: Center for Transportation Research, Argonne National Laboratory.

Wierzbicka, A., Lillieblad, L., Pagels, J., Strand, M., Gudmundsson, A., Gharibi, A., Swietlicki, E., Sanati, M., & Bohgard, M. (2005). Particle emissions from district heating units on three commonly used biofuels. *Atmospheric Environment, 39*(1), 139–150.

# CHAPTER 7

# ETHICS AND RISK MANAGEMENT

## The Cultural Perspective

**Ásthildur E. Bernharðsdóttir**

## INTRODUCTION

This chapter will discuss the relationship between culture and ethics and how that interplay shapes risk management. The Grid Group Cultural Theory (GGCT) will be used as a tool to explain and test these relationships. Morality and ethics based on moral psychology are paired with the GGCT cultural types. Icelandic case studies, including studies on crisis management at the macro level, will be used to illustrate the relationships. Risk communication, as one of the most important parts of risk management, will be especially reflected upon from the cultural and ethical perspectives. Cultural types influence the way in which decision makers perceive threat and manage risk reduction efforts in both the public and private sectors. To manage risk with regard to ethical issues, it is necessary to understand the most important values at stake for the public and to recognize the variation in emphasis of certain values in different cultures.

*Ethics and Risk Management*, pp. 105–123
Copyright © 2015 by Information Age Publishing

Risk management theories describe how rational decisions can be made and followed in order to mitigate and prepare for a probable risk. Planners are expected to consider risk and potential loss triggered by natural threats; and to apply methods to minimize risk and loss, for example, by looking at design, maintenance, and management. Risk is assessed on the basis of mathematical calculations; and it is thus measured as the probability of undesired consequences resulting from an action. Expected losses are commonly measured in numerical units, whether it is loss of lives, persons injured, property damaged, or economic activity disrupted due to a particular hazard for a given area and reference period. In order to make rational decisions, risk managers need information but often lack historical data and/or research. Lack of financial resources and information on the multiple probable effects often challenge this method of assessing risk. Even if all the needed information and resources were at hand, one could not be sure, for instance, how the risk managers' personality traits, values, or experiences would influence the way in which they would address their risk assessment and present their recommendations of how to manage the risk.

The human factor is not included in the risk-management equation, but in real life it is a non-trivial factor that greatly influences the outcome. Risk managers make errors and they might also emphasize one type of risk while avoiding other types. They are faced with different kinds of dilemmas: how to utilize cost-benefit analysis, for example, when they do not have quantifiable values, and whether they should mitigate risk in low-income neighborhoods although it is less cost-effective. These dilemmas raise ethical questions.

Increasing attention to ethical decision making has become salient over the last few decades (Tenbrunsel & Smith-Crow, 2008). According to Merriam-Webster's definition, ethics is "the discipline dealing with what is good and bad and with moral duty and obligation" (merriam-webster.com). It leaves us with the challenge of defining what is good or bad. It has been the moral duty of policymakers to protect the public from serious harm. However, even moral policymaking is not a guarantee for an ethically acceptable policy. The decision maker often may not realize the ethical aspects of their decisions. "The moral decision making that follows from moral awareness, can result in unethical decisions as well as ethical ones; likewise, the amoral decision making that follows from moral unawareness can lead to ethical decisions as well as unethical ones" (Tenbrunsel & Smith-Crowe, 2008, p. 554). However, for a risk manager, the morality seems to be the logical path in his/her aim to develop ethical risk policies or to manage risk ethically.

The stakeholders, whom the risk policy is intended to serve, should be the judges as to whether a risk policy is good or bad. Both ethics and risk management are supposed to respect people's needs. In simpler terms, it might be said that what the public judges as good risk management is risk that is ethically managed. Yet, this simplified explanation has the challenge of how the public's needs and the public's feedback can be assessed. People have different expectations, interests, and values that need to be reconciled. A real test is that once a disaster hits, it reveals the quality of risk reduction efforts and response plans that were made prior to the disaster. Good risk managers need to be able to use the practical tools available to analyze and assess the risks; they need to keep an overview of the available resources for risk-reduction measures; and at the same time, recognize peoples' psychological as well as their physical need for such measures.

## CULTURAL THEORY AS A TOOL FOR UNDERSTANDING RISK MANAGEMENT CULTURE

A risk manager who is fully engaged in understanding people's risk perceptions also needs to understand their values. What are their ideas about security and safety, and what risks do they fear the most? Different opinions on how to prioritize risk prevention or mitigation can be easily understood when interests are starkly different; for instance, if the conflict is between public safety and property protection. It is more difficult to understand differences that lie in peoples' value systems. The Grid Group Cultural Theory (GGCT) offers a tool that can help risk managers gain insight into different value systems; it can help them, not only to understand and resolve a debate, but also to predict probable debates that different risk policies are likely to trigger (Swedlow, 2002). GGCT helps assure the policymaker that cultural differences are being considered in the policymaking process (Hendriks, 2004; Thompson, 1997). Such a predisposition can be viewed as morally right (Lockhart & Franzwa, 1994).

The Grid Group Cultural Theory offers four cultural types. Since people judge the ethicality of risk policies based on their cultural values, ethical norms become constrained by those cultural types; but why four types? According to Mary Douglas (1975; Douglas and Wildavsky, 1982), the apparently unique combination of cultural bias and social relations in different social settings is most fruitfully analyzed using a simple grid-group typology of sociality. Michael Thompson, Richard Ellis, and Aaron Wildavsky (1990) further clarify this combination with their "way of life" definition. They define cultural bias as shared values and beliefs, but "social relations" as patterns of interpersonal relations. People organize their social relations, based on their values and beliefs across two fundamental dimensions of social life: boundedness/collectivity (group) and prescriptive/stratification (grid). This typology displays the four cultural types (see Figure 7.1), where hierarchy represents strong structure and strong group commitment; and individualism is at the opposite end with minimal structure and minimal group commitment. Egalitarianism prefers minimal structure, but strong group commitment; while fatalism, on the opposite end, promotes strong structure, but minimal group commitment.

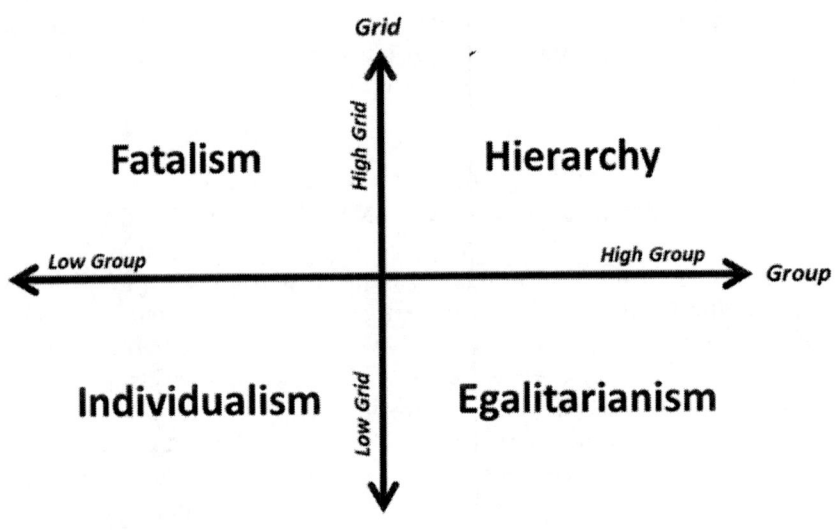

*Source:* Thompson et al. (1990, p. 8).

**Figure 7.1.**   GGCT typology of cultural orientations.

All four cultural types are present to some degree in every human group, and they are in constant tension with each other. This mutual opposition is necessary as it keeps the cultural types alive. The "impossibility theorem" states that in the jungle of cultural complexities, these are cultural archetypes that persist over time and countries "… the remaining possible mixtures are assumed to be transitional" (Douglas, 1999, p. 411)

Michael Thompson uses the "four myths of nature," which capture the cultural debate on the risks to the environment, to reflect further on human behavior and management of institutions under each cultural type (see Dake, 1991; Schwartz, 1994; Thompson, Ellis, & Wildavsky, 1990). Thompson illustrates these myths graphically by a ball on a two dimensional landscape.

The hierarchical perspective, which reflects the belief that nature can be vulnerable, but disruptors can be met with planning, holds the *Nature is Perverse/Tolerant myth*. **Risk** cannot be avoided and should be embraced by

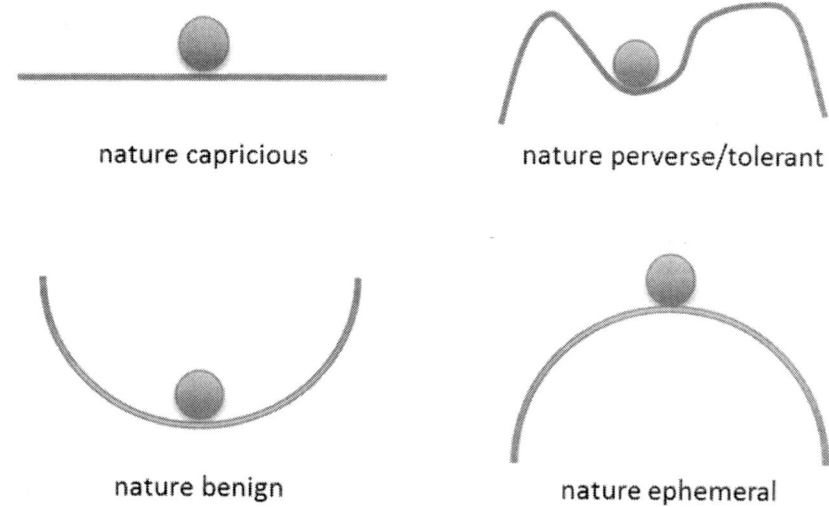

nature capricious

nature perverse/tolerant

nature benign

nature ephemeral

*Source:* Schwarz and Thompson (1990, p. 5); Thompson et al. (1990).

**Figure 7.2.**   The four primary myths of nature.

high-level decision makers, and by involving experts in the decision-making process. The cultural pattern, in cases where the management outcome is seen as a failure, is that responsibility and accountability is dispersed, and that it is hidden among different staff members or departments. A subordinate showing unwanted behavior is likely to be reprimanded in this cultural context (Thompson et al., 1990).

The *Nature is Ephemeral myth* is held by the egalitarian perspective: viewing the future as dangerous, assuming discontinuity, predicting the future will be bad, and arguing for the need to predict such a future in order to validate their warnings and thus gain political influence (Douglas & Wildavsky, 1982). However, to their credit, egalitarian cultures and groups believe in cooperative methods of solving problems (Thompson et al., 1990, p. 34); Egalitarians, furthermore, are acutely aware of, and may even exaggerate, risks in their surroundings. Risk is not viewed as an opportunity, and egalitarians will try to bring perceived risks to the attention of people they believe have caused the risk. In times of failure, the system is to blame; but egalitarians will also look for and are likely to perceive secret enemies within the group (Thompson et al., 1990).

The *Nature is Benign myth* is held by the individualistic perspective. Risk is looked upon as an opportunity among individualistic groups. New wealth should be created, and envy is not seen as a negative consequence in society since it stimulates ambition. In the case of failure, competition is not to blame; rather, failure is the result of bad luck or personal incompetence. Individuals within this culture are skeptical of politicizing and believe that the role of authority should be diminished by self-regulation (Thompson et al., 1990).

The *Nature is Capricious myth* is held by the fatalistic perspective. According to fatalism, both nature and humans are unpredictable, and disruptions resulting from this quality cannot be prevented. Risk can be avoided, but should not be confronted, as fatalists tend to lack the belief that its probable consequences can be managed or mitigated; Thus, it is useless trying to withstand crises and their consequences, much less consider mitigation or planning. Fatalists choose to avoid risk, but in times of failure they blame fate, which no individual is able to influence (Thompson et al., 1990).

Aaron Wildavsky and William Dake (1990) analyzed "what kind of people will perceive which potential hazards to be how dangerous" (p. 42). Their findings support GGCT claims that the theory can predict and explain the answer (Sheppard, Janoske, & Brook, 2012) to this question. According to their findings, individualists fear whatever impedes their freedom, and the most serious obstacle is war, when they may have to surrender to other people's control. They also show fear of developing a socialist government. Egalitarians fear developments that may increase inequalities, and they oppose risk that might harm many people or future generations. Hierarchists fear social disorder and crime, and emphasize that decisions about risk taking have to be justified by the government or experts. Fatalists try to avoid risk in general, because they think they cannot do anything about it.

In a study of culture and crisis management, both individualism and egalitarianism had an established relationship to the origin of a crisis. Natural disasters and environmental crises are the most frequent types of crises managed in egalitarian cultures or by egalitarian groups. It could be argued that because of the nature of natural and environmental disasters, decentralized operations are demanded, and that it is easy to convince people and policymakers of the necessity to prepare for them. However, as stated earlier, egalitarianism is mostly concerned with risk that could harm many people. History has shown that natural hazards are likely to have these kinds of catastrophic effects if they affect populated areas. Egalitarianism is also supposed to be concerned with the larger ecosystem. Individualistic groups most often handle fiscal and environmental crises. Hence, decentralized decision-making units with no, or few, standard operating procedures to rely on are most likely to be in charge of these types of crises. The supposed "risk-taking behavior in hope of reward" could explain why they tend to end up managing these kinds of crises, as well as the individualistic belief that "nature is benign," which suggests that society will always recover after disruptive events. Hence, costly measures to protect the environment or prepare for environmental disasters are not a priority in individualistic culture (Bernhardsdóttir, in press).

## RISK COMMUNICATION AS AN ETHICAL MIRROR

Risk communication is like the heart of risk governance that circulates information to all the stakeholders. This process includes information creation, presentation, persuasion, and strategic messaging (Sheppard, Janoske, & Brooke, 2012). One of the most important roles of risk governance, is to raise the public's awareness about the probable risks they face. It appears to be a dilemma, on the one hand, to expect risk managers to be sensitive to the public's needs; and on the other hand, to persuade people to behave in a certain way. With increasingly complex technology and their interactions, the public does not have the resources to understand the probable dangers they might face. The more their vulnerability increases, the more the public has to put its trust in the government to provide the necessary research and organization to protect it from harm. Hence, while we ask risk managers to be informed about the public's need for safety, security, and prioritization, we expect risk managers to take the responsibility for finding the best solutions and for providing the needed protection. The "perfect" way to serve this task can be hard to find, but extremes in risk communications in either direction ( i.e., negligence in raising public awareness or being manipulative in information processing) can have serious consequences.

The case of the 2009 L'Aquilla earthquake in Italy is worth reflecting on for both government officials and scientists who play a role in risk and disaster management. Negligence in raising public awareness (or more precisely not following procedures in information processing and even giving misinformation in this case), led to seven Italian scientists, one of them a government official, being convicted of manslaughter as a consequence of their public denials of the increased risk of an impending earthquake in L'Aquila (Hall, 2011). This was the first time that scientists had faced criminal charges for their own public statements regarding earthquake risk, and the charges immediately drew global condemnation. It is interesting to look at the responses in Italy through a cultural lens (Hall, 2011). Victims of the disaster reported how they themselves broke their "age-old cautionary 'culture' of living in an earthquake zone" (i.e., to stay out of their houses during impending risk), because they were swayed by the officials' assurances that there was no imminent danger (Hall, 2011, p. 264). In a survey measuring cultural dimensions, (House and Javidan, 2004) Italians showed relatively low emphasis on avoiding uncertainty, and they also valued a low-power distance. In Bernhardsdóttir's (in press) cultural framework, this behavior reflects individualistic values that tend to emphasize preparedness among individual households, over collectively focused strategies (Tierney, Lindell, & Perry, 2001). The Italian public living in the earthquake zone had been taking part of the responsibility of monitoring the risk for their own family—their own household—for decades. The "violation" of that unwritten rule must have played heavily into the public outrage in the wake of the disaster. The way in which the situation was managed was thought to be poor and unethical.

Another extreme in risk communication is exaggerated persuasion or manipulation; that, in the end, adds risk to the public instead of protecting them from harm. It can be thought of as advantageous for risk managers to imagine the worst-case scenario when predicting the risk of a disaster. By examining the worst-case scenario, plans can be made to avoid or mitigate it. However, when the danger predicted is unmanageable the question arises: what good does it do to keep people constantly vigilant and thereby risking their sense of trust and security?

Joseph Masco (2008, p. 361) has provided an example of manipulative risk governance; he argued that was evident by the way in which U.S. policymakers used the atomic bomb as "a new means of engaging and disciplining citizens in everyday life." Preparedness for the imagined nuclear warfare posed a tremendous risk to the U.S. population, both physically and psychologically. Test programs were run that transformed the country "into the most nuclear-bombed country on earth, distributing its environmental, economic, and health effect to each and every U.S. citizen" (p. 361). U.S. policymakers, Masco argued, used these collective formulations of nuclear fear in the United States as pillars of the national security policy, where the key aspects of U.S. security culture "have been formed in relation to images of nuclear devastation" (p. 362).

The United States has a very heterogeneous culture where each "state, each local community, possesses its own mix of political culture" (Elazar, as cited in Mamadouh, 1997, p. 19). Individualism has been thought of as the dominant cultural value in the United States (Tierney, Lindell, & Perry, 2001). In the GLOBE survey (House & Javidan, 2004) that measured cultural dimensions, Americans were shown to value low uncertainty avoidance, which could reflect a belief in the ability to avoid uncertainty, as expected by individualists; while they may not necessarily have thought there was a need to avoid uncertainty. What was more unexpected was how much Americans valued power distance; but the survey displayed their willingness to have more power distances than they felt they had in practice. It showed that they they preferred "... more deference and respect for its authorities and leadership" (Hoppe & Bhagat, 2007, p. 502). Mamadouh (1997, p. 18) argued that what Elazar defined as individualistic culture was "an alliance between the individualist and the hiearchist ways of life, referred to as 'the establishment' by Thompson Ellis and Wildavsky." Political parties that "serve as business corporations coordinating individual enterprise in the political arena" upheld the structure of society. "Politicians are interested in office as a means of controlling the distribution of favours and rewards of government" (p. 18). Government was restricted to necessary activities, as for instance national defense. The business elite supposedly favored the power of fear and militarism in the U.S. culture due, in part, to the economic gains it created for the weapons industry.

## Relative and Constrained Morality

Scholars have debated whether morality should be looked at from the objectivistic or relativistic perspective. Those who aim for the objectivistic morality would argue that "objective moral standards exist and that the practices of some cultures approximate these standards more closely than do the practices of others, and are accordingly morally superior" (Lockhard & Franzwa, 1994, p. 175). It would be easier to evaluate the morality and ethics of risk decision making having such standards as measurement. Protection of human lives should be expected to be the highest standard; Deaths during disasters in the 20th century listed by cause (EM-DAT) were 434.1 million, thereof 62.4% due to political violence. How many deaths of those approximately 271 million people would be justified or defined as ethical by the political leadership and/or public in the affected areas?

GGCT agrees that morality is different between cultures, but avoids defining the morality of one culture as better than another. Hence, GGCT takes the relativistic stance. According to the GGCT argument that its culture types are the only four that have stable organizational forms, the relativistic morality is constrained by those cultures. In order to provide GGCT the moral vocabulary it has been missing, Joshua A. Bruce (2013) has developed a "framework of moral concepts that are tied to social actions built from leading theories of moral psychology" (p. 37) He has tied together these theories using the GGCT "social-relational framework within which these morals direct behavior" (Bruce, 2013, p. 37). Hence, the *Ethics of Autonomy* is the moral counterpart of the GGCT grid, and usually directs the behavior of people whose ideal culture is individualism. The individuals' preferences matter. "Fairness/reciprocity and harm/care are the core individual moral concerns" (Bruce, 2013, p. 42). The *Ethic of Community* directs both group cultures (i.e. hierarchy and egalitarianism), and emphasizes that an individual ought to belong to a group; "In-group/loyalty and authority/respect" are the core group concerns. The high group and low grid of egalitarianism makes the cultures autonomy driven by both group- and individuality-based morality (p. 42).

Bernhardsdóttir's (in press) analysis on the relationship between culture and crisis managers' behavior, reveals that low-grid cultures provide decision makers who are more concerned and sensitive towards others than decision makers in high-grid cultures. It also shows when the test includes the four cultures that egalitarianism increases the likelihood of concerned decision making, while the likelihood of in-group collectivism and group loyalty increases in cultures with a hierarchical emphasis. Thus, Bernhardsdóttir's analysis supports Bruce's (2013) framework, but fine-tunes the differences between the cultural types. Hence, individualism and egalitarianism both share the individual moral concerns although displayed stronger in the latter. While the emphasis on group formation is shared among the group cultures, the egalitarianism group-emphasis can be seen by the way in which the cultural type increases the likelihood of decentralized collective decision making.

## CULTURAL CHANGES AND CHANGES IN MORALITY AND ETHICS: ICELAND AS A CASE STUDY

Crises are tests of the values of those who are affected by the crises. Crises and crisis management in Iceland will be used in this chapter to analyze and reflect on the influence of culture, especially on risk reduction, and whether and how the morality and ethics—as discussed above—relate to GGCT cultural types.

The culture of Nordic countries was measured in 1999 by using a survey of cultural types based on the GGCT (Grendstad, Jensen, Kristinsson, Sjöberg, & Sundback, 1999). It displayed that egalitarianism scored higher in Iceland than in the other Nordic countries. Factor analysis showed that the strongest factor was egalitarianism and the second was a mixture of individualism and hierarchy (Bernhardsdóttir & Kristinsson, 2003).

One of the fundamental differences between low-grid cultures is that egalitarianism emphasizes equality over freedom, while with individualism the reverse is true. According to Stefán Ólfasson (1985) the emphasis on equality relative to freedom is far greater in Iceland than in North America and other parts of Europe, even greater than in other Nordic countries.

An empirical test based on the GGCT with propositions about the expected crisis management culture in Iceland, showed an egalitarian emphasis (Bernhardsdóttir & Kristinsson, 2003). Some of the findings that especially related to the interplay between culture and risk reduction, are reflected upon in this chapter. The Icelandic civil defense structure was built in accordance with decentralized organizational control. Operative decisions were decentralized down to the level where actions must be taken, which was often in a local setting. In addition, the involvement of different responding parties was based on the nature of the crisis; and volunteer organizations played an important role in the Icelandic crisis response. Such processes demanded consensus between the parties in crisis decision making.

Important steps towards mitigation and preparedness in Iceland were taken with the establishment of the Association for Accident Prevention in 1928. This organization aims to prevent accidents at sea. The public concern about the risk of marine accidents is understandable in the light of the fact that it has taken a higher toll of human lives in Iceland, than any other type of disaster. The idea behind the association was consistent with the egalitarian perspective, but the government followed public initiative when it created new regulations regarding safety at the sea. In a short period of time, the association became one of the most powerful social movements that provided rescue teams around the country. Along with rapid social changes, the association took over prevention, preparedness, and rescue in case of accidents and disasters, both on land and at sea (Arnalds, Pétursson, & Thorkelsson, 1996; Bernhardsdóttir & Kristinsson, 2003). The dominant role of the association explains why disaster management in Iceland has kept its main focus on the safety of human lives, rather than on other types of safety, such as environmental safety.

## Five Crisis-Case Studies

The crisis studies referred to in this chapter's analysis, concern avalanches that hit the two small villages of Sudavik and Flateyri, located in the West Fjords of Iceland; the 2000 earthquakes in south Iceland; the response by Iceland to a proposal by the European Commission to ban fishmeal in animal feed in 2000; and the 1997 stranding of the cargo vessel Vikartindur on the south shore of Iceland. The banking collapse in 2008 is presented separately and used to reflect on the cultural changes pre and post that crisis.

Icelandic crisis studies show that the "system" is first and foremost blamed for inadequate preparedness in Iceland, which is consistent with the egalitarian culture. Prior to the avalanche in Sudavik, engineering consulting firms had been overseeing avalanche risk assessments on behalf of the Icelandic civil defense agency. Yet after the disaster, discussions in the Icelandic parliament centered, among other things, on having risk assessment conducted by the public sector rather than in the private sector. It was thus recommended that risk assessments, which had previously been the responsibility of the civil defense agency, be taken over by the Icelandic Meteorological office on the grounds that this would help ensure that objective expert knowledge, obtained and developed by the institution, would be digested and used in future risk assessments (Bernhardsdóttir, 2001; Bernhardsdóttir & Svedin, 2004). According to GGCT, egalitarianists do not trust the market or private institutions. Thus, the kind of distrust expressed towards the engineering consulting firm reflected the egalitarian culture (Bernhardsdóttir & Kristinsson, 2003).

In this chapter it is important to ask about the type of political culture that was dominant in the country during this period, and whether or not it was consistent with public preferences. Mamadouh (1997) defines political culture as being the specific mix of ways of life in a community. Egalitarianism, in alliance with hierarchy, creates the moralistic culture; but its alliance with individualism is likely to be a "pseudo-traditional" culture that he describes as being unstable and created when the egalitarian and individualistic "ways of life are strong, but are not able to form a stable alliance" (p. 24). It can be argued, that in the wake of the young republic of Iceland (1944), a moralistic culture with an emphasis on equality and strong political power and regulations were being developed. The public had a notion of themselves as being a member of the "group": independent Icelanders. They were seen as people who accepted the rather detailed prescriptions of how to behave in economic life; rules now made by their own politicians. Thus, the ethics of the community was strong. At that time, neither the politicians nor the public had pending questions or worries regarding ethical risk governance.

In a very broad-brush description, a part of the economic and social life developments in the latter half of the 20th century were shaped by the growing demand for a more market-driven economy and deregulation. Thus, individualism was on the rise, but it did not take the primary spot of egalitarianism. The ethics of autonomy (low grid) was the common nominator between the cultural types. Referring again to Mamadouh (1997) and Bruce (2013) the egalitarian emphasis, as measured around the last millennium in Iceland, should have reflected a moralistic culture; with the ethic of community, as well as with ethic of autonomy, both on the individual and group level. The risk management development reported above as the analysis of the five crises-cases, shows such relationships between culture, morality, and ethics

According to GGCT, culture is not static, but needs to be changing in order to keep the societal culture stable. Value conflicts resulting from the breaking and making of new alliances involve constant micro-changes; there is movement from one cultural type to another within a society. Could crisis trigger a major value change? One isolated incident or crisis affecting a limited number of people, could hardly initiate value change in society as a whole. However, a crisis that had a widespread influence on people's lives, would push value changes (Benhardsdóttir, in-press). Such a crisis was the banking collapse in 2008.

## The 2008 Banking Collapse Crisis

Everyone who has followed the global banking collapse that hit Western economies in 2008, knows that Iceland was one of the biggest casualties of that crisis. The country's three major commercial banks collapsed. The worth of the banks had grown to twelve times the country's GDP (Jónsson, 2009) How could the small nation that had for decades and centuries emphasized egalitarian values, experience such a devastating situation lead by market forces and reinforced by individualistic values? Why did the Icelandic government and the Icelandic political community not perceive the risk and why did they not give proper warnings to stakeholders; stakeholders who, in the end, turned out to be the Icelandic public and foreign creditors. In Iceland, the general public was defined as a stakeholder with their whole livelihood at risk.

The Icelandic government has been criticized for its lack of preparedness, particularly for its inability to employ measures that could have mitigated the consequences. Although it is hard to believe that the Icelandic government could have anticipated the simultaneous collapse of its three major banks, there were many warning signs before October 2008 that indicated that the Icelandic financial sector had become dangerously large for such a small nation (Jonsson, 2009).

"Thanks to a neoliberal deregulation strategy, Iceland was in one decade —from Iceland's entry into the Single European Market in the mid-1990s, until the privatization of financial institutions in the first years of the 21st century—transformed from being amongst the most heavily regulated and backward banking regimes, shut within its own borders, to being one of the most liberal and international in the world" (Bergmann, 2014, p. 65). Hence, in this relatively short time period, Icelandic culture became extremely market driven or individualistic. Instead of being a resource-based local economy, which was dependent on fishing and geo-thermal energy, it had become a global financial giant (Bergmann, 2014). How could this egalitarian nation accept the geared-up market economy that triggered such extremely high, risk-taking behavior? In this macro-level case, the government was primarily responsible for the risk governance; The government policies had surely driven Iceland in this direction.

In the 1970s, a group of young, conservative libertarians had been established with the aim to push for more economic freedom in the country. One of its members was to become a prime minister for the Independent party, and stayed in office for 13 years. The libertarian influence within the party pulled it further into an individualistic culture. The alliance between the Independence party and the Progressive party (1995–2000), gave the libertarians' air under their wings, and they pushed through the policies needed for privatization and deregulation in early 2000, as mentioned above.

The Nordic survey referred to earlier, demonstrates that egalitarianism was still the dominant culture around the last millennium. The privatization of the banking sector in 2002–2003, with the creation of a new wealthy elite with political and financial power, was the policymaking that challenged the egalitarianism values, where equal opportunity weighed heavily. Manipulation is a part of political life. Politicians and political parties use their words and deeds to try to convince people that their ideals are the most worthy to believe in and that policies should be driven by those ideals. In that sense, the big economic changes in Iceland can be looked at as a powerful manipulation. The whole economy was swept into and operated under the individualistic ideals.

Risk manipulation became a natural part of the new deal given to the public. Both individuals with high-risk preferences, as well as those who had worked hard and cautiously for their savings, had become participants in the risky game; both knowingly and unknowingly. How could so many egalitarians become participants in this development? What had become of the moralistic culture and the ethics of community that had been expected of that culture? First it should be stressed, that some people and experts voiced warnings; but they were drowned out by the conviction of those who strongly believed in the success of the new economy. We should also not forget the leaderships' risk communications that downplayed the risky situation.

According to GGCT, surprises can push for cultural change; i.e. when unexpected experiences make individuals re-evaluate their view on life. Supposedly many of those who had chosen egalitarianism as their way of life, began re-evaluating their view of the market economy. Yes, the new elite had been created, but the average Icelander was also getting richer. Thus, the myth that obstacles would always be in the way of infinite growth was perhaps wrong?

The banking collapse in Iceland in 2008 convinced many Icelanders about the truth of that myth. The crisis made Icelanders re-evaluate their values, their culture, and the ethicality of governmental policies. The outraged public stormed through the streets, armed with their pots and pans, and started a revolution that led to the resignation of the government in January 2009; the first, pure left-wing coalition government was formed, "which initiated a number of policies and programs aimed at replacing the collapsed neoliberal growth model with a resurrected Nordic welfare society" (Bergmann, 2014, p. 9).

The risk governance of this new government aimed first, and foremost, at preventing growing inequality as a result of the crisis. Thus, the moralistic culture and ethics of community bounced back forcefully. However, despite the demand for a more egalitarian culture, the blame-game that followed was more intact with what could be expected within an individualistic culture.

Although key institutions—as a part of the system—were accused of playing along with the political elite in the collapse, the blaming was turned more toward individuals. Hence, the blaming was reflecting more on the individualistic culture, which blames failure on personal incompetence and bad luck or some combination of both, and which uses ad hoc inspection or review of how crises are managed in search for explanation. The three politically appointed governors of the Central Bank were replaced, and the director and board of the Financial Supervisory Authority were sacked (Bergmann, 2014). "The new office of Special Prosecutor was established to investigate criminal activities in the financial sector leading up to the crash, and Parliament appointed a Special Investigation Research Commission (a truth committee), which was to analyze events and eventually proposed to Parliament that a hitherto dormant clause in the constitution relating to the prosecution of government ministers should be used to hold political leaders accountable" (Bergmann, 2014, p. 10). This sharpening of the cultural lens, gave the public new clarity on the ethical controversy of the development that lead to the crash. As expected, every decision made by the former government or governmental agencies was scrutinized through those new lenses (Booth, 2000). Corruption and inexcusable risky behavior were what people looked at in hindsight with disbelief and fury.

The concern of the left-wing government about the risk of inequality was shared globally; when the ongoing gap between the incomes of the richest and poorest citizens is the risk, that is most likely to cause serious damage globally in the coming decade, according to more than 700 global experts that contributed to the World Economic Forum's Global Risks 2014 report (World Economic Forum, 2014). The OECD's 2014 report, Society at a Glance, said that the socio-economic impact of the crisis showed in "lower-income households [that] have lost greater proportions of their incomes than the better-off, or benefited less from the sluggish recovery— particularly in the hardest hit countries like Estonia, Greece, Ireland, Italy, and Spain, though not in Iceland where well-off households have sustained greater income losses than poor ones" (OECD, 2014). In all fairness, we should expect that all the highly paid bankers that were out of jobs, and thus not counted in this comparison, lowered the gap, but still the report shows that the measures taken by the government were able to direct the society toward the moralistic culture of egalitarianism and hierarchy. New regulations—prescriptions—and more decisive governmental control diminished the economic freedom of individuals, but the concern and thus ethics of community increased.

In the trauma following the crash, and in the attempts to recover and raise the economy from its ruins, it was expected that the left-wing coalition government would become a convenient target. Despite the relatively rapid recovery, the government lost its public support in the parliamentary election in 2013, and the Independence and Progressive parties regained the majority they had in the 10 years around the millennium, as discussed above. Thus, the pull and push between the cultural types continues, and it remains to be seen whether the egalitarian culture in so much demand in the post-crisis period, will give way to the individualistic values.

## SUMMARY

This chapter examined the relationship between ethics and risk management from the cultural perspective. It discussed how morality and ethics are a part of the prevalent culture in a society or community. The Grid Group Cultural Theory was used to both explain and test these relationships. The theory offered four viable cultures: hierarchy, egalitarianism, individualism, and fatalism. It took the relativistic orientation toward morality, and therefore did not provide morality standards. What it did, though, was constrain the moralistic possibilities within the four cultural types. A framework of moral concepts built on moral psychology tied to GGCT (Bruce, 2013) was used to seek the needed morality guidance for the different types. It showed that Ethics of Autonomy was the moral counterpart of the GGCT grid, and usually directed the behavior of people whose ideal culture was individualism; They seek fairness and care. The Ethic of Community directed both group cultures, that is, hierarchy and egalitarianism, and emphasized that people ought to belong to a group. Besides seeking membership, they preferred loyalty and authority/respect. Egalitarianism was driven by both group and individuality-based morality (Bruce, 2013). A study of the relationship between culture and crisis managers' behavior, which showed that egalitarianism increased the likelihood of concerned decision making and hierarchy of in-group loyalty, was reported in order to show how the ethics of community was emphasized differently between the group cultures. The egalitarianism group emphasis was seen by the way in which the cultural type increased the likelihood of decentralized collective decision making (Bernhardsdóttir, in press).

Six Icelandic crisis-case studies were used to analyze and test the relationship between ethics and risk management. Since all of those crises were on the macro level, and involved the Icelandic government, it was necessary to analyze especially the political culture based on the way Mamadouh (1997) defined it as being the specific mix of ways of life in a community. Egalitarianism in alliance with hierarchy created the moralistic culture, but its alliance with individualism was likely to be a "pseudo-traditional" culture, which was described as being unstable and was created when the egalitarian and individualistic "ways of life are strong, but are not able to form a stable alliance." The Icelandic political culture fell under the "pseudo-traditional" culture, but the instability in their alliance had not been prevalent, although it could have been argued that it created fertile ground for economic and social instability. Especially not if looking at the 10-year alliance between the political parties that developed the culture that involved the high risk of financial crisis. The Icelandic case studies demonstrate how cultural changes led to changes in ethical standards.

Risk communication was especially brought into focus in this chapter due to its importance for ethical risk management. It can become a great challenge to search for the right information, understand the contents, and have it processed by stakeholders. The way in which the Icelandic government began working on risk policy to prevent harmful accidents at sea by following the initiative of the Association for Accident Prevention, was far from the complex risk policies that were needed in order to prevent the banking collapse. However, the extremity in risk communication, and the risk of serious consequences, was especially focused on: both negligence due to the lack of vigilance, and manipulation of public fear could be judged unethical. The governmental negligence in risk communication (prior to the crash) became salient in the post review; but the way it swayed the cultural emphasis away from egalitarianism to individualism, could also be looked at as a powerful manipulation. It was not driven by fear tactics, but rather by the promise of reward.

This chapter's findings should encourage risk managers to use GGCT as a tool to gain a better understanding of different cultures, their morality, and ethics. Even though the morality path does not always lead to ethical outcomes, it is the path that needs to be taken. If a risk manager is so unfortunate as to experience a crisis during his or her working life, then he/she should expect that his/her behavior and decision making will be re-evaluated by different ethical standards than those in place during the time the related risk policies were made (or not made). Such a shift in ethical standards is likely to follow a shift in cultural values, as a result of a serious crisis at the macro level.

## REFERENCES

Arnalds, E. S., Pétursson, P. A., & Thorkelsson, T. (1996). *Lansbjorg: The national life saving association yearbook.* Reykjavik, Iceland: Landsbjorg.

Bergmann, E. (2014). *Iceland and the international financial crisis. Boom, bust and recovery.* Hampshire, England: Palgrave Macmillan.

Bernhardsdóttir, Á. E. (2001). *Learning from past experiences: The 1995 avalanches in Iceland.* Stockholm, Sweden: The National Defense College of Sweden.

Bernhardsdóttir, Á. E. (in press). *Crisis-related decision-making and the influence of culture on the behavior of decision makers: Cross cultural behavior in crisis preparedness and response.* Cham, Switzerland: Springer International AG.

Bernhardsdóttir, Á. E., & Kristinsson, G. H. (2003). Kúltúrkenning um áfallastjórnun [Cultural theory and crisis management]. In *Rannsóknir í Félagsvísinum IV [Research in Social Sciences IV]* (pp. 559–579). Reykjavik, Iceland: University Press.

Bernhardsdóttir, Á. E., & Svedin, L. M. (2004). *Small-state crisis management: The Icelandic way.* Stockholm, Sweden: The National Defence College of Sweden.

Booth, S. A. (2000). How can organisations prepare for reputational crisis? *Journal of Contingencies and Crisis Management,* 197–207.

Bruce, J. R. (2013). Uniting theories of morality, religion, and social interaction: Grid-Group Cultural Theory, the "big three" ethics, and moral foundations theory. *Psychology & Society, 5*(1), 37–50.

Dake, K. (1991). Orienting dispositions in the perception of risk: An analysis of contemporary worldviews and cultural biases. *Journal of Cross-Cultural Psychology, 22*(1), 61–82.

Douglas, M. (1975). *Implicit meanings: Essays in anthropology.* London, England: Routledge & Kegan Paul.

Douglas, M. (1982). *In the active voice.* London, England: Routledge & Kegan Paul.

Douglas, M. (1996). *Natural symbols: Explorations in cosmology.* New York, NY: Routledge.

Douglas, M. (1999). Four cultures: The evolution of a parsimonious model. *GeoJournal, 47*(3), 411–415.

Douglas, M., & Wildavsky, A. (1982). *Risk and culture. An essay on the selection of technical and environmental dagers.* Berkeley, CA: University of California Press.

Grendstad, G., Jensen, L., Kristinsson, G. H., Sjöberg, L., & Sundback, S. (1999). *Nordic Cultures: Measurement, Consequences and Comparisons, Study Description and Fequencies.* Bergen: LOS-senteret.

Hall, S. S. (2011). Scientists on trial: At fault? *Nature, 477,* 264–269.

Hendriks, F. (2004). The poison is the dose: Or how "more egalitarianism" may work in some places but not in all. *Innovation, 17*(4), 349–361.

Hoppe, M. H., & Bhagat, R. S. (2007). Leadership in the United States of Amerika: The leader as cultural hero. In J. S. Chhokar, F. C. Brodbeck, & R. J. House, *culture and leadership across the world. The GLOBE book of in-depth studies of 25 societies* (pp. 475–544). Mahwah, NJ: Lawrence Erlbaum.

House, R. J., & Javidan, M. (2004). Overview of GLOBE. In R. J. House, P. J. Hanges, M. Javidan, P. W. Dorfaman, & V. Gupta, *Culture, leadership, and organizations. The GLOBE study of 62 societies* (pp. 9–28). Thousand Oaks, CA: Sage.

Jónsson, Á. (2009). *Why Iceland? How one of the world's smallest countries became the meltdown's biggest casualty.* New York, NY: McGraw-Hill.

Lockhart, C., & Franzwa, G. (1994). Cultural theory and the problem of moral relativism. In D. J. Coyle, & R. J. Ellis, *Politics, policy and culture* (pp. 175–189). Boulder, CO: Westview Press.

Mamadouh, V. V. (1999). Grid-Group Cultural Theory: An introduction. *GeoJournal, 47*(3), 345–409.

Masco, J. (2008). Survival is your business: Engineering ruins and affect in nuclear America. *Cultural Anthropology, 23*(2), 361–398.

OECD. (2014). Society at a glance 2014: OECD social indicators. OECD Publishing.

Ólafsson, S. (1985). *Hvernig eru Íslendingar? Nokkrar vísbendingar um gildi í menningu Íslendinga* [How to describe Icelanders? A few indications about values in Icelandi culture]. Reykjavik, Iceland: Department of Social Sciences, University of Iceland.

Schwartz, S. H. (1994). Are there universal aspects in the structure and contents of human values? *Journal of Social Issues, 50*(4), 19–45.

Sheppard, B., Janoske, M., & Brooke, L. (2012). *Understanding risk communication theory: A guide for emergency managers and communicators.* Washington, DC: U.S. Department of Homeland Security.

Swedlow, B. (2002). Toward cultural analysis in policy analysis: Picking up where Aaron Wildavsky left off. *Journal of Comparative Policy Analysis, 4*(3), 267–285.

Tenbrunsel, A. E., & Smith-Crowe, K. (2008). Ethical decision making: Where we've been and where we're going. *The Academy of Management Annals, 2*(1), 545–507.

Thompson, M. (1997). Rewring the precepts of policy analysis. In R. J. Ellis, & M. Thompson, *Culture matters: Essays in honor of Aaron Wildavsky* (pp. 203–216). Boulder, CO: Westview Press.

Thompson, M., Ellis, R., & Wildavsky, A. (1990). *Cultural theory.* Boulder, CO: Westview Press.

Tierney, K. J., Lindell, M. K., & Perry, R. W. (2001). *Facing the unexpected. disaster preparedness and response in the United States.* Washington, DC: Joseph Henry Press.

Wildavsky, A., & Dake, K. (1990). Theories of risk perception: Who fears what and why? *Daedalus, 119*(4), 41–60.

World Economic Forum. (2014). *Global risks 2014: Insight report* (9th ed.). Geneva: Author.

CHAPTER 8

---

# CIVIL SOCIETY ORGANIZATIONS AND RISK MANAGEMENT

## The Case of Japan

**Aya Okada**

---

## INTRODUCTION

For anyone living in Japan, feeling an earthquake is not an unusual event. Every time I feel the shake, I immediately look around to secure a route to escape, turn on the television to get the latest information, and make sure I have my cellular phone with me. I take such series of actions, because I am aware that an earthquake is a serious risk in Japan, and that taking these actions is necessary to protect my life once the risk turns into reality. By contrast, I did not take the same series of action when I felt a shake in Pennsylvania in August 2011. My first thought was, "Was that an airplane crash?" All I did, aside from going online to learn what happened, was simply to look around and see how other people were reacting. The difference in my response to an earthquake in two contexts comes from whether

---

I had pre-considered the disaster as a potential risk in the respective circumstances.

The way human beings manage risks is closely related to their *risk perception*. In other words, we characterize the situation as a risk based on what we perceive as a potential danger, our knowledge of how dangerous the situation could be, how likely the incident is to take place, and what we can do in responding to the risk.

For every kind of risk—be it an earthquake, tsunami, or terrorist attack —our perception is shaped by past experiences and practices, as well as information that we have been exposed to. There are multiple sources of information that provide knowledge about the danger we might encounter. These range from government agencies (local, national, and international); mass media, including television and newspapers; to individuals, like our family and friends.

This chapter will shed light on civil society organizations as the key actors influencing people's risk management behaviors. These organizations include neighborhood associations, residents groups, voluntary organizations, and nonprofit organizations.[1] The chapter will highlight three roles that civil society organizations play in the context of Japan, and discuss ethical questions that these organizations face. The roles they play in Japan include: (1) spreading common knowledge and ideas; (2) providing knowledge and facilitating knowledge creation as experts; and (3) capitalizing lessons learned for future disasters. This chapter will examine actor-centered ethics (Svedin, 2011, p. 13) and discuss value conflicts and judgments that civil-society organizations face in making decisions as they influence people's risk-management behaviors. I will discuss the ethical questions that these organizations face as providers of information, such as deciding what information is *effective, correct*, and *appropriate* in protecting people's lives from potential risks. I also will discuss the unique situation civil society organizations face in attempting to be accountable for their decisions.

## SETTING UP THE CONTEXT

### Japan, a Disaster-Prone Land

In discussing the role of civil society organizations in risk management, this chapter will look at Japan. A small island nation located on the Pacific Rim, Japan has experienced several major natural disasters, such as earthquakes, volcano eruptions, typhoons, and tsunamis. Between 1984 and 2013, Japan was home to 18.5% of the world's earthquakes larger than magnitude 6.0, and it has 7.1% of the world's active volcanoes (Cabinet

Office, 2014). Some of the recent disasters have included: a magnitude 7.3 earthquake in Kobe in 1995 (known as the Great Hanshin-Awaji Earthquake); a magnitude 6.8 earthquake in Niigata (Niigata-Ken-Chuetsu Earthquake) in 2004; and the triple disasters of earthquake, tsunami, and nuclear threat that struck northeastern Japan on March 11, 2011 (the Great East Japan Earthquake or Tohoku disasters).

Japan expects to face another major disaster in the near future. Seismologists predict that the chance of an earthquake larger than magnitude 7.0 (or higher) striking Japan in the next 30 years is 70%. If such an earthquake strikes the capital city of Tokyo, it is estimated that 23,000 persons will be killed with an economic loss of approximately $950 billion (USD).[2] Another potential risk is an earthquake in the Tokai region, which is expected to possibly reach 9.0 in magnitude. A governmental working group predicts that in a worst-case scenario, the Tokai earthquake could claim 323,000 lives (Cabinet Office, 2014).

Given past experiences and predictions, the Japanese people have developed their own risk perceptions of these natural disasters. When a national Japanese survey asked for citizens' image of a disaster, 80.4% of the respondents answered earthquake. This was followed by wind disasters including tornadoes and typhoons (48.1%), river floods (19.6%), tsunami (17.8 %), and landslide (13.2%). Only 8.8% of the respondents said that they had no specific image of a disaster (Cabinet Office, 2013a).

## Emerging Expectations Toward Civil Society Organizations in Managing Risks

Preparing for the risk of natural disasters has long been a key priority in Japan. The Japanese government has invested around 5% of the national general account budget for disaster prevention, response, recovery, and reconstruction. The government has also established its disaster management system after the passage of the Disaster Countermeasures Basic Act of 1961 (Cabinet Office, 2011, 2014).

One interesting characteristic of the Japanese disaster management system is the assumption that public-sector organizations (mainly national and local governments) serve as the key actors in a disaster (Comfort, Okada, & Ertan, 2013). This assumption and experience has undergone a significant change based on the experience of two major disasters in the past two decades: the 1995 Kobe earthquake and the 2011 Tohoku disasters. What has emerged is an expectation, both within the official disaster-management framework as well as among the general public, that civil society organizations play a vital role in managing risks.

The 1995 Kobe earthquake was the first key momentum for such change. Contributions by volunteers and voluntary organizations in disaster response and reconstruction came to be widely recognized. This lead to what Honma and Deguchi (1996) called a Japanese "volunteer revolution." In response to the claim that effectiveness and efficiency of these organizations will greatly enhance with official recognition, the government of Japan enacted its first law for nonprofit organizations in 1998 (Law to Promote Specified Nonprofit Activities). The number of organizations that have gained legal status under this new law has steadily risen. The term "NPO" is now widely used around Japan.

When the earthquake and tsunami struck northeastern Japan in 2011, civil society organizations were again very active. Contributions made by these organizations were widely evident. Many local governments, who were initially designed to take the initiative in response operations, did not function. In some cases, the mayor had lost his/her life in the disaster or was missing during the first few days. In other cases, the disaster directly hit municipal governments and left them with heavily damaged offices. From these experiences, the national government began to reconsider the limitation of disaster management led by the public sector or "public help" (*kojo*).

The government of Japan is now taking steps to recognize the role of civil society organizations in its disaster management system and plans. One reflection of this trend can be seen in the latest white paper on disaster management titled *Strengthening Regional Disaster Prevention Power through Mutual-Help* (Cabinet Office, 2014).

The shift toward recognizing the contributions of civil society organizations was also observed in amendments to the Disaster Countermeasures Basic Act passed in 2013. For example, "arranging environment for disaster prevention activities by volunteers" was no longer considered an "item for consideration" for national and local governments; the amendment clearly stated that both national and local governments were "to partner" with these organizations while respecting their autonomy.

Expectation toward civil society organizations are also on the rise among the Japanese public. Figure 8.1 shows the change in what the Japanese people view as necessary in responding to disasters (Cabinet Office, 2013a). The questions posed dealt with three different aspects of help in disaster management: self-help, or protecting oneself (*jijo*); mutual-help, or cooperative efforts among local residents and volunteers (*kyojo*); and public help, or efforts by public organizations including national and local governments (*kojo*). Respondents that placed emphasis on traditional public help decreased from 24.9% to 8.3% over 10 years. More people preferred to emphasize a balance between public-help, mutual-help, and self-help.

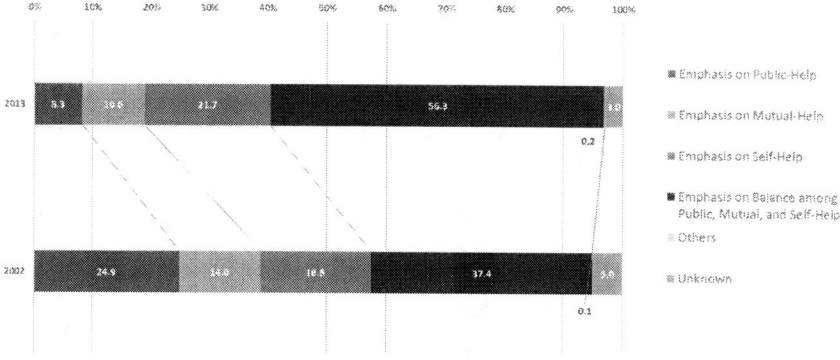

*Source:* Cabinet Office of Japan (2013a)

**Figure 8.1**

## TYPES OF CIVIL SOCIETY ORGANIZATIONS

Multiple types of civil society organizations are engaged in risk management in Japan, from loosely organized resident groups, to highly organized and institutionalized nonprofit organizations with formal legal status. This section will highlight two key types of civil society organizations in Japan.

### Voluntary Organization for Disaster Prevention

The first type of civil society organization is called *jishu bosai soshiki*. These voluntary organizations are made up of local residents who work specifically on disaster prevention. In many cases, the basis of these organizations is neighborhood associations or self-governing community associations. As Figure 8.2 shows, the number of voluntary organizations for disaster prevention in Japan has increased consistently over the past decade. The percentage of households covered by these organizations has also been steadily increasing, reaching to 77.9% of all Japanese households in 2013. The expansion of *jishu bosai soshiki* is a reflection of a key characteristic of Japanese civil society. That is, while there are few large, professionally managed organizations that engage in lobby-type activities to influence national policy debates, interactions among the people at grassroots level, like these voluntary organizations for disaster prevention, are quite active (Pekkanen, 2006).

### Specified Nonprofit Organizations

Although limited in number, more institutionalized type of voluntary organizations also that influence people's risk management behaviors in Japan. A prominent example of such are what is called specified

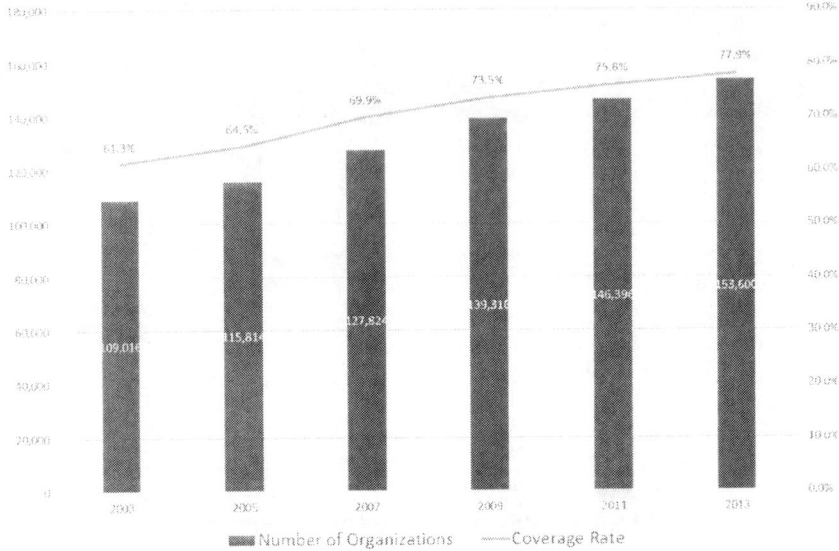

*Source:* Cabinet Office (2014)

**Figure 8.2**

nonprofit organizations or *tokutei hieiri katsudo hojin*. These are nonprofit organizations that have acquired legal status under the aforementioned nonprofit law. Disaster prevention is one of the 14 fields that the law allows for these nonprofit organizations. According to the database of the Japanese Cabinet Office as of September 14, 2014, there were 3,822 specified nonprofit organizations in Japan that had officially claimed to be engaged in disaster-prevention efforts.

It is also worth noting that the 2011 Tohoku disaster became a trigger for nonprofit organizations originally engaged in other fields of activities to expand their scope to include disaster management. Figure 8.3 shows the original field that specified nonprofit organizations were engaged in before they entered into disaster-related efforts after the triple disasters in northeastern Japan (Cabinet Office, 2012). We have learned that many organizations previously had engaged in health, medical care, welfare, social education, and nurturing children, expanded their activities to disaster prevention. We can thus predict that the number of specified nonprofit organizations engaged in disaster prevention is likely larger now than what is cited above.

There are other types of voluntary and nonprofit organizations that operate under a different legal category, such as public interest incorporated associations (*koeki shadan hojin*), public interest incorporated foundation

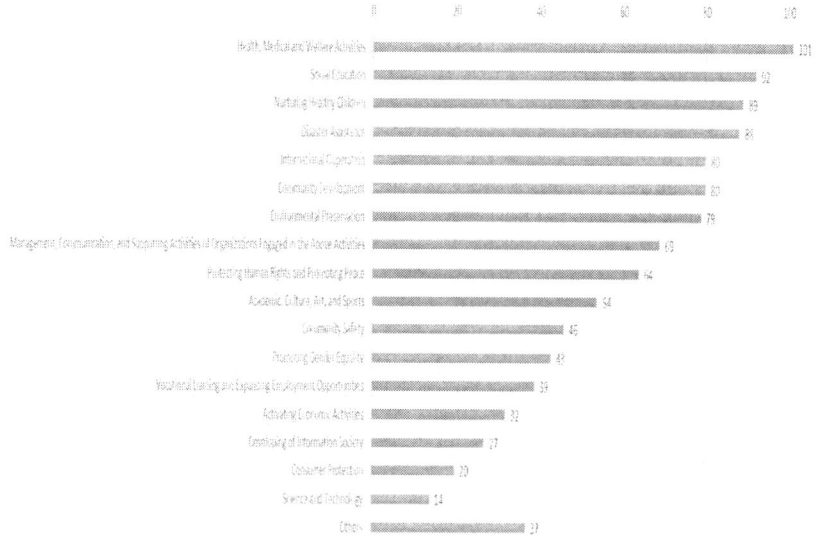

*Source:* Cabinet Office (2012)

**Figure 8.3**

(*koeki zaidan hojin*), general incorporated associations (*ippan shadan hojin*), and general incorporated foundations (*ippan zaidan hojin*). There are also groups and organizations that operate without any legal status.

## Three Roles of Civil Society Organizations in Managing Risks

What roles do these civil society organizations play in risk management? In other words, how do these organizations contribute to how people perceive risk and prepare for potential dangers? Among multiple ways these these organizations contribute, this section will highlight the following three roles: spreading common knowledge and ideas, providing knowledge/facilitating knowledge creation as experts, and capitalizing on lessons learned for future disasters.

## Spreading Common Knowledge and Ideas

Taking advantage of its closeness to the everyday lives of people, civil society organizations sometimes play a key role in spreading knowledge and ideas about risk. The aforementioned voluntary organizations for disaster prevention, for example, often organize disaster drills. Nonprofit organizations may also host a workshop on potential risks of earthquakes and tsunamis and provide the latest predictions and information to residents.

Local neighborhood associations also pass down local traditional lore, together with local municipalities and schools. One symbolic example of such is the teaching of *Tsunami Tendenko* in the Sanriku region of Japan. This region consists of a set of coastal communities that have experienced multiple tsunamis in their history, such as the Meiji Sanriku Tsunami of 1896 and the Showa Sanriku Tsunami of 1933. *Tendenko* in the local dialect means individuals or separate. The phrase implies that once an earthquake is felt, there is a risk of tsunami, and thus everyone should run to higher ground *individually* to protect their lives. One should not worry about other family members or friends, but rather evacuate *separately* (Yamori, 2012).

The story was widely taught and shared within the communities, and was put in practice when the tsunami struck the Sanriku region in 2011. The case of Kamaishi Elementary School is a prominent example. While more than 1,000 people lost their lives in the city of Kamaishi, 99.8% of the students survived the deadly tsunami. Students who were at the school building, as well as those who were at home, made decisions to run to higher grounds *separately*. Experts and mass media praised the teaching of *Tsunami-Tendenko* for saving countless students in the city (Sankei Shimbun, March 10, 2014). The case of Kamaishi is often contrasted with the case of Okawa Elementary School, where 74 out of 108 students died (Mainichi Shimbun, March 10, 2014). The teaching of *Tsunami-Tendenko* was not widely spread among the students and teachers of the Okawa district. Instead of running immediately to the mountains on the backside of the school building, teachers took some time after the first shake to discuss where to evacuate to, and decided to direct the students to the delta near the breakwater along the river, opposite from the higher grounds nearby.

## Provision of Knowledge/Facilitating Knowledge Creation as Experts

Civil society organizations are not only effective at the grassroots level, but also at a societal level, where they appear as experts that provide professional know-how. Ever since the 1995 Kobe earthquake and especially after the 2011 triple disasters, nonprofit practitioners have appeared in mass media along with scientists from academia. Figure 8.4 shows an increase in the number of newspaper articles in which nonprofit organizations were featured. In many of these articles, nonprofit practitioners provided professional knowledge and advice on risk management as experts.

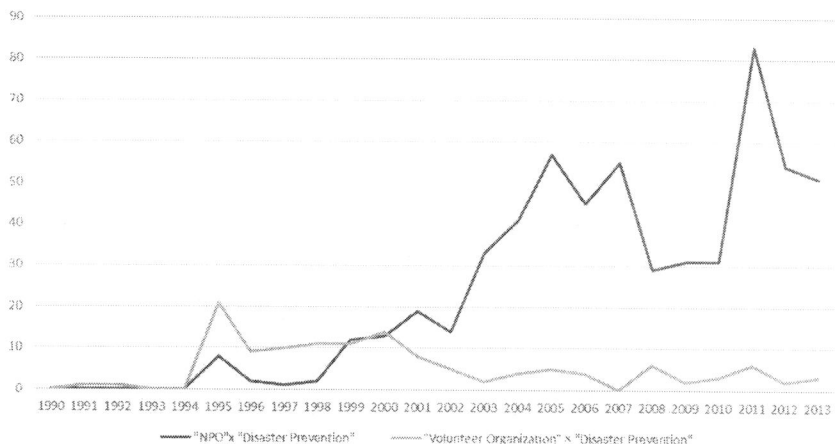

*Source:* Created with Data Acquired from Asahi Shimbun Database KIKUZO II Visual..

**Figure 8.5**

Knowledge not only comes from experts, but also from residents with rich local knowledge. Matsuda and Okada (2006) highlight this bottom-up perspective, emphasizing the importance of "community diagnose." While recognizing the importance of hazard information, mostly provided by the government, a nonprofit organization called the Rescue Stock Yard holds a series of workshops and conducts surveys in communities to check current knowledge and identify hidden ones among the residents. They provide a space for face-to-face meetings to elicit and collect local knowledge, and to facilitate the development of solutions or prescriptions to enhance preparedness for potential risks.

## CAPITALIZING ON LESSONS LEARNED FOR FUTURE DISASTERS

The degree to which people directly experience disasters can vary greatly. Some experience major earthquakes and tsunami, while others only come across smaller ones. Despite the variation, the experience of the former is often shared with the latter, and the lessons learned are widely diffused. This is exactly the process taking place in northeastern Japan today, three years after the 2011 catastrophe. There are two ways in which civil society organizations are engaged: archiving the memories and organizing storytelling.

Efforts to collect and preserve records and memories have been undertaken by various actors, including the *Hinagiku* by the National Diet Library and *Mirai no Kioku* (meaning memories of the future) by Google. Civil society organizations are also active in collecting data, archiving the disaster experience, and keeping records. For example, a nonprofit organization called 20th Century Archive Sendai has developed an archive web to preserve and record citizens' disaster experiences. They collect photos taken by citizens in Miyagi Prefecture, assuming that these records represent a different view of the disaster than those taken by professional cameramen from the media. The organization intends to develop a "memory legacy" to be utilized in the future.

Storytelling is another way in which civil society organizations have played an active role in capitalizing on lessons learned for future disasters. Residents that directly experienced the disasters are now tour guides who take the visitors around the town. In multiple municipalities across the disaster-affected regions in northeastern Japan, such efforts are organized by civil society organizations. In the case of Minami-Sanriku Town in Miyagi Prefecture, it is a nonprofit organization called Minami-Sanriku-Cho Tourism Association that organizes disaster tours. The guides include those who used to volunteer for tourism in town. In Kesennuma City in Miyagi Prefecture, Kesennuma Tourism & Convention Bureau organizes a storytelling club for disaster reconstruction, and provides various tour options for visitors. The Miyagi Reconstruction Supporting Center (also known as Ganbaro Miyagi) provides training for Sendai Chuo Taxi drivers, who then serve as guides for disaster tours around the city. As these cases imply, civil society organizations contribute to the expansion of what has come to be called disaster tourism. They capitalize on disaster experiences and diffuse lessons learned to the visitors who come to the region.

## ETHICAL DIMENSIONS IN QUESTION

In the three roles discussed above, civil society organizations in one way or another play the role of information providers in influencing people's risk management behaviors. In the process, these organizations face multiple ethical questions that involve value conflicts and judgments. This section will discuss two intertwined ethical dimensions that civil society organizations face: quality and quantity of information, and accountability. Arguments are drawn from studies on disaster information as well as from nonprofit studies.

## Quality and Quantity of Information

The primary question that civil society organizations face is how to select what information to disseminate. What risks should they highlight, and what prescriptions should they propose? What information is *correct* and what information is *appropriate*? On what criteria should civil society organizations base their decisions?

Messages related to risks and disasters, by their very nature, have a tendency to eliminate ambiguity and complexity (Yamori, 2013). The underlying rule for enhancing effectiveness is to formulate a clear message that involves an "if-then" structure. A simple example would be, if a certain risk takes place (materializes), "then" certain actions should be taken (e.g., "if " an earthquake occurs, a tsunami is likely to come; "then" run to the higher ground immediately). In order to maximize effectiveness, messages provided are often streamlined, necessarily limiting the focus and ultimately excluding alternatives. Deciding on what to retain and what to eliminate is a constant dilemma that civil society organizations face.

One example of such an information selection dilemma was observed in a discussion about the teaching of *Tsunami Tendenko* after the 2011 Tohoku disasters. As explained before, *Tendenko* refers to *individuals* and *separate*, leading people to run as individuals in case a tsunami comes and not to worry about others as they will do the same. While the effectiveness of the teaching was much praised with the "Miracle of Kamaishi," arguments remain as the teaching contradicts spirit of mutual-help, or the primary intent of voluntary organizations for disaster prevention.

In a newspaper article, a survivor in Kamaishi City recalled his experience of not being able to refuse a request to go help the others (Mainichi Shimbun, July 3, 2011). The man himself had evacuated to the higher ground immediately after the initial shake. However, he heard a women screaming for help, claiming that there were elderly still at home, not being able to evacuate themselves. Among several men went out of the evacuation center to help, only two survived. He states, "As a human being, I would definitely go out and help if I am asked to. I learned that I can't do *Tendenko*." Having faced the contradiction of the teaching of *Tsunami Tendenko*, this survived is now engaged in developing a strategy for local disaster prevention strategy as a community leader. Civil society organizations may face the same ethical dilemma as they contemplate what message to articulate and promote in the society.

If civil society organizations transmit *incorrect* information about the risk and desired responses, message might produce negative information effects. These may include the emergence and spread of false rumors, that may trigger unnecessary anxiety and panic (Sekiya, 2008a). Another danger for civil society organizations may be that they may become complicit in stereotyping certain aspects of disasters. Organizations may end up taking part in spreading information that only highlights certain regions or certain damage. This leads to convergence of specific types of information being diffused to the public (Sekiya, 2008b).

In addition to the content or quality of information, quantity is also an issue. While sending out messages is a necessity, too much information on disaster prevention can turn out to be ineffective. One such phenomenon is "normalcy bias," where people become familiar with the content of the provided information and become less eager to put the information into practice once a risk materializes.

Another unintended and undesired consequence of too much information is what Tanaka (2008) calls "dependency on information." That is, as people are exposed to information, they lose their capacity to make autonomous decisions on risks. People begin to "wait" for the information to come, before they consider making their own decisions.

Related to this is what Yamori (2013) highlights as dependency on experts. He points out that through provision of disaster-related messages, another meta-message is being articulated: that there are experts who create and disseminate the message, and those who receive and translate the message into practice. Civil society organizations, when they appear as experts on risk management, face the possibility of reproducing such meta-message.

Recently, there is a movement to break away from this tendency, such as the shift from the focus on public-help to the increased expectation of mutual-help and self-help. Nonprofit organizations, like Rescue Stock Yard, promote participatory activities that engage community members in diagnosing risks and in developing potential strategies. These efforts imply that the ultimate agent of risk management may be citizens, not experts.

In providing and promoting information on risk management, civil society organizations must decide what is *effective*, *correct*, and *appropriate*. Decision making on quantity and quality of information is thus a problematic question that civil society organizations must consider.

## Accountability

Who holds civil society organizations accountable for their decision making regarding what information to disseminate? Who assesses their performance and judgments? The uniqueness of voluntary and nonprofit organizations makes this issue of accountability a tricky question.

As has been discussed extensively in nonprofit studies, civil society organizations suffer from a "multiple accountabilities disorder" (Ebrahim, 2010). That is, they tend to work with multiple kinds of organizations and are supported by various stakeholders that demand different accountability in different ways.

> ... all nonprofit organizations have an ethical responsibility to be accountable to their supporters, their members, and their donors; and most of all, the public benefit organizations have a larger responsibility to be accountable to the broader public for how they undertake to fulfill their philanthropic purposes. (Jeavons, 2010, p. 194)

In playing the role of information providers, civil society organizations indeed work with, and work for, various stakeholders. They often partner with national and local governments, but also with schools that have their own set of rules. Some civil society organizations are funded by governments or foundations, and/or by individual donors.

The question of being accountable, *to whom* and *for what*, is a recurring question that civil society organizations face. Studies agree that it is not feasible or even desirable for these organizations to be accountable to everyone for everything. As Ebrahim (2010) points out, "the challenge for leadership and management is to prioritize among competing accountability demands" (p. 101).

Another difficulty of accountability stems from the fact that not all obligations and responsibilities that civil society organizations are expected to meet, are prescribed. Because expectations for their performance are not all stated in written laws or in codes of conduct, civil society organizations rely on internally "felt responsibility" and express their conduct through organizational missions and actions (Ebrahim, 2010, p. 102). Fulfilling accountability is sometimes a self-motivated commitment for civil society organizations, rather than something enforced by rules and regulations.

Reaching agreement on what risks to emphasize or what strategies to propose for various stakeholders is not a clearcut task for any civil-society organization. Dilemmas remain about what criteria to depend on in selecting information, how to justify the decision, and whose judgment to respect.

## CONCLUDING DISCUSSION

Questions on ethical dimensions discussed in this chapter will always stay with civil society organizations, as long as they play the role of information providers on risk as non-public, non-private organizations. If so, how can civil society organizations better deal with the questions of what information to present, and how to explain the validity of their judgments? I argue that one potential way is to enhance trust and win credibility with the public. Whether the efforts of civil society organizations are perceived to be beneficial in shaping people's risk perceptions and practices of managing risks depends on how much the people trust these organizations. Trust also determines whether engaged stakeholders and constituencies accept and consent to organizational decision making, thus regarding civil society organizations as being accountable.

Fortunately, the level of trust towards civil society organizations in Japan has improved in this past decade. In a survey that asked citizens what degree of trust they had toward nonprofit organizations, the percentage of respondents who expressed *strong* trust increased from 6.5% in 2005 to 11.4% in 2013. Similarly, those who articulated *some* trust increased from 24% to 52.9% (Cabinet Office, 2005, 2013b). While it is ironic that the occurrence of natural disasters, such as the 2011 Tohoku disaster, become the momentum for civil society organizations in Japan to win public recognition and trust, leveraging the situation may be the key for these organizations as they tackle the difficult questions of value and judgments in influencing people's risk management behaviors.

## NOTES

1. As has been pointed out by number of scholars, including Anheier (2005) and Lewis (2014), there are multiple terms that refer to these types of organizations. While recognizing the importance of respecting the differences, I use the term "civil society organizations" in this chapter to refer to a wide range of non-public, non-private organizations that affect how people perceive and respond to potential risks.
2. Calculated with an exchange rate of 1 USD = 100 JPY

## REFERENCES

Anheier, H. K., (2005). Nonprofit organizations: Theory management, policy. London, England: Routledge.

Asahi Shimbun. (n.d.). *Database KIKUZO II visual.* Kyoto, Japan: Doshisha University. Retrieved September 15, 2014, https://database.asahi.com/library2/

Cabinet Office, Government of Japan. (2005). *NPO (Minkan Hieri Soshiki) ni Kansuru Yoron Chosa* [Opinion survey on npo (private non-profit organizations)]. Retrieved September 1, 2014, from http://www8.cao.go.jp/survey/h17/h17-npo/index.html

Cabinet Office, Government of Japan. (2011). Disaster management in Japan. Retrieved September 10, 2014, from http://www.bousai.go.jp/1info/pdf/saigaipanf_e.pdf

Cabinet Office, Government of Japan. (2012). Higashi Nihon Daishinsai ni Kakaru Saigai Borantelia Katsudou no Jittai Chosa [Survey on disaster volunteer activities on the great east japan earthquake]. Retrieved September 10, 2014, from http://www.bousai.go.jp/kyoiku/volunteer/pdf/120625jittaichousa.pdf

Cabinet Office, Government of Japan. (2013a). Bosai Ni Kansuru Yoron Chosa [Opinion survey on disaster prevention]. Retrieved September 10, 2014, from http://www8.cao.go.jp/survey/h25/h25-bousai/index.html

Cabinet Office, Government of Japan. (2013b). NPO Hojin ni Kansuru Yoron Chosa [Opinion survey on specified nonprofit corporations]. Retrieved September 10, 2013, from http://www8.cao.go.jp/survey/h25/h25-npo/

Cabinet Office, Government of Japan. (2014). Heisei 26 Nendo Bousai Hakusho [2014 white paper on disaster management]. Retrieved September 10, 2014, from http://www.bousai.go.jp/kaigirep/hakusho/h26/

Comfort, L. K., Okada, A., & Ertan, G. (2013). Networks of action in catastrophic events: The 11 March 2011 Tohoku Disasters. *Earthquake Spectra*, *29*(S1), S387–S402.

Ebrahim, A. (2010). The many faces of nonprofit accountability. In D.O. Renz, & Associates (Eds.), *The Jossey-Bass handbook of nonprofit leadership and management* (pp. 101–121). San Francisco, CA: Jossey-Bass.

Honma, M., & Deguchi, M. (1996). *Borantia Kakumei: Daishinsai no Keiken wo Shimin Katsudo-e* [Volunteer revolution: Experience of the great disaster to citizen activities]. Tokyo, Japan: Toyo Keizai Shinposha.

Jeavons, T. H. (2010). Ethical nonprofit management. In D.O. Renz, & Associates (Eds.), *The Jossey-Bass handbook of nonprofit leadership and management* (pp. 178–205). San Francisco, CA: Jossey-Bass.

Kesennuma Tourism & Convention Bureau. (n.d.). Retrieved September 15, 2014, from http://www.kesennuma-kanko.jp/

Lewis, D. (2014). *Non-governmental organizations, management, and development*. London, England: Routledge.

*Mainichi Shimbun.* (2011, July 3). Shogen 3.11: Higashi Nihon Daishinsai Kotae Denai Tendenko [Testimony 3.11: The great east Japan earthquake no clear answer for Tendenko]. Retrieved September 15, 2014, from Maisaku, database http://mainichi.jp/contents/edu/maisaku/login.html. Kyoto, Japan: Doshisha University.

*Mainichi Shimbun.* (2014, March 10). Higashi Nihon Daishinsai 3-Nen: Okawa-Sho Jiko, Daisanshai no "Shippai" [Three years after the great east Japan earthquake: Accident at Okawa Elementary School, "failure" of the third party committee]. Retrieved September 15, 2014, from Maisaku, database http://mainichi.jp/contents/edu/maisaku/login.html. Kyoto, Japan: Doshisha University.

Matsuda, Y., & Okada, N. (2006). Community diagnosis for sustainable disaster preparedness. *Journal of Natural Disaster Science*, *28*(1), 25–33.

Minami-Sanriku-Cho Tourism Association. (n.d.). Retrieved September 15, 2014, from https://www.m-kankou.jp/tour/storyteller/

*Mirai e-no Kioku* [Memories for the future]. (n.d.). Retrieved September 15, 2014, from https://www.miraikioku.com/

Miyagi reconstruction supporting center (Ganbaro Miyagi). Retrieved September 15, 2014, from http://www.ganbaro-miyagi.com/

National diet library of Japan. NDL Higashi Nihon Daishinsai Archive Hinagiku (Great east Japan earthquake archive Hinagiku). Retrieved September 15, 2014, from http://kn.ndl.go.jp/

Pekkanen, R. (2006). *Japan's dual civil society: Members without advocates*. Stanford, CA: Stanford University Press.

*Sankei Shimbun*. (2014, March 10). Seizonritsu 99.8%, "Kamaishi no Kiseki" wo Furikaeru: "Tsunami Tendenko" no Oshie [Survival rate 99.8%, looking back the "miracle of Kamaishi": The teaching of "Tsunami Tendenko]." Retrieved August 20, 2014, from *sankei.jp.msn.com/science/news/140310/scn14031009350003-n1.htm*

Sekiya, N. (2008a). Saigai Hodo no Funo Koka [Negative effects of disaster broadcasting]. In A., Tanaka, & H. Yoshii, (Eds.), *Saigai joho ron nyumon* [Introduction to studies on disaster information] (pp. 218–227). Tokyo, Japan: Kobundo.

Sekiya, N. (2008b). Saigai Ryugen [False rumors in disasters]. In A. Tanaka, & H. Yoshii, (Eds.), *Saigai joho ron nyumon* [Introduction to studies on disaster information] (pp. 232–242). Tokyo, Japan: Kobundo.

*Sendai chuo taxi*. Retrieved September 15, 2014, from https://www.sendaichuotaxi.co. jp/charter/kataribe.html

Svedin, L. (2011). Introduction. *Ethics and crisis management*. (pp. 1–20). Charlotte, NC: Information Age.

20th century archive sendai. (n.d.). *Hajimeni* [Introduction]. Retrieved September 14, 2014, from http://www.sendai-city.org/311.htm/

Yamori, K. (2012). Tsunami Tendenko no Yottsu no Imi [Four meanings of Tsunami Tendenko]. *Shizen Saigai Kagaku, 31*(1), 35–46.

Yamori, K. (2013). *Kyodai Saigai no Risuku Komyunikeishon: Saigai Jouhou no Atarashi Katachi* [Improving disaster risk communication: A paradigm shift in disaster information research]. Tokyo, Japan: Minerva Shobo.

# CHAPTER 9

# ETHICAL PERSPECTIVES ON VOLUNTEER PARTICIPATION

## Training CBRN Incidents Live

**Erna Danielsson, Erika Wall, and Susanna Öhman**

### INTRODUCTION

Risk in this chapter will be studied along the lines of sociology. From this perspective, focus will be placed on the integration between the context and the individual. This means that our focus on ethical issues will be on what is planned and how it affects those planned for (or not planned for); for example, how plans affect both professionals and role-play volunteers during live exercises. We also will discuss the effect of live exercises on how professionals deal with real incidents, specifically with regards to ethical attitudes towards a multi-cultured society.

The importance of civil contingency training exercises for the effective handling of crises has been well documented; and a number of established management techniques have been developed during such exercises, to support decision makers at times of crisis, including standard operating procedures and checklists. However, studies of the ethical management

*Ethics and Risk Management*, pp. 141–158
Copyright © 2015 by Information Age Publishing
All rights of reproduction in any form reserved.

of role-play volunteers, who take part in live training exercise, have been lacking. Furthermore, there has been a reluctance among professionals to evaluate real crises from an ethics perspective; and when such assessments are attempted,they often descend into hunts for scapegoats (Svedin, 2011). The result has often been that lessons about ethical management that need to be drawn from actual crises, are not folded into the planning of training exercises; nor are ethical dilemmas regarding role-play volunteers.

In academia, meanwhile, researchers have faced ethical dilemmas and ever since the early 1960s have received much training to avoid unethical research conduct. Academic researchers have a duty to detail any possible ethical problems associated with their work, in their mandatory ethical review of proposed research that involves people as subjects. Yet in many countries, among them Sweden, there is no requirement for other public organizations to undergo a similar ethical review when developing, and before conducting, internal development activities or training exercises where personnel in a very real sense function as subjects in the training (SFS, [2003:460] om etikprövning av forskning som avser människor; SFS, 1998:204).[1] In fact the planning of such exercises, is in many ways similar to the planning of many academic data-gathering activities; such as human subject experiments for example. In both the practical and academic setting, questions that need to be raised regarding training and data collecting, include what are appropriate and good ways to gather information, to learn from experience with new information, as well as how best to report on the results of the exercise or experiment.

In recent years, a new type of ethical discussion has emerged among scholars; it is one in which ethics are considered from a longer term perspective. Brown and Peek (2014) examined ethics in disaster studies and have asserted that ethics need to be a consideration throughout the whole study at hand, not merely at the outset when the original application for an ethical review is made. A similar problem can arise when planning for a training exercise involving volunteers: It is hard to know when contacts with the volunteers will cease, and what responsibility the management of the exercise has long term (i.e., after the exercise) to monitor and possibly ensure the participants well-being.

We would argue that the same difficulties in determining potential harm and establishing appropriate parameters for responsible conduct and follow-up in disaster research, is also true in practice in the run-up to live training exercises of the type intended to prepare participants to handle crises. It is important not to ignore the ethical ramifications of a training exercise, since how participants deal with ethical dilemmas in the exercise will have consequences on how they will manage real crises.

In this chapter, we will take an ethical perspective on leadership in the planning and execution of live training exercises; we will look specifically at two exercises—one held in 2013 in the United Kingdom, and one in 2014 in Sweden.[2] In doing this we will address the ethical issues of working with role-play volunteers; and we will argue that training exercises can be made even more relevant if ethical dimensions are included, especially since experience teaches us that difficult ethical dilemmas arise in the acute phase of a crisis (Svedin, 2011). During a live training exercise, the situation is not acute, which means that ethical dilemmas can very well be incorporated into the exercise, and thereby contribute to a more effective management of real crises.

## CONCEPTUAL FRAMEWORK

Strategic managers are responsible for preventing crises. Part of this work is to stage different types of training exercises designed to give their organization the opportunity to practice handling crises. Preventive measures can include such things as informing and educating the general public, prioritizing between different preventive measures, and practicing the organization of various kinds of crisis management (see Boin & t'Hart, 2003). The importance of practicing ethical expertise and of raising the question of ethical dilemmas, particularly in leadership training, is also stressed by Frunză (2012). Training exercises become a way of relating to the risks the organization chooses to prioritize.

The ethical ramifications of live training exercises, however, have rarely been studied. The studies that exist are mainly confined to medical research, such as studies of emergency healthcare and incidents involving medical treatment and triage. Studies on ethics and education can be found: for example, a study of police officers' attitudes toward intellectual disability (Bailey, Barr, & Bunting, 2001) shows that participation in an 'awareness exercise' significantly reduces participants' ethnicity-based attitudes towards people with intellectual disabilities. Another study by Wittmer (1992), uses an experiment to increase ethical sensitivity in education and training, to show that it can have an impact on decision-making.

As will have been noted, it is primarily in education that the ethical problems are most pressing, yet it is difficult to find studies that have looked closely at how ethics can be addressed during larger live training exercises.

The importance of trust is highlighted by Stephenson (2005). He argues that trust can be achieved if managers introduce collaborative ways of thinking in their staff training. Trust is also a key element in any communication with the public (Coombs & Holladay, 1996; Rosenthal & Kouzmin, 1997; Veil, 2008) in order to send the right signals at times of threat or crisis; but is also important in situations when the experts do *not* see any risk but the public does, as with genetic engineering in the 1990s (Olofsson et al., 2006). Thus it is crucial to build trust in advance (Seeger, 2006). These same studies have demonstrated how important it is to the success of training exercises to have the active participation of other groups, over and above the people actually being trained.

The need for training exercises is well documented, and studies have shown that practice is important for effectiveness when handling crises (Kapucu, 2008b; Ödlund, 2007; Stephenson, 2005; Uhr, 2009). A study of the Manchester bombings in 1996 (Batho, 1999), for example, showed that a national exercise that had been held in the recent past had built up a working partnership between private and public organizations, and had fostered institutional skills in managing crises. The importance of holding training exercises to practice how to manage major crises has been evident in many studies, and in particular the importance of getting to know one another and establishing everyday routines (Batho, Williams, & Russell, 1999; Kapucu, 2008a, 2008b; Kendra & Wachtendorf, 2003; Wise & McGuire, 2009).

## Live Training Exercises

Unlike academic research, as mentioned previously, training exercises do not need to undergo an ethical review. In planning a training exercise, the focus is on the participants to be trained and what they need to be able to cope in a real incident.

The ethical dilemmas that relate to the public welfare, and the right to be treated fairly are rarely considered when constructing these exercises. When public participants are included, it is in the form of role-play volunteers; they are invariably recruited as extras to be "practiced on" or to be deliberate annoyances for decision makers rather than valuable representatives of the general public. As such, the focus of the exercises is wholly on the professional participants and their need to be drilled in certain procedures. Yet the volunteers' needs, actions, and standpoints as the "practiced-on" public, ought to be of far greater concern (Enander & Hede, 2004).

Volunteers are often students and young people from colleges, or NGOs such as Red Cross and Civil Defense. To recruit people with disabilities or from minority ethnic backgrounds or different age groups for training exercises, is more difficult. This means that not all groups will be practiced with, or have the opportunity to make their needs and wishes clear under that set of circumstances, when the vulnerable groups are role-played by students or other volunteers. This brings its own set of ethical problems, when professionals and crisis management will not get information on needs from these groups directly.

### Ethical Guidelines for Live Training Exercises

Ethical guidelines stress that the freedom of the individual should only be curbed when it is essential and appropriate to do so, and in proportion to the nature and scale of events. The leadership that has to decide on such measures must assess what it is absolutely necessary to expose volunteers to, and training leaders should be able to justify their decisions in terms of their wider benefit. Moreover, their decisions must be open to scrutiny.

In a CBRN event, it is of equal importance that society offers special assistance to those who, in their efforts to protect the public, are affected particularly badly by events. The ethical guidelines do not mention how to manage volunteers during training exercises, although human rights and recognized ethical principles are observed in major international exercises.

### Study Method

The data analyzed in this study is based on observations carried out during two training exercises conducted within the PRACTICE project in 2013–2014. Under the aegis of the project, an ethics advisory committee was appointed to oversee the planning and implementation of the exercises, to ensure these trainings adhered to the ethical guidelines agreed upon in advance. In its work, the ethics committee followed the EU's ethical guidelines on data protection, health and safety, privacy, racial and sexual discrimination, and the more specific requirements for ethical controls in force in the particular countries where the exercises were conducted (The European Convention of Human Rights [ECHR], n.d.). An evaluation form covering all the ethical guidelines specific to the exercise, was used as the basis for monitoring (Stănciugelu & Danielsson, 2013). Some of the most important objectives were the informed consent of all participants, so that appropriate permits to hold the exercise were obtained and the relevant laws and regulations were followed.

In analyzing the two exercises we have examined the ethical aspects of *proportionality* (whereby restrictions on the freedom of the individual should be limited to what is absolutely necessary, given the risks posed by the incident), *privacy* (the privacy of the individual should be respected as far as possible), *reciprocity* (society has a special duty of care for those who are most at risk because of their work to protect the public), *respect for person* (all individuals should be respected for their own sake, regardless of age, gender, ethnicity, or socioeconomic status), and *stewardship* (leadership should be characterized by trust, ethics, and sound decisions). We would argue that proportionality and privacy are central when it comes to training for CBRN events, and for this reason we focused on these two aspects.

### Empirical Sources

The source material used here is comprised of the evaluations compiled by the ethics committee after the exercises. The questions we posed as we examined the material were: the extent to which volunteers were briefed about the exercises in advance; whether they received answers to their questions; whether there was routine monitoring of their well-being during and after the exercises; and how were they treated during the exercises.

## THE CASE STUDIES

The two exercises were designed to give emergency participants the skills needed to take preventive measures at a serious chemical, biological, radiological, or nuclear (CBRN) event. In both countries, ethical reviews are not required for training exercises—there is no duty to inform or to obtain informed consent from participants or role-play volunteers.

### The Training Exercise in the United Kingdom

The purpose of the British exercise was to test the tools developed to assist emergency services in managing the general public during a CBRN event. This was a live exercise, with an emphasis on social encounters with the public and cooperation between the emergency services. The specific incident was a sarin attack in a conference hall by a suspected terrorist. The exercise involved some 230 people, of whom approximately 80 were role-play volunteers who acted as victims of the gas attack (i.e., pretending to be the general public). There were around 150 participants from the emergency services, and about 70 CBRN-trained professionals as well as observers from the EU project's ethics committee who monitored the various parts of the exercise. The exercise fell into 12 phases: it ran from preparations for the exercise, through the alarm being raised, events in the conference hall, evacuation, then care for the victims, to the subsequent evaluation by the ethics committee.

The objective of the phase of the exercise that involved the role-play volunteers, was to prepare the public mentally and emotionally for a CBRN event, and in particular the necessary decontamination procedures. This was done through a *human behavior user manual* (developed by Kings College London) for the public in which they could follow the procedure for decontamination and gain knowledge and awareness about the processes and procedures at sites affected by CBRN events.

The volunteers were divided into three groups representing the general public, and each group received different amounts of information. This variation was designed to determine how detailed the information had to be to be most effective in ensuring a safe evacuation of the conference hall and a successful decontamination of those affected. Group 1 received a full human behavior user manual, Group 2 received a shortened version, and Group 3 received no information. After the exercise, groups were assigned to two kinds of focus group interviews.

## The Training Exercise in Sweden

The Swedish exercise took a different approach, being held in two stages. We chose to concentrate on the first exercise, which itself was made up of two phases. The first phase took place in the morning with 20 police officers and emergency service personnel participating; and the same exercise was then carried out again in the afternoon with police and rescue personnel replaced by 20 students of fire and rescue, and emergency health care.

The exercise commenced with some CBRN training in addition to a diagnostic test of the professionals' CBRN knowledge. After the test, the exercise was conducted with the two groups in turn. The scenario event was a radiological incident with adolescent victims in a public place. The role-play volunteers came from the College of the Swedish Contingency Agency (MSB College). The exercise was observed by CBRN-trained professionals as well as observers from the EU project's ethics committee. During the exercise, volunteers were required to act as the victims of a radioactive bomb in a public place, where they were tended to by the emergency services. They had been given instructions before the exercise on how to behave according to their injuries and roles (some played the part of the hearing impaired or visually impaired).

### Information and Consent

The ethical management of volunteers prior to the training exercises, involved providing information that spelled out what was expected of the volunteer role-players, and giving them the opportunity to ask questions immediately before the exercise. Participants in both the British and the Swedish exercises were informed, both verbally and in writing, and in conjunction with the exercise. This information was provided when they signed the informed consent form, which included a reference to each country's laws on personal data protection. They were informed prior to the exercise that participation was voluntary, and that they had the right to withdraw from participating in the exercise at any time. At the British exercise, there were hot drinks available, as well as information about what would be provided in the form of food and drink. When it came to the kind of information given beforehand, we would argue that it was essentially the same kinds of information that would be given to participants in a research project.

The information to the volunteers was very consistent (Danielsson et al., 2014). In both countries they were informed that they might undergo a decontamination process in the form of a shower. They were also told that they would be videotaped and observed by appointed observers, and that at the incident site they would encounter the participants, the exercise leaders, other role-play volunteers, and authorized observers. In terms of the risks, the exercise leaders felt there was little to endanger or inconvenience the volunteers. The video recording was mentioned, as was the fact that it might be felt to be an irritation, but that it was arranged in such a way as to minimize any unpleasantness. It was also explained that the exercise would be held outdoors, so the weather might be found stressful; but they were told that equipment to protect them from the cold would be available. They were also informed that if anyone was injured, there was medical staff on site.

Other information concerned the data gathered during the exercises, and that personal details (such as their identity) would be protected. However, volunteers were informed that individuals might be identifiable in photographs used in presentations, in information about the project, and in subsequent educational materials.

## ANALYSIS

In the analysis, we examined the ethical responsibilities of the exercise leaders and managers at the planning stage; and the acceptable treatment of volunteers during and after a training exercise (acceptable by the standards of a normal ethical review, that is). We discuss the ethical dilemmas that individuals face and how an ethical approach could be applied in practice, in the sense that if the exercise leaders put themselves in the volunteers' place, they would be more likely to understand the nature of their involvement in a longer perspective—an issue rarely discussed.

Our content analysis uncovered four themes that were particularly prominent in the material. We have grouped these findings under the headings of roles, communication, expectations, and publicity.

### Roles

Two central ethical problems encountered in the course of the training exercises pertained to the question of roles. Both exercises involved individuals, professionals, students, and volunteers recruited from the general public, who participated in the training in a variety of functions. The participants took part in the training exercises in their professional capacity —they played themselves. The volunteers were there to play the general public, but in doing so had to play the role of other people: they did not play themselves. This meant that some volunteers were required to act disabled, and thus acted according to their idea of what this meant. This is not unusual for live training exercises, as it is easy to get hold of students or members of NGOs (such as the Red Cross and civil defense forces) to serve as volunteers.

The first ethical dilemma was the contradiction between the ambition of taking a heterogeneous approach to the training exercise by including people with disabilities, and the reality on the day of the exercise, when the inclusion of disabled people generally came to consist of volunteers instructed to play the part of the disabled public. The ethical regulations on discrimination, which hold that groups should not be favored or disadvantaged, but rather that all should be guaranteed access to equal opportunities and obligations, are thus not being followed. There may be good reasons for not enlisting actually disabled persons, but if this is the case, it should be discussed openly and all involved should be prepared for this discriminatory practice.

The second ethical dilemma was that live training exercises are planned specifically to instruct participants, and the volunteers' perspective was scarcely considered. The data suggest that human resource management was not a priority at the planning stage, but that it became an obvious factor as the exercises proceeded. One example was that while the professional participants' safety and well-being were borne in mind at the planning stage, the demands to be placed on volunteers were not considered. The weather was chilly for the Swedish exercise, 5–7 °C, and the volunteers were left sitting outside in the freezing wind for more than 20 minutes. They also had to shower, outdoors, in icy water in order to be decontaminated, with one person being drenched for several minutes. All this could have been avoided if the planning had also had a thought for the volunteers' well-being. The ethical rule applicable in this instance says that research must not endanger human health, and that one should not expose test subjects to any greater stress than strictly necessary. In this instance, volunteers were subject to far greater stress than the situation required. The objective of training the participants, would still have been served with better plans for the treatment of volunteers.

### Communication

Our examination of the sources showed that communication with the volunteers was a specific theme in the British exercise; and although it did feature in the Swedish exercise as well, in Britain special attention was paid to communicating both before the event and during the exercise.

The data showed that, in both countries, the volunteers were given ample information about what they could expect to experience during the exercises, and the ways in which this might prove unpleasant. Above all, they were informed that they would be decontaminated by taking a decontamination shower. Meanwhile, information about the future uses of the data gathered during the exercises, was not made available to them to the same extent. An example of this was that there had been no indication in the material that the volunteers were informed how images and videos might be used in the future, for example when planning training, instruction, and preventive measures long after the training exercises were completed.

The data showed that in the course of the exercises, two types of difficulties arose that had not been identified at the planning stage. First, the professional participants wore gas masks because of the nature of the exercise, but these made verbal communication virtually impossible. A great many misunderstandings arose when the professionals tried to speak to the volunteers through the masks. Not only did the volunteers find it difficult to understand the information, but the masks contributed to the drama of staged incident. The dilemma was how to keep the volunteers fully informed while sticking to the rules about wearing gas masks, which would have been non-negotiable in the event of a real incident.

The second unforeseen problem was the lack of information given to volunteers about the fact that photographs and videos might be used in the future, and the contexts in which they were likely to figure. They had been told that photographs and videos might be used for training and presentations, but they still did not have a clear idea of what those contexts might be or which images might be featured. To give an example, the decontamination area where volunteers showered wearing only swimwear was photographed and filmed. It would not have detracted from the exercise to let the volunteers dress in lightweight exercise clothes instead.

The dilemma here was that immediately relevant practical information had to be set against information about the possible long-term ramifications of participation. The data showed that the focus at the planning stage was wholly on the volunteers' participation *during* the exercises, ensuring they were given adequate information so they would find it a positive experience. Information about the future consequences of their presence seemed to have been handled as if it were less relevant. This has been a problem in academic research too; in other words, the duty to inform does not extend to informing research subjects about the future impact of their participation, for instance figuring in instruction videos. When considering whether to volunteer or not, and whether to accept being photographed and filmed, people need to be informed about the situations in which they will figure in the future.

### Expectations

A thematic analysis of the documentary sources and observations yielded interesting results on the topic of expectations. For the participants, the training exercises seemed to have met their expectations. However, there was evidence, especially in the U.K. exercise, that there were contradictions between the volunteers' and the participants' expectations, and also between how the different groups experienced the actual exercise. On the day of the exercise, a decision had to be made about who should be prioritized for the decontamination shower, as there was not enough time for everyone to undergo the procedure. This meant that some volunteers showered, while others were not allowed to join in this part of the exercise. One unanticipated effect of this was that the volunteers who did not shower felt disappointed and "unfairly treated." They thought the decontamination shower was central to the exercise, and had expected to be included. Instead, their participation was limited to only a short phase in the evacuation of the conference hall. They felt their participation as volunteers was of little importance, and that most of the time they had just sat around and waited.

What we had here was a dilemma where the need for participants to practice prioritizing between different groups was set against the volunteers' need to feel important during the exercise. While handling members of the public who felt excluded should be seen as a very realistic and relevant aspect of the decontamination process during a CBRN event, it can become of the highest importance to manage volunteers in such a way that they feel that their presence has been meaningful. The ethical dilemma was that the information the volunteers had received did not correspond to the commitment they displayed by taking time off for a full-day training exercise. They had thus not received all the relevant information that would have enabled them to decide whether they wanted to participate in the exercise or not.

### Publicity

Both live training exercises were designed to mimic real events as closely as possible. This meant that they were not held in enclosed areas, but rather were partly in public. Crucially, both called for the use of decontamination showers, which were set up—in accordance with idea of keeping things as real as possible—in a public place. This proved to be key in the Swedish exercise, as the decontamination shower was set up next to a public path across from an emergency services training ground that was used by a large number of students taking other courses. During the decontamination, passers-by who were not part of the exercise stopped and photographed volunteers showering. There was no place for the volunteers to change in private. Indeed, during the morning exercise they initially did not even have blankets to keep them warm.

This type of training exercise is not common, which explains the degree of interest from passersby. Neither exercise leaders stepped in to prevent excessive gawking and photographing. This was seen as a violation of the volunteers' personal integrity.

Live training exercises held in public view present a clear ethical dilemma between the desire to proceed as if it were a real emergency, when it would be absolutely crucial for those who had been exposed to contaminants to shower, and the volunteers' right to privacy when joining in the exercise—especially when it is not the volunteers who are practicing the procedure, but are being subject to the practice.

### The Treatment of Volunteers

Clearly, there were a number of ethical dilemmas posed by live exercises that were due to the presence of role-play volunteers. Much of what the volunteers went through was decided at the planning stage, and we would argue that the exercise leaders, along with the strategic upper management, bear the greatest responsibility for any ethical problems that arose. Sometimes greater planning resources are required; sometimes the problem can be addressed by training those responsible for the planning. Yet it can also be a matter of attitudes and mindfulness, as we have pointed out. Suppose, for example, that the volunteers had been allowed to take shelter while waiting for the emergency services to arrive at the scene, sparing them an unnecessary and chilly wait in the wind. Certainly, blankets should could have been made available much sooner to protect the semi-clad volunteers from the cold, and it would have made little difference if the same volunteers had worn thin exercise clothing instead of swimwear for the decontamination shower, or if they had not stood around barefoot waiting. After all, it was an exercise in handling a radiation incident and not mass hyperthermia. The area could have been cordoned off properly, with signs forbidding unauthorized photography. The information given to the volunteers could have been clearer on what to expect, and they could have been warned that the logistics might change (be it the focus group interviews, meals, or their participation in different elements of the exercise), so that waiting could have been avoided. On the plus side, the exercise in Sweden was divided into two sessions, and better shelter was offered to the volunteers during the afternoon, suggesting that the exercise leaders learned from one session to the next that the volunteers needed to be protected from the cold.

## DISCUSSION

Academic research today offers standard routines for those conducting studies that use human subjects. But the same is not true of live training exercises or intra-organizational development activities. The themes evident in our findings—the particular dilemmas associated with roles, communication, expectations, and publicity—can be viewed from many different angles. As mentioned above, we employed the standards of proportionality and privacy in our analysis of the ethical perspectives on the leadership of civil contingency training exercises. Looking at the training exercises themselves, the information distributed to role-play volunteers in advance, and the evaluation of the project concerned by the ethics committee, it was evident that the responsibility for the planning falls on the exercise leaders and their managers, and they too were accountable for the treatment of the volunteers during and after the training exercises.

In the case of the two training exercises examined there were several instances in which the exercise leaders failed in their responsibilities. The decontamination process was filmed and photographed, leaving volunteers depicted in a vulnerable situation in images over which the exercise leaders had no real control. Even authorized material may come to be used in ways that are difficult to foresee at present. Moreover, the public—which in the Swedish example meant police cadets passing by—were able to take pictures of the exercise unhindered, and there was no way to prevent them from being publicized. The only type of representation the exercise leaders had any say over, was their own documentation; but even then the information given to volunteers about how it would be used in the future was outlined in only the thinnest of terms. The exercise leaders ought to have ensured that this type of material did not spread unchecked, and out of consideration for all participants should have done its utmost to minimize it. The choice of location for decontamination showers, for example, or the correct cordoning off of public spaces could have limited how exposed the volunteers were. Normally, emergency services takes great care to minimize the public's view of the scene of an accident, and they often arrange their vehicles around a site to block it from view, or they otherwise employ the terrain to screen it off. It is recognized that it is desirable for all concerned to be protected from the public gaze. Even so, they did not follow the same procedure when setting up training exercise scenarios, when through a few simple measures they could easily have accomplished this, and thus minimized public viewing and protected the volunteers' privacy.

Another dilemma stems from the use of students to play a heterogeneous public, which left different groups in society excluded, their needs unlikely to be met or their questions answered. A workshop in the U.K. before the 2013 exercise, was attended by people with sight and hearing impairments, with disabilities, and from different age groups (Usher, 2012). During the actual exercises, however, these groups were played by young students or members of organizations such as the Red Cross, which again could not provide professional participants in the exercises with a realistic reference point in the event of a real crisis.

Our focus in this chapter has been the volunteers who make it possible for the professional participants to practice various procedures. We believe that volunteers should be put in harm's way as little as possible—the minimum needed for the participants to get a reasonable idea of what a real incident might entail. Do the volunteers really needed to wait such a long time in the cold? Surely, realism would not have suffered if greater attention had been paid to the volunteers' physical well-being, providing them with a hot drink or having them shower for a shorter time for example. It is also important to prepare volunteers for what will actually happen—in the United Kingdom, several were disappointed to find their active participation was only required for a brief time. It is also important to give a realistic picture of what will happen during the training exercise. After each exercise there was also a short debriefing for the volunteers at the end of the day, where issues raised during the exercise were discussed. However, sometimes questions took awhile to emerge, sometime after the actual exercise event, in which case the volunteers' contact information would have been needed if one was to offer them the opportunity to ask. That kind of preparedness has to be planned for before an exercise takes place.

If we look at the volunteers' performance during and after the two training exercises and the ethical responsibility, it can and should be placed at the door of the exercise leaders. These responsibilities can be summarized as follows: an ethical stance must be included in the planning of any training exercise; realistic participation requires a realistic plan; and the harm to volunteers must be minimized as they are not professional participants there to practice emergency procedures. This assertion has consequences for managers at the strategic level, who must support those who work with ethical considerations, and provide the infrastructure for their implementation. One possible approach to remedying the lack of ethical consideration, would be to include an ethical review at the planning stage specifically to address this type of issue. An ethical review could concentrate on the ethical dilemmas that will confront the individual and how they might be addressed on the ground; in other words, the exercise leaders must reflect on these questions in the individual volunteer's place, given that they are more likely to understand the longer-term ramifications of participation. And they should ensure that social heterogeneity is reflected in a relevant way when recruiting volunteers.

In recent years, there has been a great deal of research on the importance of advance planning to prepare for crises (Boin & t'Hart, 2003; McConnell & Drennan, 2006). However, training exercises have not been included in these studies even though they raise many ethical questions that speak to proportionality: Who is to participate and what procedure will they practice; What are the power relations between the participants, and whose perspective will be considered; What groups will actually have their needs accurately portrayed in the exercise; How should role-play volunteers be selected to better represent the public? It is important to accurately cover the entire community when planning for how to manage risks; for example by identifying vulnerable groups and highlighting their needs and wishes in any training exercises, if only to understand the underlying causes of crises. Far greater social diversity would only benefit such exercises, as would knowledge of how other organizations have handled similar events.

## CONCLUSION

The analysis presented in this chapter relates to the three themes described by Svedin (2011): inherent ethical challenges in crises and disasters (can the government really protect all citizens if certain groups are excluded from exercises designed to practice its civil contingencies management?); the ethical dimensions of decision making and individual or organizational behavior; and, above all, the ethical dimensions of institutional processes. The proper scrutiny of government agencies' leadership is needed to allow the public to judge whether that leadership will promote fairness and ethical behavior in a crisis (Svedin. 2011). We believe that this is also true of training exercises.

The planning of training exercises needs to be critically assessed, as it forms the basis of behavior then seen during any real crisis. Are exercises designed to take proportionality into account, for example? Are all groups in society included and able to express what their needs will be in the event of a real crisis, and are volunteers treated in an ethically acceptable manner during training exercises? An ethical review of training exercises would strengthen public confidence in the public authorities, and would probably enhance relations between professional participants and role-play volunteers during the exercises. In the research world, an ethical review requires that groups in the community being sampled are treated equally, while ensuring they are able to express their different needs. The same should be demanded of training exercises, as they often form the behavioral basis for the allocation to the community of the resources, knowledge, and professional skills intended to support citizens during a crisis or disaster. It is the authorities' risk managers who decide what resources are made available for a training exercise; they are the ones who set down the guidelines. Their decisions, expressed in guidelines and demands, determine what procedures will be practiced. These decisions and other considerations that are routinely examined in ethical reviews of research are also important for training exercises. It is therefore odd that training exercises can be conducted without any requirement for an ethical examination to be undertaken, especially given that the knowledge produced though exercises is often used as the basis for standard operating procedures and the planned allocation of resources for society's management of civil contingencies. The strategic administrative leadership must be given a realistic opportunity to identify what risks may arise and at which point all groups in society ought to be heard. How to regard ethical issues applies equally to professional participants and volunteers when it comes to live training exercises (Nohrstedt, 2011; Parker, 2011).

The need for ethical reviews in training exercises is pressing. Guidelines for this type of review must be developed, and while the ethical considerations that have a direct bearing on training exercises must be fully charted, the longer-term use of materials generated by such exercises and the monitoring of volunteers' participation in the exercises also calls for greater thought. A move toward a more consciously ethical attitude, will in time prove of utmost importance for the development of civil, contingency, training exercises as a tool for improving risk and crisis management in the community at large.

## NOTES

1. Swedish law on ethical examination and law on data protection.
2. This chapter is based on data from the project Preparedness and Resilience Against CBRN Terrorism Using Integrated Concepts and Equipment (PRACTICE), founded by the European Union's Seventh Framework Programme for research, technological development and demonstration, under grant agreement no. 261728. The project was led by Dzenan Sahovic, Eurpoean CBRNE Center Umeå University. http://www.practice-fp7-security.eu/

## REFERENCES

Bailey, A., Barr, O., & Bunting, B. (2001). Police attitudes toward people with intellectual disability: An evaluation of awareness training. *Journal of Intellectual Disability Research.* 45(4): 344–350.

Batho, S., Williams,G., & Russel, L. (1999). Crisis management of controlled recovery: The emergency planning response to the bombing of Manchester City Center. *Disasters, 23*(3), 217–233.

Boin, A., & 't Hart, P. (2003). Public leadership in times of crisis: Mission impossible? *Public Administration Review, 63*(5), 544–553.

Brown, K. E., & Peek, L. (2014). Beyond the IRB: An ethical toolkit for long-term disaster research. *International Journal of Mass Emergencies and Disaster, 32*(1), 82–120.

Broz, D., Levin, E. C., Mucha, A. P., Pelzel, D., Wong, W., Persky, V. W., & Hershow, R. C. (2009). Lessons learned from Chicago's emergency response to mass evacuations caused by hurricane Katrina. *American Journal of Public Health, 99*(8), 1496–1504.

Chia, J. (2010, January). Engaging communities before and emergency: Developing community capacity through social capital investment. *The Australian Journal of Emergency Management, 25*(1).

Clifford, G. C. (2003). Ethics and politics in qualitative research. In K. D. Norman, & Y. S. Lincoln (Eds.), *The landscape of qualitative research. Theories and issues.* Thousand Oaks, CA: Sage.

Coombs, W. T., & Holladay, S. (1996). Communication and attributions in a crisis: An experimental study in crisis communications. *Journal of Public Relations Research, 8*(4), 279–295.

Danielsson, E., Stănciugelu, I., Torstensson, M., & Johansson, P. (2014). Exercise umeå/sandö ethics and data protection evaluation report. FP7 project PRACTICE, WP6 deliverable. (WP6 deliverable to the European Union's Seventh Framework Programme for research, technological development and demonstration, under grant agreement no. 261728)

Enander A., & Hede, S. (2004). *Förväntningar och erfarenheter hos aktörer.* KBM:s forskningsserie nr 4. Stockholm: Krisberedskapsmyndigheten . [Expectations and experiences of actors. KBM's Research series number 4. Stockholm: Swedish Emergency Management Agency.]

The European Convention of Human Rights. (n.d.). Retrieved from http://www.hri. org/docs/ECHR50.html

Frunză, S. (2012). Increasing competence – an ethical duty of civil servants. *Transylvanian Review of Administrative Sciences*, [special issue], 32–41.

Hashimoto, N. (2000). Public organizations in an emergency: The 1995 Hanshin-Awaji earthquake and municipal government. *Journal of Contingencies and Crisis Management, 8*(1), 15–22.

Kapucu, N. (2008a). Collaborative emergency management: better community organising, better public preparedness and response. *Disasters, 32*(2), 239–262.

Kapucu, N. (2008b). Planning for disasters and responding to catastrophes: Error of the third type in disaster policy and planning. *International Journal of Public Policy, 3*(5/6), 313–327.

Kendra, J. M., & Wachtendorf, T. (2003). Elements of resilience after the World Trade Center disaster: Reconstructing New York City's emergency operations center. *Disaster, 27*(1), 37–53.

McConnell, A., & Drennan, I. (2006). Mission impossible? Planning and preparing for crisis. *Journal of Contingencies and Crisis Management, 14*(2), 59–70.

SFS (2003). Act (2003: 460) concerning the ethical review of research involving humans. Stockholm.

Nohrstedt, D. (2011). Uncertainty, accountability, and the conduct of postcrisis inquiries. In L. Svedin (Ed.), *Ethics and crisis management* (pp. 183–209). Charlotte, NC: Information Age.

Ödlund, A. (2007). *Interorganisatorisk samverkan som nationell resurs i krishantering* [Inter-organizational collaboration as a national resource in crisis management.]. Stockholm, Sweden: Totalförsvarets Forskningsinstitut. FOI-R-2425-SE.

Olofsson, A., Öhman, S., & Rashid, S. (2006). Attitudes to gene technology: The significance of trust in institutions. *European Societies, 8*(4), 601–624.

Parker, C. (2011). The purpose, functions, and ethical dimensions of post crisis investigations. The case of the 9/11 commission. In L. Svedin (Ed.), *Ethics and crisis management,* (pp. 199–216. Charlotte, NC.: Information Age.

Rosenthal, U., & Kouzmin, A. (1997). Crises and crisis management: Toward comprehensive government decision making. *Journal of Public Administration Research & Theory, 7*(2), 277–304.

Seeger, M. (2006). Best practices in crisis communication: An expert panel process. *Journal of Applied Communication Research, 34*(3), 232–244.

SFS. (1998). Personal Data Act (1998:204) Stockholm.

Stănciugelu, I. & Danielsson, E. (2013). Exercise ARDEN ethics and data protection evaluation report. (WP6 deliverable to the European Union's Seventh Framework Programme for research, technological development and demonstration, under grant agreement no. 261728.)

Stephenson Jr., M. (2005). Making humanitarian relief networks more effective: Operational coordination, trust and sense making. *Disasters, 29*(4), 337–350.

Svedin, L. (Ed), (2011). *Ethics and crisis management.* Charlotte, NC.: Information Age.

Uhr, C. (2009). *Multi-organizational emergency response management* (Dissertation). Lund University, Lund, Swedin.

Usher, D. (2012). D8.4 Stakeholder Workshop. PRACTICE (Deliverable D8.4 to the European Union's Seventh Framework Programme for research, technological development and demonstration, undergrant agreement no. 261728)

Veil, S. R. (2008). Civil responsibility in a risk democracy. *Public Relations Review, 34*(4), 387–391.

Wise, C. R., & McGuire, M. (2009). Wildland fire mitigation networks in the western United States. *Disasters, 33*(4), 721–746.

Wittmer, D. (1992). Ethical sensitivity and managerial decision making: An experiment. *Journal of Public Administration Research Theory, 2*(4): 443–462.

CHAPTER 10

# THE ETHICS OF A GLOBAL RESPONSE TO THE GOVERNANCE OF MIGRATION

**Adam Luedtke**

## ABSTRACT

Human migration in contexts of economic crisis or ethno-religious conflict, poses social and economic risks both for migrant-receiving and migrant-sending states. This chapter will explore the ethical gains that would come from the establishment of a global institution for governing migration issues. The chapter will outline the ethical basis for a negotiating forum and dispute settlement mechanism for migration, similar in function to the World Trade Organization. The proposed World Migration Organization (WMO) would allow for both ethical and practical gains by minimizing the wide variety of acute risks facing all actors associated with migration. The chapter will show how such a regulatory scheme would not only satisfy utilitarian ethical concerns in optimizing practical benefits and minimizing immigration-related risks, but would also make world migration outcomes fit better (if not perfectly) with other ethical frameworks like human rights. The establishment of a WMO would, in theory, benefit all parties concerned (immigrants themselves, employers, host country voters, law enforcement agencies, and

*Ethics and Risk Management*, pp. 159–175

politicians in both sending and receiving countries). However, the very acuteness of migration as a social risk—seen by many receiving-country citizens as threatening national identity, security, and economies—makes the establishment of a WMO unlikely in practical reality, despite the variety of ethical/utilitarian gains that could be realized from such a scheme.

## MIGRATION AS A "SOCIAL RISK," AND ETHICAL APPROACHES TO REGULATING IMMIGRATION

Dominant ethical approaches to regulating immigration, I will argue below, have only served to enhance the "taboo" problem as outlined by Svedin (2014), which blocks effective risk regulation on this issue. Political theory on migration has paradoxically served to maintain a distinction between citizens and "the other," through privileging the abstract *rights* of immigrants, over any pragmatic, cost-benefit analysis that could resolve the acute conflicts of interest at stake (see Francis, this volume). More specifically, the "cosmopolitan egalitarianism" of scholars like Carens (1987), has been a dominant ethical approach toward migration that, I will argue, leaves us poorly equipped to regulate the problem in the real world.

The remainder of this section will explain why migration, as an acute "social risk," does not easily bend to ethical frameworks based on abstract rights. But first, I will briefly explain the cosmopolitan egalitarianism of Carens (1987), who is a leading proponent of such abstract rights. In short, Carens applies John Rawls's (1971) "veil of ignorance" argument as an ethical device to advocate the opening of borders and the loosening of immigration controls. Like Rawls does with economic equality and social class, Carens argues that since we cannot choose *a priori* what country we are born into, but since the country of our birth profoundly affects our life choices, closed borders essentially perpetuate a world system of deep inequality; inequality based on nothing but pure luck.

As Carens (1987) writes, "citizenship in Western liberal democracies is the modern equivalent to feudal privilege—an inherited status that greatly enhances one's life chances. Like feudal birthright privileges, restrictive citizenship is hard to justify when one thinks about it closely" (p. 252). Thus, cosmopolitan egalitarians see a policy of open borders as the only possible ethical response.

However, this stance is based on a simplistic model of national sovereignty, which ignores both the exceptional qualities of contemporary human migration as a multi-dimensional social risk, as well as the complexity of regulating migration in the 21st century. Indeed, immigration is a political problem that spans national boundaries, in ways that are difficult for a moral philosophy based on traditional national sovereignty to grasp.

In an age of globalization, governments have eased restrictions on movements of goods, services, and capital. Yet movement of people continues to provoke intense political backlashes.

However, improvements in communications and transport technology, along with falling prices, have made human migration easier (Weiner, 1995); yet immigrant-receiving governments are still punished politically for allowing human flows to cross national borders, despite the potential economic gains accruing to all parties in the exchange.[1] As James Hollifield (1998) has argued, migration is the political mirror of trade and finance. The wealthier states push hard for protection (to keep labor flows out), whereas many poorer states (if rarely explicitly stated) push for openness; whether to export workers to gain remittances (money sent home by workers abroad, which is a sizable chunk of GDP in many countries[2]) or to use as a social safety valve, as shown by Bearce and Laks (2011).

In presenting the real-world challenges of ethically regulating migration, and proposing a solution, this chapter necessarily defines the concept of "immigrants" broadly, to include labor migrants of all skill levels, refugees/asylum-seekers, family migrants, students, and, perhaps most importantly, those from any of the above categories who at one time or another are considered "illegal" due to a lack of proper documentation or a failure to comply with immigration laws, even if they might technically be eligible for legal status. It is especially when one considers the experience of such "illegal" migrants, who are often at the mercy of human trafficking mafias, unscrupulous employers, and xenophobic hostility in their host countries abroad, that it becomes evident that human migration poses acute social and economic risks for all parties concerned. No matter what the circumstances, significant risks are taken by any migrant who opts to leave his or her home country, not to mention the perceived risks faced by their communities and their family members who are left behind. Emigration also poses risks for the governments of migrants' home countries, since at home these governments are often accused of failing to protect fellow citizens from exploitation in foreign countries, even as they are simultaneously accused by governments in immigrant-receiving countries of failing to cooperate on issues like stemming illegal immigration.

The intensity and frequency of these accusations show that on the receiving-country side, the perceived risks are no less acute. Governments in host countries have lost elections over the immigration issue, and new political parties have arisen and been successful with a platform focused on the restriction of immigrants' entry, rights and freedoms. Native-born workers in host countries fear that their jobs will be "taken" by foreigners willing to work for lower wages, and immigrants are often seen as threatening national security, or even the cultural, linguistic, or ethnic identity of the host nation itself.

Anxieties are already high regarding the entry of foreign goods, services, or capital. However, the entry of foreign people, trumps these other forces in terms of perceived risk. Indeed, in every developed country, the median voter is against more immigration (Cornelius & Rosenblum, 2005). Increasingly since the 9/11 attacks on the United States, and the growth of fears over terrorism, immigration is perceived to be a grave security risk for states and publics alike (Givens, Freeman, & Leal, 2008). In the EU, a *Eurobarometer* survey showed that citizens ranked the importance of the immigration issue higher than pensions, taxation, education, housing, the environment, public transport, defense, and foreign affairs (EEIG, 2003).

Yet despite the risks perceived by all parties involved, immigration continues to increase. According to the United Nations, the number of migrants around the world rose 46% in the 1990s, from 120 million to 175 million, and it is estimated today to be well above 200 million people. How is this possible? First, the work of Portes (1995) has revealed how global social networks of migrants and their ethnic kin take advantage of normative and economic factors to perpetuate migration even in the face of harsh objective conditions (e.g., the hostility and exploitation risks, including the fact that prices for human smuggling can run as high as $80,000 USD). Secondly, and perhaps counter-intuitively, research has shown that economic development and globalization—rather than allowing citizens of developing countries to enjoy less incentives to "stay home"—actually uproot communities and cause emigration (de Haas, 2005). In the economic realm, one cannot separate trade and capital flows from migration. The movement of goods, services and capital not only entails inherent, accompanying movements of people, but free trade has empirically been shown to lead to increased emigration from emerging economies. Paradoxically, the middle stages of economic development, even when GDP is growing rapidly, lead to human flight (emigration). As farmers leave small-scale agriculture and move to cities, there are not enough jobs in the medium-term to absorb this new exodus. With increased expectations of wealth and easy urban access to transport technology, human smuggling mafias and social networks of past migrants (often family members or people from the same home region), economic growth thus serves to increase emigration (de Haas, 2005).

These contradictions, with accompanying mismatches in risk perception and incentives, thus lead to a status quo mired in political hypocrisy, in which everyone is worse off, and politicians pretend to be able to limit migration despite their knowledge to the contrary. Due to the hostility against immigrants on the part of the public, however, foreign workers are frequently pushed into illegal status, and their exploitation goes unnoticed or is even encouraged. Businesses in developed countries continue to lack needed labor in many sectors, while developing countries face a "brain drain" of their best and brightest. Receiving-country publics are angry over the perceived loss of control of national borders, and the abuse of immigration laws, and this anger is felt by their governments, who have few options available to them since immigration is obviously continuing apace despite the political risks of allowing it. On the other hand, sending-country governments feel the heat from their own citizens' accusations of allowing foreign exploitation of their citizens, even as they feel the heat from receiving-country governments for their perceived failure to "stem the tide." In such a situation, sending and receiving countries see no reasons to trust each other, or to work together on regulating migration.

Ethically, the main philosophical approaches to migration have not helped to resolve this dilemma, and indeed have even served to heighten the perceived social risks. Democratic theory privileges the will of the voters, a group that is usually hostile to increased migration based on the preferences of the median voter (Cornelius & Rosenblum, 2005). Developments in both Europe and America reflect a political struggle where anti-immigration publics face political and business elites who take a more positive view on immigration. In both polities, though, anti-immigration sentiment is fueled by populist politicians who capitalize on the perception of threat and an often amorphous set of fears. Political elites in both Europe and America see the economic benefits of immigration, as well as see the ethical dangers in overregulating this "risk" (Freeman, 2002; Hollifield, 1992). Notably, as in many issues where majority preferences are ethically problematic, the standard ethical approach is to rely on human rights theory, which on immigration is usually grounded in international law. Indeed, international migration law based on human rights, such as conventions on the sanctity of family reunification, or on states' obligations to take in refugees post-World War II, has been a major mechanism by which migration continues despite public hostility. And unfortunately, this has made human-rights theory part of the problem, in a sense; as avenues for legal migration were closed off in the developed world, it was only through refugee or family reunification laws that immigrants continued to arrive. Thus, migration that is based on human rights, such as asylum-seekers' continuing ability to arrive in Europe—and to stay for years even if thought to be false claimants—has become central to the "problem," since there is a great deal of perceived abuse of the refugee system; not to mention perceived abuse of family migration and other legal protections grounded in human rights.[3]

Thus, despite EU-level moves toward liberal regulation, where European policymakers seem to have accepted that immigration cannot be restricted in the way the average voter wants, immigration is an area of considerable controversy in the EU; this is because of its ties to hot-button issues such as national identity and the loss of national sovereignty. The latter two issue-areas have been characterized by McLaren (2002, 2003) as areas of deep social risk; and De Vreese and Boomgaarden (2005) have shown that the fear of immigration is strongly correlated with this perceived "cultural threat." In the current climate, despite a pressing awareness of the economic and demographic benefits among political elites, migration is continually perceived as a worrying, even destabilizing, phenomenon (den Boer, 1995). Den Boer (2005, pp. 1–2) draws a strong connection between immigration and Beck's (1992) "risk society" concept; he argues that, "anxiety seems to be one of the core drivers of current domestic and European politics." Den Boer (2005) highlights the fact that terrorism is a new element of social insecurity surrounding immigration:

> In the risk society, catastrophe—being the exceptional condition—becomes the norm. Nowadays, the fight against terrorism—whether incidental or structural in nature—has become the norm in the organization of safety and security. The perception of risk and anxiety is based on the relative loss of security and trust, to the exposure to a society which becomes more anonymous and more globalized. (Den Boer, pp. 1–2)

Since 9/11, terrorism has become the number one security item on many Western agendas, and this perception of terrorism as an "existential" security threat is exceedingly difficult for liberal states to negate in the face of a global economy.

Given the failures of democratic theory and human-rights theory to resolve these ethical dilemmas, and in the face of the acute social risks associated with the unstoppable tide of human migration, the remainder of this chapter will posit that immigration can only be ethically regulated by adopting a utilitarian approach at the international level. A prototype of such a solution already exists in the European Union, which has increasingly become involved in regulating migration, ever since the passage of the Lisbon Treaty in 2009 made immigration an area of EU law. Despite public hostility in Europe to both immigration and European integration, there is good evidence that such worries can be overcome through a utilitarian ethical framework. Indeed, Kritzinger's (2005) research shows that an EU citizen's utilitarian expectations of Europe, determine the strength with which he or she feels attached to Europe (and thus less prone to feel threatened by foreigners, or by international cooperation, on a basis of perceived risks to cultural/national identity). Based on Lipset (1960), Kritzinger argues that a political system that is expected to be efficient can create identity. For Kritzinger, identity is believed to encompass different dimensions, including efficiency. Thus, for Kritzinger:

> It is possible to use utilitarian reasoning to observe affective (identity) variations. As utilitarian expectations we use citizens' policy preferences. We

observe whether they favor a national handling of the policy or whether they prefer the EU to be the main policy actor. The results of factor and multinominal logit analyses confirm the existence of a "utilitarian identity" at the European level indicating that the development of a European identity is closely connected to the EU's ability to deliver policy outputs. (p. 50)

The implication here is that if a hypothetical World Migration Organization is able to deliver tangible benefits—like the World Trade Organization (WTO) aims to do in the realm of goods and services—including mitigating immigration-related risks for all parties involved, not to mention bringing migration policies more in line with democratic theory and human rights, then this might be enough to overcome the deep skepticism and even hostility that publics in both developing and developed countries feel toward international organizations like the WTO.

## ETHICAL AND PRACTICAL INCENTIVES FOR GLOBAL IMMIGRATION POLICY COOPERATION

Human migration is one of the last frontiers of international cooperation. Despite massive gains that could result from creating institutions to regulate migration flows between states, such institutions have been rare and weak in terms of binding states to commitments. This section of the chapter uses a utilitarian approach to analyze the normative and economic gains that could result from international cooperation on immigration, in terms of reducing the perceived economic, political, social and security risks associated with migration.

As mentioned above, economic development and globalization are inextricably linked to migration, and indeed often serve to increase immigration, which is counter-intuitive to many. Thus, even as global economic institutions have multiplied, expanded, and strengthened, the accompanying effects of increased migration have been ignored due to false assumptions or political hypocrisy (paying lip service to xenophobia or "getting tough", even while pushing policies that allow migration flows to increase). For instance, the North American Free Trade Agreement (NAFTA) supposedly originated as an attempt to slow Mexico-U.S. migration, yet it actually ended up boosting this migration substantially. According to Miller and Stefanova (2003):

The origins of NAFTA can be traced to the creation of the Commission for the Study of International Migration and Cooperative Economic Development (CSIMCED) authorized by the [Reagan] Immigration Control and Reform Act of 1986. Essentially, CSIMCED examined alternative or complementary strategies for prevention of illegal migration ... [but] so sharp were differences between the United States and Mexico over illegal migration that a decision was made to exclude the "poison pill" of migration from NAFTA ... paradoxically, then, only one minor formal clause of the NAFTA treaty pertains to migration while, in fact, migration control concerns figured centrally in the diplomatic initiative. Indeed, both President Salinas and President Clinton would argue in support of signature and ratification of the NAFTA treaty that it would reduce illegal Mexican migration to the United States. To paraphrase President Salinas, either the United States would get Mexican tomatoes or Mexican workers.

After the passage of NAFTA, however, Mexican migration to the United States surged, and it grew every year until the 2008 financial crisis.

This case illustrates the difficulties that states face in attempting to cooperate on migration. While the post-war liberal order, founded on an international framework of human-rights law, empowers the United Nations to safeguard the movement of refugees, these flows are modest in number compared with labor and family migration; and the incentives for cooperation on managing refugee flows by liberal states were closely linked to the politics of the Cold War (e.g., American willingness to embrace refugees from communist countries). Until the economic slowdowns of the 1970s, liberal states had little incentive to create multilateral regimes for managing labor migration, as bilateral arrangements tended to suffice under conditions of rapid economic growth and minimal political controversy.

Freeman (2002) characterizes this period as being marked by "client politics." According to his definition, under "normal" conditions (low political salience of immigration), business and ethnic lobbies formed an alliance of convenience to manage immigration away from the public eye. However, the increasing political salience of immigration in recent years has punctured this equilibrium, putting governments (and economies) at greater perceived risk. Yet despite these risks, as explained above, immigration levels never decreased. As legal avenues for labor migration were closed, more asylum-seekers and family migrants (both protected under international human rights law) and more illegal migrants continued to arrive. Thus, as economies slowed and immigration became more politically controversial, the incentives for international cooperation on trade versus those for cooperation on migration diverged. As Hollifield (1998) argues that with respect to trade, groups tend to follow their market interests; but with migration, this is often not the case. If a state can be sure of reciprocity, it is easier to convince a skeptical public to support free trade. However, with migration, purely economic arguments are usually overshadowed by political, cultural and ideological arguments. Thus, developed states are caught in a "liberal paradox" (Hollifield, 1998). The rules of the market require openness and factor mobility, but the rules of the liberal polity require some degree of closure, since polls show that the median voter in OECD countries opposes increased immigration (Cornelius & Rosenblum, 2005). This opposition is rooted in many things, from post-9/11 security concerns, to worries over national identity, to perceived crises of immigrant integration, to economic scapegoating during recession, or increased unemployment.

Establishing a multilateral process for regulating and controlling migration, offers one possible way out of this dilemma that could achieve an "orderly" movement of people that would balance economic gains, rule of law, and public opinion concerns. This is already taking place inside the European Union, to some degree, but is limited by the same worries that would face any prospective World Migration Organization. At the global level, the possibility of states putting their trust in a WMO, could seem to be jeopardized by excess opportunities for defection from any common agreements, to put it in game-theoretic terms (Putnam, 1988; Rotte & Zimmerman, 1998; Vaubel, 1994; Vink, 2001). Indeed, the capacity of states to monitor and enforce "orderly" movements of people, would seem to be minimal given the tenacity of illegal immigration in the face of expensive efforts at control, as well as the lack of incentives and resources for developing countries to stop emigration.

The only realistic solution to this collective action problem, would seem to be tactical issue linkage; in effect "rewarding" sending states for their cooperation in controlling migration. Receiving states, however, might face credibility or reputational problems with their own citizens or fellow receiving states in pursuing these strategies. Of course, multilateral international organizations could lessen the transaction costs and perceived risks that bilateral agreements (e.g., between a sending and a receiving country) might produce. But, as Hollifield (1998) warns:

> This may entail some short-term loss of control (larger numbers of visas, higher quotas, etc. for the sending states) in exchange for long-term stability and more orderly regular migration. The ultimate payoff for liberal states is the establishment of a liberal world order based upon rule of law and respect for state sovereignty. The payoff for sending states is greater freedom of movement for their nationals, greater foreign reserves and a more favorable balance of payments (thanks to remittances), and increases in cultural and economic exchange, including technology transfers. (pp. 190–191)

International organizations do things for countries that countries cannot or will not do on their own (Keohane 1984). For an international organization to work, however, all countries that participate need to gain something tangible, enough to "sell" to their own publics. This has been well analyzed as the "two-level game" problem in international relations, wherein negotiators are "playing" strategically in opposite directions: against other countries, as well as their own publics (Putnam, 1988; Rotte & Zimmerman, 1998; Vaubel, 1994; Vink, 2001). In this type of two-level game, all parties need to gain enough perceived benefits to overcome the particularly salient social risks posed by immigration and international cooperation.

How, then, could a WMO accomplish this? The key goal would have to be a "grand bargain" in which more effective enforcement of immigration rules is balanced with liberalization of migrant flows. Currently, these migrants are pushed underground or outside the law, thereby benefitting human trafficking organizations, exploitative employers, and reducing immigrants' incentives to cooperate with host country police, or to feel an increased "stake" in terms of wanting to contribute to the host society. In other words, the flows that are already occurring, would potentially be regulated and coordinated, to the benefit of all. For receiving countries, the rewards of cooperation would include less overlap or duplication of effort (whether in the current difficulties posed by deporting illegal immigrants, to the "beggar-thy-neighbor" efforts to recruit certain categories of immigrants, such as high-tech workers). Additionally, receiving countries would reap the benefits of increased sharing of migration data (law enforcement databases, for instance) and increased pooling of border control resources, which would result in better enforcement through economies of scale.

For sending countries, the benefits would be no less tangible in ethical or risk-management terms, not to mention in increased utilitarian or economic benefits. First, sending countries' citizens would receive the increased protection of having the law on their side, allowing them to step out of the shadows and end their reliance on informal or criminal networks to get around the law. Furthermore, sending countries would also benefit from increased remittance flows; side payments for cooperating with receiving countries on issues like deportation and enforcement, as well as a more orderly and predictable system of temporary migration. This is because, paradoxically, making it more difficult to cross borders makes an immigrant more likely to try and stay in the host country permanently, rather than follow the predilection of many to migrate seasonally or on a short-term basis, since the probability of capture and deportation increases in tandem with the number of border crossings.

Thus, an international organization for migration governance could move the world some distance towards the following positive outcomes:

1.   Ensure more orderly migration flows, which would strengthen rule of law and transparency.
2.   Fight human smuggling and human trafficking, and protect the rights of migrants while sapping criminal mafias of a lucrative source of income.

3.  Minimize any "race to the bottom" or negative externalities caused by lack of coordination, as in the example of the "asylum-shopping" problem in Europe, where a prospective refugee (lacking identification documents) would apply to one country, stay for years at taxpayer expense while awaiting the hearing and any appeals, and then simply move on to another country and apply again (often under a different name) if the first claim was ultimately denied.

4.  Coordinate the recruitment of high-skilled immigrants and other "desirable" categories in order to avoid a counter-productive competition for the same people.

5.  Assist with the "brain drain" and other development problems in sending countries through the increased use of seasonal or temporary migration, which would mitigate the social costs to communities that depend on emigrants sending home remittances.

6.  Reduce economic distortions like overcrowding in slums and rural depopulation in developing countries through issue linkages and side payments, such as helping mitigate the destruction of small-scale agriculture in the face of cheap, subsidized food coming in from the developed world, making peasants in developing countries more likely to emigrate even in the face of incredible risks and costs.

7.  Conduct re-admission agreements to coordinate deportation of illegal immigrants between sending and receiving countries (currently many sending countries often refuse to accept the return of their own citizens, thus putting migrants in a stateless limbo of detention in the host country at taxpayer expense).

8.  Allow receiving countries to pool their resources and information as regards border control, deportation, and immigration law enforcement.

## EXISTING COOPERATION, THE EU PROTOTYPE, AND THE RISKS OF REGULATING MIGRATION GLOBALLY

The only existing global, multilateral institution that plays a significant role in regulating migration (albeit only with one category of migrants) is the United Nations High Commission for Refugees (UNHCR), which enforces the 1951 Geneva Refugee Convention (drawn up to prevent another situation like that faced by Jewish refugees from the Nazis in the 1930s and 40s). Like the World Trade Organization, the International Monetary Fund, and the World Bank, the UNHCR's initial success was rooted in the Cold War (it was a politically convenient way for liberal states to gain moral leverage over the Soviet Bloc). However, it then became more broadly useful at a global level in the 1990s and beyond, as a way for a diverse array of states (e.g., Iran and Pakistan regarding Afghan refugees) to coordinate the management of refugee flows with minimal political costs and increased sharing of financial burdens (compensation from wealthier states given to refugee-hosting countries). Such "burden-sharing" is currently being attempted at the bilateral level as well (e.g., Australia's deal with Malaysia to take their Vietnamese refugees in exchange for Malaysian interdiction of seaborne asylum-seekers headed to Australia), but would be far more effective if done multilaterally; this would open the options and opportunities available for cooperation. To wit, an Australian court struck down the deal with Malaysia on human-rights grounds, thus upholding a principled ethical standard that let Vietnamese refugees continue to languish in Malaysian camps, and let boatloads of asylum-seekers continue to reach Australian shores. In utilitarian terms, international cooperation would have reduced risks and increased overall gains for all parties concerned, but a domestic court saw things differently. Such blockages could be overcome by a new set of international agreements on migration that could be drafted from a utilitarian point of view, rather than a purist human-rights framework that in practice is violated daily.

In terms of other existing international forums, the International Labor Organization (ILO, another U.N. body) drafted a 1990 International Convention on the Protection of the Rights of all Migrant Workers and Members of their Families, as well as two agreements in 2000: the Protocol to Prevent, Suppress and Punish Trafficking in Persons, and the Protocol Against the Smuggling of Migrants by Land, Sea, and Air. However, these agreements have not been ratified by any major migrant-receiving country; this is probably due to a perception that developed countries would "bear the burden" of increased rights protection, without gaining any accompanying enforcement cooperation from sending countries. Again, no real compromise or grand bargain has been reached by these bodies, due to their ethical focus on the sanctity of human rights versus politico-economic pragmatism.

One completely different type of global body that regulates migration is the International Organization for Migration (IOM, 2014), which is seen as somewhat credible by receiving countries, since it largely serves their aims (in contrast to the perception of the U.N. bodies and the agreements they promote). The following quote from the IOM's website (2014) nicely sums up the potential gains from global migration governance; but the fact that it is seen as a tool of developed, immigrant-receiving countries also highlights the reluctance to abandon a human-rights-based view in favor of a practical utilitarian approach. Here is what the IOM has to say:

Governments and societies have an interest in knowing who is seeking access to their territories. The objective is to take measures that prevent access by those who are not authorized to enter, while facilitating speedy access for those who are. IOM assists governments in the development and implementation of migration policy, legislation, and administrative mechanisms. To this end, IOM provides technical assistance and training for governmental migration managers on border management, visa systems, regulating entry and stay, and collecting and using biometric information. Replacing irregular flows with orderly, regular migration serves the interests of all governments, and IOM can offer a broad range of programs to counter trafficking and smuggling in human beings, from prevention to assisting the victims. IOM also implements programs to facilitate the voluntary return and reintegration of displaced and stranded persons and other migrants, taking into account the needs and concerns of local communities.

In terms of an ethical framework based on utilitarian risk management, this comes very close to the essence of what a future WMO would have to do, if it is to succeed in mitigating risk and realizing gains for all parties. However, just as the U.N. is trapped in a perception (right or wrong) that its human-rights agenda serves migrants at the expense of host government interests, the IOM is trapped in a perception (right or wrong) that its law enforcement agenda serves host government interests at the expense of migrant rights (and thus at the expense of human-rights ethics in principle).

Thus, since global cooperation has been confined to these few limited fora, the question arises regarding the possibility of regional cooperation (which was the vanguard for free trade, as in the case of NAFTA providing the impetus for the WTO to expand and deepen cooperation). However, on immigration, there has been only minimal cooperation in regional associations like NAFTA or the Association of Southeast Asian Nations, mostly regarding liberalization agreements on narrow categories of immigrants perceived as less risky, like students or high-skill professionals.

As stated above, the only possible prototype for a WMO at the regional level would be the EU's recent progress in terms of cooperating on immigration governance (both among EU countries, and also in terms of negotiating agreements with non-EU, immigrant-sending countries). After Ireland's approval of the EU's "Reform Treaty" in 2009, immigration policy has finally become a "normal" area of EU law, meaning that the European Commission proposes new immigration legislation, the European Council votes by qualified majority instead of unanimity, the European Parliament has a right of amendment and veto on immigration legislation, and the European Court of Justice has jurisdiction over immigration law. There are now more than forty EU-level immigration laws which have been passed and are enforced throughout the Union (as well as beyond its borders, through the EU's border enforcement agency, known as FRONTEX, which operates in international waters and also in some third countries through negotiated agreements). This array of EU-level immigration laws is admittedly less favorable to immigrant rights and freedoms than some of the previous national-level laws in members states that it replaced, but it is certainly more liberal than the immigration laws that existed in the EU's newer member states. That being said, it is true that the laws passed thus far do tend to highlight restriction and control—notable examples being the empowerment of FRONTEX as well as the creation of three EU-wide identity databases for tracking unwanted immigrants: EURODAC (a biometric database of asylum applicants, to prevent multiple applications as per the "asylum-shopping" worry mentioned above); the Schengen Information System, which allows authorities to share information on any person seeking to enter the Schengen Zone (Europe's area of free travel with no internal border checks); and the Visa Information System, which gathers information on any applicant for a Visa in any EU country.

However, since 2009 there have been many positive developments in terms of EU-level laws and policies raising the level of immigrant rights and freedoms, while increasing the rule of law and the transparency of policy. The European Court of Justice (ECJ) has taken action against EU member states for failing to respect migrants' fundamental rights. New laws on liberalizing and coordinating the admission of skilled workers, students and researchers have passed at the EU level. Re-admission agreements have been concluded with a growing number of countries. Furthermore, any future legislation promises to be more balanced in terms of liberalization versus restriction; most of the existing laws were passed in 2009 and thus were not subject to ECJ jurisdiction, European Parliament amendments and veto power, or qualified majority voting in the Council.

Thus, the EU offers us a good blueprint for how a global organization might be able to legislate migration in a balanced manner; one that minimizes risks for all, while increasing utilitarian gains overall. The increased rule of law will assist law enforcement, but will also bring stronger protections for immigrant rights and freedoms by allowing them to step out of the underground economy. Of course, international organizations, paradoxically, might have more liberal preferences on immigration, because many of their staff are unelected and technocratically-minded. However, if they succeed in providing absolute gains for all parties and mitigating risks associated with immigration, then international organizations can gain the public's loyalty, as evidenced by the work of Kritzinger (2005). When international organizations are effective, they can protect human rights and realize utilitarian gains overall, while at the same time respecting popular sovereignty by gaining support from voters. On the immigration issue, this would be an extreme challenge indeed. However, the failure of existing policy, coupled with the failure of existing ethical frameworks (human rights, democratic theory) to help resolve the dilemmas, means that the potential rewards are greater than in possibly any other policy area. Hundreds of millions of potential and actual migrants (not to mention their families, communities, and governments) face tremendous risks and dangers every day. At the same time, immigrant-receiving countries pay lip-service to "cracking down" and "getting tough," while engaging in wholesale dishonesty and unrealistic policies. The gap between stated policy goals and actual policy outcomes, is larger when it comes to immigration than perhaps any other policy area (Hollifield, Martin, & Orrenius, 2014). The only way to bridge this gap is with a realistic compromise between sending and receiving countries; and this can only happen in a multilateral, global organization with the ability to increase enforcement of realistic immigration laws, which are in line with the overlapping preferences of both migrants and their hosts. As Rodrik's (2002) research shows, even a small step in this direction could provide economic gains far greater than those achieved by free trade.

## NOTES

1. According to Dani Rodrik (2002), even a marginal liberalization of immigration flows would create gains for the world economy far larger than prospective gains from trade liberalization.
2. A World Bank study estimated that in 2004 remittances were the second largest source of external financing in developing countries, after foreign direct investment, and totaled more than twice the size of official aid. The equivalent percent of *total* GDP sent home as remittances by emigrants in Haiti was 26%, in Bosnia 23%, in Jordan 20% and in Jamaica 18% (Ratha, 2006).
3. One example is the worries over a perceived phenomenon of immigrant men bringing spouses from their home countries via arranged marriages, meaning that in some cases they are thought to have never met or to barely know their wives. Denmark's law banning the importation of foreign spouses under certain conditions (age and length of relationship) is a notable example.

## REFERENCES

Bearce, D. & Laks, J. (2011, September). *International labor mobility and domestic political liberalization.* Presented at Annual American Political Science Association Conference, Seattle, WA.

Beck, U. (1992). *Risk society: Toward a new modernity.* London, England: Sage.

Cornelius, W., & Rosenblum, M. (2005). Immigration and politics. *Annual Review of Political Science, 8,* 99–119.

Carens, J. (1987). Aliens and citizens: The case for open borders. *Review of Politics, 49*, 251–273.

Cornelius, W. A, & M. R. Rosenblum. (2005). Immigration and politics. *Annual Review of Political Science, 8*, 99–119.

de Haas, H. (2005). International migration, remittances, and development: Myths and fact. *Global Migration Perspectives, 30*. Global Commission on International Migration: Retrieved from http://www.gcim.org

De Vreese, C. H., & Boomgarden, H. G. (2005). Projecting EU referendums: Fear of immigration and support for European integration. *European Union Politics 6*, 59–82.

den Boer, M. (1995). Moving between bogus and bona fide: The policing of inclusion and exclusion in Europe. In R. Miles & D. Thränhardt (Eds.), *Migration and European integration: The dynamics of inclusion and exclusion* (pp. 92–111). London, England: Pinter.

den Boer, M. (2005). Ins and outs of an EU integration policy: The position of migrants in the era of security. *Lecture for Cicero Foundation Seminar*. Retrieved from http://www.cicerofoundation.org/pdf/presentation_DenBoer.doc

EEIG, European Opinion Research Group. (2003). *Eurobarometer 60: Public opinion in the European Union*. Ann Arbor, MI: Inter-University Consortium for Political and Social Research.

Freeman, G. P. (2002). Winners and losers: Politics and the costs and benefits of migration. In A. Messina (Ed.), *West European immigration and immigrant policy in the new century* (pp. 77–96). Westport: Praeger.

Givens, T. E., Freeman, G. P., & Leal, D. L. (2008). *Immigration policy and security: U.S., European, and Commonwealth perspectives*. New York, NY: Routledge.

Hollifield, J. F. (1992). *Immigrants, markets and states: The political economy of postwar Europe*. Boston, MA: Harvard University Press.

Hollifield, J. F. (1998). Migration, trade and the nation-state: The myth of globalization. *UCLA Journal of International Law and Foreign Affairs, 3*(2), 595–636.

Hollifield, J. F., Martin, P. L., & Orrenius, P. M. (2014). *Controlling immigration: A global perspective*. Stanford, CA: Stanford University Press.

International Organization for Migration. (2014). What we do. Retrieved October 30, 2014, from https://www.iom.int/cms/nepal

Keohane, R. O. (1984). *After hegemony: Cooperation and discord in the world political economy*. Princeton, NJ: Princeton University Press.

Kritzinger, S. (2005). European identity building from the perspective of efficiency. *Comparative European Politics, 3*, 50–75.

Lipset, S. M. (1960). *Political man: The social basis of politics*. Baltimore, MD: Johns Hopkins University Press.

McLaren, L. (2002). Public support for the European Union: Cost/benefit analysis or perceived cultural threat? *Journal of Politics, 64*, 551-66.

McLaren, L. (2003). Anti-immigrant prejudice in Europe: Contact, threat perception, and preferences for the exclusion of migrants. *Social Forces, 81*, 909–936.

Miller, M. J., & Stefanova, B. (2003). NAFTA and the European referent: Labor mobility in European and North American regional integration. *Jean Monnet/Robert Schumann Paper Series, 3*(1), 559–560.

Portes, A. (1995). *The economic sociology of immigration: Essays on networks, ethnicity, and entrepreneurship.* New York, NY: Russell Sage Foundation.

Putnam, R. (1988). Diplomacy and domestic politics: The logic of two-level games. *International Organization, 42*(3), 427–460.

Ratha, D. (2006). *Global economic prospects 2006: Economic implications of remittances and migration.* Washington, DC: World Bank.

Rawls, J. (1971). *A theory of justice.* Cambridge, MA: Harvard University Press.

Rodrik, D. (2002). Comments at the conference on Immigration Policy and the Welfare State. In T. Boeri, G. H. Hanson, & B. McCormick (Eds.), *Immigration policy and the welfare system* (pp. 314–317). New York, NY: Oxford University Press.

Rotte, R., & Zimmermann, K. (1998). Fiscal restraint and the political economy of EMU. *Public Choice, 94*(3/4), 385–406.

Svedin, L. (2014, April 17–19). *American taboos: Regulating what we feel we cannot talk about.* Paper presented at the Western Political Science Association annual meeting, Seattle, WA.

United Nations. (2013). The number of international migrants worldwide reaches 232 million (P. Division, Trans.). In Department of Economic and Social Affairs—Popultion Division (Ed.), *Population facts* (p. 4). New York, NY: Author.

Vaubel, R. (1994). The public choice analysis of European integration: A survey. *European Journal of Political Economy, 10*(1), 227–249.

Vink, M. (2001). The limited Europeanization of domestic citizenship policy: Evidence from the Netherlands. *Journal of Common Market Studies, 39*(5), 875–896.

Weiner, M. (1995). *The global migration crisis: Challenge to states and to human rights.* New York, NY: HarperCollins.

# CHAPTER 11

# CONCLUSIONS

**Lina Svedin**

The empirical chapters in this volume have covered a lot of ground and reflect a number of disciplinary perspectives: business, law, philosophy, healthcare professions, psychology, international relations, public policy, non-profit organizing to mention a few. This concluding chapter will discuss the assertions and findings in the empirical chapters around a core set of themes. The intention is to underscore what the chapters have in common as they relate to both the underlying, fundamental challenges of ethical risk management, as well as possible solutions and ways forward. The ethical management of risk is not only under-researched and a subject of a nascent conversation, it is also a difficult thing to accomplish practically. However, the contributors to this book are not uniformly pessimistic about the prospects of an ethical way to manage risk and risk mitigation. In fact, the reason they took on the challenge of examining their core research on risk from an ethics perspective, is because they feel strongly that things can be done to improve the state of affairs in this regard. As such, the concluding chapter of this volume will provide some suggestions for ways to improve the practice of ethical management, for those in the trenches as well as for those at a strategic policy level. While far from exhaustive, we feel this book provides a foundation, a first building block, on the path toward public discourse about risk: who takes it, who manages it, and how and what we think is most important to protect today and for the future.

## RISK AND CULTURE

Why policymakers and citizens think and approach risk the way they do is a central underlying theme of this book. Several chapters give clues and specific examples of the rationales behind public preferences, and of the many competing obligations policymakers encounter. Culture, as presented by Ásthildur Bernharðsdóttir in Chapter 7 makes a strong claim for how different countries view and approach risk regulation. In considering the impact of culture, we have looked to Iceland and Japan, two countries with perhaps the greatest number of naturally occurring hazards and risks of disaster in the world. They are also two countries with pronounced cultural norms that shape the approach they take to the risks they encounter.

In Bernharðsdóttir's case studies of how culture shapes risk perception and risk management, we are presented with the fiercely independent Icelanders and their somewhat fatalistic view of nature as unpredictable and full of fury. Consequently, Icelanders tend not to prepare, perhaps as much as would be expected, for the risk of avalanches and accidents at sea. The egalitarian side of Iceland's culture, however, had left the government in charge of making sure large numbers of citizens are not seriously harmed, and with making sure that whatever risks did materialize did not unnecessarily harm those already worse off. In the early 2000s when the influence of individualistic culture, which was aided in large part by American banking consultants, started to shape Iceland's financial risk regulation policies, the structural changes created an invisible gap between reality and the Icelandic public's expectations of risk management. When the global financial crisis in 2008 nearly destroyed all of Iceland's economy, the public outcry was not about the fickle nature of financial flows, but about the government's failure to protect a majority of the Icelandic population from severe harm.

In Chapter 8, Aya Okada introduces us to a closer encounter with the Japanese. Japan is a traditional society, where patterns of cultural values and roles of institutions are not easily reshaped. Their respect for hierarchy and strong group affiliation is privileged over individual considerations, creating conditions where individuals often have a hard time helping themselves first by separating themselves from the group, even when this may be the most beneficial in an acute situation. However, following the 2011 triple disaster in eastern Japan, Okada documents a significant surge in non-profit and community organizational involvement in the response to the disasters, and in the communication of risk and effective civil protection procedures. As such, Japanese society has started to allow a new actor a greater role in the assessment, communication, and response to solution the many risks the country faces.

Ragnar Löfstedt (2005) asserts that in order to effectively manage risks, risk communication is paramount, but so is trust. He has foreshadowed some of Bernharðsdóttir's and Okada's findings in this volume. Löfstedt argues that; while *which* specific risks to regulate and *how* to regulate will and should vary according to national and regional cultures, all regulation is built on trust. Regulatory agencies can only operate effectively, if there is some trust (a perception of competence, fairness, and efficiency) in the institutions charged with this task (Löfstedt, 2005). By extension, how governments like Iceland's or non-profits in Japan communicate about the risks the public faces, and the extent to which they involve the public in the decision-making process as they take on risk management responsibilities, will likely be extremely important for building and mainlining public trust around risk.

Matthew Adler reflects in Chapter 2 on value priority in policymaking around risk, which is intrinsically tied to the ethics of value and resource allocation, and on how to calculate benefit when pursuing risk reduction. Adler's formal proof that cost-benefit analysis is neither value-neutral nor consequence-neutral, suggests that policymakers may want to consider a deliberate choice of how we allocate value and benefit among those they design policy for. Whether we as a society want to lift those who are at the bottom of the socio-economic ladder, or simply want to maximize the production of benefits based on individual preferences and risk baseline, Adler leaves as an open question. He does, however, make a thorough and convincing argument that policymakers can use benefit-calculation formulas much better if they consider using weighted prioritarian formulas, instead of hiding behind the deceptive neutrality of cost-benefit analysis. The widespread practice of using cost-benefit calculations to develop risk reduction policies, Adler cautions, is even worse than the theory of it; using an averaged value of a statistical life baseline for the benefit calculation is even less correct and a clumsier proxy for what would actually create the most benefit in society. However, the political minefield associated with actually stating whose risk we are willing to live with, and whose we are willing as a society to pay to reduce, and how this is tied to wealth, is the reason to use both: for the use of the seemingly value-neutral, cost-benefit analysis and the praxis of using an average-statistical-life value, instead of actually talking about whose life and value we are actually prioritizing.

For those who design and participate in exercises aimed to reduce risk and improve the response to hazardous material events, a persistent challenge is how to incorporate the public in these exercises in an ethical way. The realism that comes from working with public volunteers in live training exercises, can be beneficial for professional emergency managers. However, depending on how the public volunteers are selected, it may set the wrong expectations for practitioners into place and may inadvertently cause policymakers to design policy and praxis that do not adequately take vulnerable populations' needs into account. Because of their vulnerabilities, disabled persons, very young or old people, as well as persons from ethnic and language minority groups, are often not asked to participate in these trainings; trainings that in many ways pre-program professional emergency managers' response to high pressure and high risk situations. Consequently, public volunteers are often recruited from student groups and volunteer cadres in organizations like the Red Cross; they are not a representative sample of the population as a whole. When students are asked to role-play persons with disabilities or other challenges, there is a false sense that these vulnerable and/or minority populations are actually being represented in the emergency planning process; their particular needs and preferences may in fact not be adequately represented by these volunteers. The risk of miseducating these professionals is significant, in terms of the public they are going to be protecting, helping, and communicating with.

## Risk Management in a Comparative Perspective

There are many issues that remain a challenge with regard to effective and legitimate risk management. First, the difference between the risks the public perceives as threatening and the ones that risk-assessment policymakers receive from scientific sources, is as far apart as it has ever been. What the public perceives as risky technology and behavior, and what the public wants the government to mitigate to reduce the likelihood of severe events and societal consequences, are frequently risks that governments have little control over, know little about, and have few economic incentives to invest in preventing.

David Vogel (Chapter 3) and Adam Luedtke (Chapter 11) illustrate how this works in the European Union, the United States, and on the international arena. Citizens raise concerns and want what they perceive as unacceptable threats and risks regulated. In the case of global financial and economic systems, policymakers have to walk the tightrope of maintaining public approval; supporting an industry, that bankrolls segments of the political machinery; while finding effective solutions to risks that have developed. In the EU, genetically modified organisms (GMOs) are strongly opposed by consumers, despite a wealth of science suggesting that these products are not harmful. Consequently, the European Union policymakers have been forced to respond to this public preference; and as a result, have mounted a near ban on GMOs being sold or produced in the EU. The fallout from this has been costly trade disputes with the United States. In the separate case of migration being perceived as a social and economic threat by the average voter, strong public perceptions have forced both the EU and the United States to perform policy acrobatics, appeasing the public that the government is not being soft on illegal immigration, and is keeping a tight grip on what immigration is allowed, while simultaneously trying to capture as much of the economic benefit of migration as possible.

The other side of the equation is both a public and industry that is reluctant to change its ways, habits, and understanding of risk. The less risky behaviors or consumer preferences that governments would like the public to adopt, do not always meet with a positive response or support. The Japanese have a historical understanding of the real threat posed by earthquakes and tsunamis. Yet, as pointed out by Okada, it has taken much retraining and communication to get the majority of the Japanese public to respond independently, without regard for other family members or classmates, and to move to the safety of higher ground when an earthquake is felt (Chapter 6). In considering greener energy consumption and production, consumers have consistently settled for renewable energy that is only less polluting in part because the public wants immediate solutions; they have little patience for what is entailed in ambiguious, partial solutions, and the complex interdependencies and radically different structure of the energy sector that could result with the development of new energy technologies.

Kristin Shrader-Frechette (Chapter 6) points out the ethical dilemmas these dynamics can present to policymakers in the case of biomass incineration. While biomass fuel is seen as a renewable, greener way to produce energy, policymakers risk actually exposing the public (and the environment) to larger quantities of more harmful substances than those produced with coal fuel incineration, an energy-production method that most people now perceive as dangerous and antiquated. Because the science of biomass incineration has been neither well communicated nor understood by policymakers and the public, poor policy choices are being implemented. In Shrader-Frechette's account, we witness the lack of patience and the unwillingness of both the public and policymakers to take in complex scientific information; they are mapping out interdependencies and accepting that partial and evolving solutions are perhaps the best they can do as the energy sector restructures to meet changing technological and environmental considerations. The result thus far has been a failure to regulate this growing industry in a way that limits harmful exposure; and a subsidization and prioritization biomass energy production and energy security instead of agricultural production, which is less resource demanding and that supports our food security.

The ethical dilemmas associated with managing risk, such as biomass energy production, include how to communicate the virtues, but also the increased risks and measurable harms that come with new technology and new processes. In the case of biomass, there is also the complicating factor that the harmful particulate matter that raises the risk of harm, cannot be see with the human eye. Relationships between a harmful substance/process and the actual harm that cannot be seen (readily), are harder to advocate for (or around) in a policy setting where experts and stakeholders are fighting for their side of the argument. Regulating and creating policy around "invisible" risks is more difficult and more contested, than when engaging other clearly tangible and measurable risks of harm. Research also shows, paradoxically, that the public is actually more afraid of dangers that they cannot see, touch, or smell (e.g. invisible threats such as radiation and carcinogenic food substances produces greater fear), than visible and readily identifiable threats like poisonous snakes or riding a motorcycle (Fischhoff, Slovic, & Lichtenstein, 2000; Slovic, Fischhoff, & Lichtenstein, 2000). As such, if the "invisible" but not immeasurable harm that can come from a new technology or process, such as biomass incineration, can be better communicated, then it is more likely that there will be strong and urgent support between the public and policymakers for regulating these risks effectively.

The biomass incineration example also illustrates a larger ethical challenge: how to find a balance between competing strategic priorities, such as energy security and independence versus food security and good stewardship of scarce resources like water. This is an ethical challenge faced not only at a state or federal level in the United States, but globally. While a country like Iceland may be able to make sound and effective choices about whether or how much to invest in avalanche risk reduction, it is much harder to choose whether (or to what degree) to keep an open financial market, to allow foreign direct investment, or adjust financial regulation to stay competitive in a global economy (Bernharðsdóttir's Chapter 7). Furthermore, what is considered an ethical practice or policy today, may not be so tomorrow. While strong consumer preferences make it easier for the European Union and the United States to take either a precautionary or an innocent-until-proven-guilty approach to risky substances and procedures, history has shown that public preferences can be reversed based on particularly poignant and salient events in which risks have either materialized or failed to materialize (Vogel's Chapter 3). Consequently, what may seem like a clear choice for policymakers on how to prioritize major strategic approaches (a choice that has substantial consequences going into the future), may change; all it takes is a few highly publicized and vocalized failures to protect the public or perceived overprotection and costly red-tape.

## PATH DEPENDENCY AND THE FUTURE OF TODAY'S RISK MANAGEMENT

Time perspective is one of the challenging parameters of successful risk analysis and risk management. Estimating what risks will occur within a timespan is one of the baselines upon which we choose to prioritize mitigating some risks over others. The estimation of the timeline in which some negative event or threatening condition will occur is one of the false certainties often generated when using statistical analysis as the basis for decisions about risk. Consider for instance the 100-year flood, the 700-year earthquake or the one-in-a-million chance of a space shuttle O-ring breaking under cold conditions. Because of the way these statistical averages or estimations get used in everyday policy discussions, policymakers and the public actually expect these events *only* to take place every hundred years or once after a million usages.

This is but one of the potentially devastating ways in which the pronounced scientific and number-driven approach to risk assessment and risk management can placate us into thinking that "it will not happen here" or "it will not happen for another hundred years." Such approaches also make it easier to ignore the ethical consequences, and implications, of our risk-management strategies, or our lack of strategies. Objectifying and abstracting risk into numbers helps us deal with our fear of risk and the lack of control we may feel. It is often easier to put the discussion of ethics aside, when our methodology of choice discourages consideration of the human impact that can result from crises. Yet, as has been discussed here, such security is often misleading and ultimately distorts our moral perception; it undermines the conscious effort that is necessary to deal with conflicting values and priorities in an ethically conscious and conscientious way.

As Chapter 9 shows us, even as we are preparing to deal more effectively with adverse events, we may in fact be exporting harm into the future if we fail to consciously consider the ethical aspects of what we are doing. Erna Danielsson, Erika Wall, and Susanna Öhman discuss the treatment of live volunteers, who play the threatened or injured public during professional emergency responders' large training exercises. While volunteers may have agreed to participate in the exercise, and even to be filmed for the purposes of maximizing the learning from the exercise, these tapes and photographs are frequently used after the event in other contexts; training other people or even in larger conference presentations. A person who has volunteered to help local firefighters practice decontamination in the case of a chemical spill, may not have considered or implicitly agreed to have revealing photos and video of themselves being showered spread around in different forums or posted on the internet. Compared to live events, the context of a prepared training is a highly controlled environment where good ethical judgment should be relatively easy to apply and implement. Yet even at this foundational stage of risk management, decision makers can fail in their ethical obligations if they are not actively mindful of the values at stake for all groups involved.

Much about the current practice of risk assessment and risk management is deeply problematic and holds potentially severed consequences for the future. The chapters that speak most clearly to this situation are Chapter 5 (Simon's consideration of fossil fuel development and extraction in the United States and Canada), and Shrader-Frechette's investigation of biomass incineration (Chapter 6).

In the current debate over energy extraction and production, the growing consensus has been that past choices have led to a precarious environmental situation today. Such circumstances present important ethical considerations with regard to the type of world we wish to leave (or are capable of leaving) to future generations. Simon discussed both the social and the environmental costs associated with the surge in fossil-fuel extraction as well as nuclear, and renewable energy development over the last 10 to 15 years. He stated that while the externalities associated with fossil fuel use are well known and significant, the negative long-term effects on public lands, water, and wildlife, of renewable energy development have tended to be undervalued by policymakers who lump them together with green-energy development (which has more positive short-term and long-term impacts). By undervaluing the risks associated with all domestic energy production (including fossil fuels, uranium extraction and green energy development), policymakers are not necessarily pushing policy development on key public concerns (energy security, sustainability, and serious commitment to future generations) in a positive direction.

Shrader-Frechette echoed many of Simon's points, but approached the problem from a biochemistry point of view. She argued that the risks associated with exposure to, even the smallest particles released in the air from burning biodegradable fuel, was actually *worse* than some of the existing bad practices. The result of her study, surprisingly, was that what had long been touted and perceived as greener energy, had significant potential to do way more harm than good. If the biofuel industry continues to ramp up installation and usage, politicians and policymakers may well be committing our limited resources into structural energy solutions that are too poorly regulated, and not nearly as cost-effective as previously suggested. While our current policy of generous subsidies for biofuel production (growing biofuel crops) supports fast growth, we may actually be growing faster than we can regulate the inherent risks; all the while we may be sinking massive amounts of money into an industry that may have less to offer for the future than we have hoped.

As we consider the future effects of policy choices today, policymakers need to keep in mind that society with its diverse cultures, is continually evolving. Just as yesterday's enthusiasm over gasoline and electricity is now seen as limited and problematic, the values and priorities we collectively hold will change over time. Likewise, our perception of risk itself may change, as will our perception of the division of roles and responsibilities between the government and the governed. In the United States, confidence and trust in government today is at an all-time low. How we see the government, and our own role as consumers and potential risk victims, is shaping much of our risk management strategies. As Luedtke pointed out (Chapter 11), what Ulrich Beck characterized as our "risk society" catastrophe, was once considered the extreme and unusual, but it has now has become a social norm. With the emergence of a risk society, are we becoming desensitized to the risk that others face? Or are we now, more than ever, driven by our fears? "The perception of risk and anxiety is based on the relative loss of security and trust, to the exposure to a society which becomes more anonymous and more globalized" (Den Boer, as cited in Chapter 11). With policy rhetoric that has actors from governments to charities waging war on drugs, war on terror and war on want, are we in the United States living in a culture so characterized by violent problem solving, that the ethical assessment of how we manage risks has no place or no space?

## POLICY ADVICE FOR ETHICS IN PRACTICE

While ethically dealing with risk appears a daunting task, there is some hope presented in this book. Several chapters offered options for better conduct, better rationales for prioritization, and better structures for dealing with politically charged risk.

Adler (Chapter 3) makes the case for weighing and prioritizing the calculated benefit that different groups of people get from policy that reduces the risk they face. He also highlighted the advantages associated with policy choices that are the most beneficial (effective), but for those who start out worse off (a normative prioritization of reducing risks for those worst off in society). Adler crafted a profound indictment of unweighted cost benefit analysis, our most frequently used tool for calculating which government policy we should adopt when looking to reduce risk as a form of public benefit. In elegant ropes of formal logic and reasoning, Adler demonstrated how straight-forward, cost-benefit analysis (and some of the prioritarian methods of calculation), fall short on desired outcomes.

Another chapter that lent some concrete hope to the idea of a more ethical management of risk, was Luedtke's vision of a "World Migration

Organization" (Chapter 11). The challenge Luedtke pointed to still remains, with regard to the median voter in the United States being averse to immigration and the subsequent lack of incentives for elected U.S. representatives to encourage immigration reform. However, the increased fairness, predictability and accountability that could be brought to the area of migration, would not only strengthen the ethical treatment of migrants, but could also bring a greater sense of control to receiving countries whose voters are worried about large migration flows undermining their prosperity and way of living. Those voters and policymakers who support a liberal policy on migration on humanitarian or economic grounds, may perceive institutionalizing migration regulation at the international level as the wrong way to go; however, they would likely feel that the consequences of the current approach to global migration are a worse alternative.

It may be that on issues that are so closely tied to a community's sense of culture, such as immigration and food, it may not be possible to reach a point of policy consensus. Europeans and Americans may never see eye-to-eye on genetically-modified food products; and *sending* and *receiving* countries in the migration flow may never agree on what is a fair rate of acceptance and rejection when considering movement across borders. Luedtke's chapter introduced as an important factor that could support cooperation around these thorny value issues (the principle of relative gains). He argued that if the World Migration Organization he proposed to establish could ensure that each stakeholder in the process felt they benefited from participating in this structured process for resolving individual claims and disputes, the cooperative venture had a chance of leading to better and safer treatment of migrants. This same principle has applicability in the area of green-energy development as well. Governments could more effectively manage the risk posed by new technologies and production modes if both industry and consumers felt they gained enough by remaining open to scientific developments and adjusting their behaviors in accordance with best-known risk practices.

Francis (Chapter 4) provides practical strategies for industries that regularly face the ethical challenge of balancing a responsibility to their clients, consumers, or supporters while simultaneously limiting the liability exposure to the own organization when things go wrong. Looking at large hospitals and their risk managers, Francis argued that informal conflict resolution and doing what we might call a "poodle,"[1] may not be an ethically sound way to deal with their obligation to patients. Outlining a more effective way forward, Francis suggested three additions to the disclosure process to help mitigate conflict of interest risks: (1) remind the patient that they can and should perhaps seek outside counsel, (2) do not keep settlement agreements confidential (which makes it more difficult to determine what has been considered fair pay for harm done), and (3) institute an impartial review process for all hospital disclosures, apologies, and compensation offers. While publishing settlement amounts in individual cases can pose a potential risk to patient privacy, it may also increase transparency in a way that supports improved care and fairness for all patients.

The larger lesson drawn from Francis' empirical case was that when there are perverse incentives that encourage people, organizations, or states to act unethically, there is a legitimate need to instituting checks and balances; and they are needed even if those checks come in the form of self-disclosures and self-policing primarily through transparency. If the financial risk that ultimately put Iceland on the brink of financial ruin (Chapter 7) had been subject to more transparency, to more self-disclosure it: (a) may never have materialized into the crisis it did; and (b) Icelanders might have been better prepared psychologically for the fact that their government no longer held the reins of public protection.

Ethics is ultimately about values, about doing what is "right" and avoiding what is "wrong." Yet, if ethics is based on values, the question remains: whose values determine the ethical norm? Bernharðsdóttir, addressed this very issue in her consideration of culture, risk, and approaches to risk management in different societies. She argued that the central values of a society are manifest in its culture, in its understanding of nature, in its ontological perspective, and in the institutions it crafts to protect those values. Consequently, a more ethical way to analyze risk and manage it, either in its frequency or its impact, is necessarily based on that society's cultural values. Looking to societal cultural values can help policymakers manage public expectations, provide a value base: one upon which to ask for behavioral adjustments and changes, and can predict what people will do if and when risks materialize into acute crises.

## WHY WE SHOULD CARE ABOUT
## THE ETHICS OF RISK MANAGEMENT

Ethical risk management is possible. The authors in this book have shown some good guidelines for determining what values are appropriate for guiding this process, as well as what are some sound strategies for effectively prioritizing competing claims and sought benefits. However, such ethics-based approaches do require sustained thought, attention, and careful consideration of the implications and consequences of promoting some risks (encouraging certain modes of production, industry relationships, regulation or deregulation), while demoting other products, practices, relations, or forms of control. As reflected by the scholarly diversity of our authors, we believe an interdisciplinary conversation presents an ideal forum to engage in careful analysis, and to consider the values involved from a various stakeholders' perspectives. Our hope is that this volume is a small start on that conversation; a conversation we need to have, and we need to have soon.

As a society we are making critical decisions every day in the areas of energy, healthcare, disaster preparedness, and food production; these decisions can have far-reaching consequences for the future and future generations. Yet there are many people today struggling under the fallout of risk-distribution policies and practices. Those groups that have greater than average needs, fewer resources, or who cross geographic boundaries to increase their chances of survival, are just some of those left unaccounted for by dominant rational-choice models.

How we ethically allocate our communal resources and communal values through our institutions, is of critical concern to us all; From the isolated groups who are smuggled to countries where they are forced to live without a voice, to the international populations that need their governments to regulate industry to sustain healthy living environments. To paraphrase what V. O. Key (1940) once said about public budgeting, we are now at a point (in the evolution of the administrative state) where we are sufficiently skilled at crunching the numbers; what we need now is a theory that tells us *why* we should spend x amount of money on activity Y instead of activity Z. We believe that ethical management of risk is the beginning of just such a theory; one that requires continued collaboration and a cross-disciplinary conversation to succeed.

## NOTE

1. Apologizing profusely or intentionally groveling in front of the offended or harmed party in order to get away with a lesser punishment for harm done. In Chapter 4 this behavior comes out as "[a] recent, highly praised strategy for healthcare institutions to reduce costs of malpractice litigation is to encourage early settlement through disclosure, apology, and offer to patients" (pp. 52–53).

## REFERENCES

Fischhoff, B., Slovic, P., & Lichtenstein, S. (2000). Weighing the risks: Which risks are acceptable? In P. Slovic (Ed.), *The perception of risk* (pp. 121–136). London, England: Earthscan.

Key, V. O. J. (1940). The lack of a budgetary theory. *American Political Science Review, 34*(06), 1137–1144.

Löfstedt, R. E. (2005). *Risk management in post-trust societies*. Basingstoke, England: Palgrave Macmillan.

Slovic, P., Fischhoff, B., & Lichtenstein, S. (2000). Facts and fears: Understanding perceived risk. In P. Slovic (Ed.), *The perception of risk* (pp. 137–153). London, England: Earthscan.

# ABOUT THE AUTHORS

**Matthew D. Adler** (JD, Yale University; MA, literature, Oxford University) is a Richard A. Horvitz Professor of Law and a professor of economics, philosophy and public policy at Duke Law School, Durham, NC, United Tates. Dr. Adler clerked for U.S. Supreme Court Justice Sandra Day O'Connor and Judge Harry Edwards, District of Columbia Court of Appeals, and is currently an editor of the journal *Legal Theory.* http://law. duke.edu/fac/adler/

**Ásthildur E. Bernharðsdóttir** (PhD, University of Iceland; MA, political science, University of Iceland; BA, University of Iceland) is a research scientist at the Earthquake Engineering Research Centre at the University in Reykjavik, Iceland. http://jardskjalftamidstod.hi.is/en/%C3%A1sthildur_elva_bernhar%C3%B0sd%C3%B3ttir

**Erna Danielsson** (PhD, sociology, Umeå University) is an associate professor of sociology at Risk and Crisis Research Center at Mid-Sweden University in Östersund, Sweden. www.miun.se/en/Research/Our-Research/Centers-and-Institutes/RCR/About-RCR/Staff/Erna-Danielsson/

**Leslie Francis** (PhD, philosophy, University of Michigan; JD, University of Utah; BA, philosophy, Wellesley College) is associate dean for faculty research development at the college of law; distinguished professor of law and philosophy; as well as adjunct professor of political science, family and preventative medicine, and internal medicine at the University of

Utah. Salt Lake City, UT, United States. http://faculty.utah.edu/u0035587-LESLIE_FRANCIS/bibliography/index.hml

**Adam Luedtke** (PhD, political science, University of Washington; MA, political science, McGill University; BA, political science, Antioch College) is an assistant professor in the department of social sciences at Queensborough Community College, City University of New York, **NY, United States.** www.qcc.cuny.edu/socialSciences/faculty.html

**Susanna Öhman** (PhD, sociology, Umeå University, Sweden) is an associate professor of sociology and head of the department of social science at Mid Sweden University in Östersund, Sweden. www.miun.se/en/Research/Our-Research/Centers-and-Institutes/RCR/About-RCR/Staff/Susanna-Ohman/

**Aya Okada** (PhD, University of Pittsburgh, PA; MA, Hitotsubashi University, Tokyo, Japan; BA, Keio University, Minato, Tokyo, Japan) is an assistant professor in the department of policy studies at Doshisha University, Kyoto, Japan. https://kenkyudb.doshisha.ac.jp/rd/html/english/researchersHtml/113139/113139_Researcher.html

**Kristin Shrader-Frechette** (Post-doctoral, biology, University of Florida) economics and hydrogeology; Post-doctoral, economics and hydrogeology, University of California–Santa Barbara); PhD, philosophy of science, University of Notre Dame; BA, mathematics, Xavier University) is the O'Neill Family Professor of Philosophy, concurrent professor of biological sciences, and director of the Center for Environmental Justice and Children's Health at the University of Notre Dame, South Bend, IN, United States. www.nd.edu/~kshrader

**Christopher A. Simon** (PhD, political science, University of Washington) is a professor in the political science department, University of Utah, Salt Lake City, UT, United States. http://faculty.utah.edu/u0722430-CHRISTOPHER_A_SIMON/teaching/index.hml

**Lina Svedin** (PhD, political science, Syracuse University; MA, international relations, Stockholm University) is an associate professor in the political science department, the associate director of the master's of public administration program, and affiliated with the masters of public policy program, University of Utah, Salt Lake City, UT, United States. http://faculty.utah.edu/u0586845-LINA_M._SVEDIN/research/index.hml

**Brendon Swedlow** (PhD, University of California, Berkeley; JD, University of California, Hastings) is an associate professor in the department of political science and a founding faculty associate of the Institute for the Study of the Environment, Sustainability, and Energy at Northern Illinois University, DeKalb, IL, United States. Dr. Swedlow is a research associate of the Center for Analysis of Risk and Regulation at the London School of Economics and a fellow of the Center for Governance at the University of California, Los Angeles. www.niu.edu/polisci/faculty/profiles/swedlow1.shtml

**David J. Vogel** (PhD, politics, Princeton University; BA, political science, Queens College, City University of New York) is the Solomon P. Lee Chair in Business Ethics and professor in the political science department at the University of California, Berkeley. He also is the editor of the *California Management Review* and is affiliated with the Haas Business and Public Policy Group. http://facultybio.haas.berkeley.edu/faculty-list/vogel-david

**Erika Wall** (PhD, sociology, Mid Sweden University) is a postdoctoral candidate at Mid Sweden University's Risk and Crisis Research Center in Östersund, Sweden. www.miun.se/en/Research/Our-Research/Centers-and-Institutes/RCR/About-RCR/Staff/Erika-Wall/

CPSIA information can be obtained
at www.ICGtesting.com
Printed in the USA
FFOW01n0531131015
17635FF